Dear Rea

Some cri ... he jury has returned its verdict. Violent in the extreme, the David Parker Ray case is one of the most shocking of all.

Beside New Mexico's Elephant Butte Lake stood a windowless trailer that Ray called "the Toy Box." The homemade torture chamber was lavishly equipped with whips, chains, pulleys, surgical blades—and a camcorder, set up for making "snuff" videos.

On March 22, 1999, a desperate victim escaped from the Toy Box, clad only in a slave collar and padlocked chains. Another brave survivor came forward to describe her ordeal. And soon authorities uncovered horrifying evidence of an orgy of bloodshed that may have taken more than sixty lives.

Yet, the David Parker Ray story did not end with his trial, conviction, and sentencing—or with his death in prison. As recently as 2012, new evidence pointed to additional victims.

Sadly, author Jim Fielder did not live to update the story to which he devoted so many years of research and writing. Having had the privilege of getting to know Jim while we prepared his book for publication, I knew he would want his saga of crime and justice to reach a new audience through an updated edition.

Fortunately, veteran crime writer Sheila Johnson was able to step in on Jim's behalf. Her new update will fascinate all who have followed the Ray story over the years—and anyone, too, who is interested in the good and evil in human nature.

Already a long-term bestseller, *Slow Death* will enthrall and amaze you. Sit back and enjoy a page-turning story, told by two of America's finest investigative journalists.

If you would like to comment on *Slow Death,* we'd love to hear from you at marketing@kensingtonbooks.com.

With my best wishes,

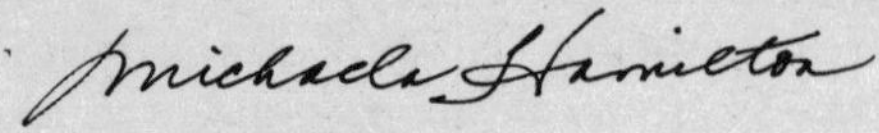

Michaela Hamilton

Executive Editor, Pinnacle True Crime

SLOW DEATH

JIM FIELDER

PINNACLE BOOKS
Kensington Publishing Corp.
http://www.kensingtonbooks.com

Some names have been changed to protect the privacy of individuals connected to this story.

PINNACLE BOOKS are published by

Kensington Publishing Corp.
119 West 40th Street
New York, NY 10018

ISBN-13: 978-0-7860-2926-6
ISBN-10: 0-7860-2926-9

First Printing: January 2003
20 19 18 17

Printed in the United States of America

DEDICATION

To my mother, Marjorie Fielder,
who never lost faith in me.

To my father, Jim "Ed" Fielder,
who taught me how to fight back.

ACKNOWLEDGMENTS

Thanks to all my friends in New Mexico, especially Jim Yontz, Lee McMillian, Frances (Baird) Sanchez, and Connie Burch.

I worked on this book for nearly four years. I could not have finished writing such a difficult book without the help and support of my family and friends. Thanks to M'Lissa Fielder, Sydney Trussler, Nichole Lungren, Tommy Moreno, Terry Eggers, Jonathan Stenberg, Eric Larsen, Terry Lee Walker, Melissa Danforth, Karl Blatt, Stu Dixon, Bob Pyle, Dick Smith, Gary Schaefer, David Mack, Joel Seidel, Bob Westling, Greg Coy, Larry Hoof, Kevin Huff, Rebecca Kelly, Janet Lizop, and, finally, my dear friend Allen Nickelson.

Over the years I've studied with many fine writing teachers. Thanks to Fan Gates, Leon Arksey, Leonardo Bercovici, and Al Hikida.

Every writer needs a big break to get published. I want to thank the following editors and writers who helped me find my way through the "dog-eat-dog" world of publishing: Craig Lewis, Gregg Olsen, Judy Alexander, Paul Dinas, and Michaela Hamilton.

Books don't get written without coffee. I spent many hours at a local Starbucks dreaming up my approach to telling the David Parker Ray story. Thanks to the people who poured my Colombian "short drip" every day—Courtney, Rachael, Lindsey, Joey, Jill, Liz, John, Ken, Ashley, Kristen, Andrea, and Mary.

And, finally, thanks to Ernest Hemingway and Truman Capote—the guys who made me want to be a writer someday.

PROLOGUE

The black mask in the storage shed appears from the description given to be the mask or similar mask which (David) Ray has been observed wearing in video tapes which were seized from his residence and which were viewed by officers pursuant to previous search warrants.

—Police search warrant, 4/13/1999

Smoke was pouring out from between her legs, the sacred place where God had intended for this young woman to give birth to a baby someday.

Eight Federal Bureau of Investigation (FBI) special agents watched the homemade videotape with a growing sense of horror crossing their somber faces. Their eyes followed the two people torturing the faceless victim—David Parker Ray, fifty-nine, and his girlfriend, Cynthia Lea Hendy, thirty-nine. The criminals hovered over the naked woman and stuck a hot cattle prod inside her vagina, watching her body writhe in pain. The agents kept their eyes on Ray and Hendy.

The federal investigators were sitting inside an eight-by twenty-five-foot white cargo trailer where the crime had taken place. The trailer was parked on the edge of Bass Road, along the shoreline of the largest lake in New Mexico—Elephant Butte Lake. The partners in crime lived on the outskirts of a small town cradled in the high, dry desert country of southern New Mexico—a strange place called Truth or Consequences.

The cops couldn't take their eyes off the torture unfolding in front of them. The naked woman, spread-eagled on her back, was anchored to a black leather medical table by the red nylon straps on her wrists and her ankles. Her eyes and mouth were covered with silver duct tape. She could barely move.

David Ray was wearing a long black robe and his face was covered by a black leather mask sprinkled with gold glitter. He looked out through two large eyeholes. He laughed as he rammed the cattle prod inside the terrified woman. Cindy Hendy was waving a small handgun, threatening to kill the woman if she didn't let the couple have their way with her.

Patty Rust and her fellow FBI agents watched the dying girl struggle to get free. It was clear to all of them that she'd been drugged out of her mind and frightened into submission by her dominating captors. The duo took off the duct tape and she screamed for help as the car mechanic and his welfare-cheating girlfriend continued to make her beg for her life.

The two sadists continued to molest the young woman until blood oozed out of her mouth and her ears. A moment later, her head slumped to the side and her body went limp.

The FBI agents turned off the videotape recorder and walked out of the torture chamber, one by one. Several agents threw up in the hot desert sand. Others sat on the steps of David Ray's white cargo trailer and talked among themselves.

For the next four days, Rust went back in the place David called his "toy box" and did her job, making a series of highly detailed black-and-white drawings of all the whips and chains and gigantic dildos and other devices used by David Parker Ray to hurt women. When she was done, she submitted her work to the Evidence

Recovery Team in Albuquerque. On Friday morning, April 2, 1999, she met with her boss to discuss the drawings. He told her she'd done a "fantastic job." Then he told her to go home and relax and try not to think anymore about what she'd seen in the trailer.

Later that night, Patricia E. Rust, thirty-six, drove home to her family in El Paso, Texas. Just before midnight, she got out of bed and went downstairs to get her personal handgun.

She put the barrel of the gun to her head and pulled the trigger.

CHAPTER 1

He put gravy on me and then let a dog lick it off.

—Cyndy Vigil, describing her torture by David Ray, 4/16/1999

Cyndy Vigil, twenty-two, ran down the narrow hall and out the door of the mobile home—fleeing for her life. It was late in the afternoon on March 22, 1999, and she had no idea where she was. She didn't know she was running down Bass Road in Elephant Butte, New Mexico. She just knew she had to get away from the two people who'd kept her in captivity for the last three horrible days and nights. She was naked from head to toe, except for the padlocked metal collar around her neck attached to a four-foot swinging chain dangling in the wind over her shoulder.

One local motorist saw her "running in circles" in the Hot Springs neighborhood overlooking the giant turquoise blue lake and the woman wanted to help. Doris Mitchell was driving home from afternoon grocery shopping, but the sight of the naked woman made her freeze in fear. She rolled up her windows and locked all her doors. She would not soon forget the frightened woman who ran beside her car and tried desperately to open her locked doors that day.

"She didn't say anything. She didn't say anything at all," Mitchell later told Frances Baird, a young reporter for the *Sentinel*, the local Sierra County newspaper. "She just looked wild."

By the time Vigil rounded the corner of the dusty dirt road and turned to flee down a patchy asphalt road leading to the lake, she was looking for shelter. The neighborhood was a jumble of mobile homes and looked to her like every yard was empty. As the road started to veer downhill, she got lucky and spotted a double-wide trailer on her left with a small grassy green yard surrounded by a tiny white picket fence. It was the home of Darlene and Donald Breech, who had worked and lived near Elephant Butte Lake for almost twenty-three years.

Without knocking, Vigil barged through the front door and started yelling at the top of her lungs. "Help me! Help me!" she shrieked.

Darlene Breech was standing in her kitchen pouring herself a glass of water when the hysterical girl suddenly appeared in her living room, stark naked and nearly out of her mind with fear.

"She didn't knock; she just burst in," Darlene later told Assistant District Attorney James A. Yontz. "As she was walkin' in the door, she just started screaming, 'Don't let them get me! Please help me!' She grabbed my arms and she didn't want to let go. I looked at her body and I couldn't believe my eyes.

"Her wrists looked like hamburger meat. She had beautiful long brown hair and it was all matted with blood. She was dirty all over and it looked like she had pooped in her pants. Her poor little boobs were black and blue and there were bruises all over her arms and legs.

"For some reason I didn't tell her to get out of the house. Donald and I are both retired, and we have four grown daughters, and to us she didn't look like she could hurt a flea. She couldn't have weighed over a hundred pounds, dripping wet.

"She held on to me real tight while she was talking and I had blood all over me. I tried to calm her down and a second later she ran over to the front door and dead-bolted it from the inside so nobody could snatch her. My husband, Don, was outside, watering the backyard.

"She ran back from the front door and grabbed my arm and started talking—very, very fast. She was terrified. She said some guy named David and his girlfriend, Cindy, had kept her locked up in a trailer for three days and nights, and during this time, they did nothing but torture her.

"She said on the third day David woke up and put on some kind of ranger uniform and went to work, leaving Hendy to watch her. She was chained to a wall while her captor watched a soap opera on television. Cyndy somehow managed to get a key and unlock herself from the wall, but the woman caught her and yelled, 'Hey, bitch, you're not going anywhere!' [She] hit [Cyndy] over the head with a big glass lamp.

"She escaped by stabbing this other woman in the back of the neck with an ice pick.

"Then she jumped through a window and ran for her life.

"Right away I called the nine-one-one operator. The first time I called, I told the operator what was going on, but not where I lived. I've lived here a long time and I know there are too many 'creepholes' living around Truth or Consequences, so I just hung up.

"Cyndy sat down in the kitchen. I've got this wet bar in my trailer and the bar stools are covered with a white Naugahyde kinda leather. I'm a smoker and I remember having a cigarette in the ashtray. I remember her sittin' there, smoking my cigarette, sitting on a stool."

Darlene listened to Vigil tell her that the man and the woman who hurt her were probably driving around the neighborhood looking for her, and Darlene told the young girl not to worry—Darlene Breech had a shotgun. What she didn't tell Vigil was the shotgun probably hadn't been fired in over fifty years.

"My husband, Donald, come in the back door and I explained what was going on. I told him to go to the closet and get my pink robe. Cyndy is just a little bitty thing and that pink bathrobe just swallowed her up. Right after she put it on, she hugged herself and went over and sat in the corner, cuddling herself, kinda like a little kid.

"She was real quiet, just whimpering.

"I called nine-one-one again and told them we lived next to Elephant Butte Lake, and a few minutes later, the deputies drove down Hot Springs Landing Road and the fools drove right past the house! Don went outside and waved them down. When Vigil saw the police, she just went outside and threw herself at them. They never came inside the house.

"They took her away and I went inside the house and started shaking all over. Right away I called my oldest daughter, who works as a nurse at the local Sierra Vista County Hospital. She told me to clean everything with Clorox.

"I must have cleaned the house for three hours, nonstop.

"I found out later the police picked up the kidnappers, Ray and Hendy, driving around less than a block from my house. If I had waited any longer to call back to the nine-one-one operator, they would have been at my door. . . ."

Sierra County sheriff's deputy Lucas Alvarez picked up Cyndy Vigil in front of Don and Darlene's double-wide and rushed her to the Sierra Vista County Hospital, where the dog collar and chain were cut off in the emergency room and doctors and nurses began to care for her banged-up body. His partner, David Elston, drove the three blocks to Ray's mobile home to search it.

The rutted wood sign out in front read DAVID P. RAY. There was a six-foot-high chain-link fence surrounding the entire piece of lakeside rental property. Ray's long brown-and-white mobile home was set far back from the dirt road and it was surrounded by two sheds, a bait trailer and a large white cargo trailer just off the northern end of the front porch. There were two sailboats and a car garage in the front yard.

Elston stepped through the open sliding glass door in the back of the building and "cleared" the house for any other persons. It was deserted.

He walked through a hallway into a middle bedroom and the first thing he saw was broken shards of green glass on the floor, next to a broken lamp, next to a broken window. There were smears of blood on the tangled sheets of the bed. A large dildo stood on a counter nearby. There was a long coffinlike box next to one wall, and when he looked up at the ceiling, he saw a pulley device with hooks and chains that slid along half-inch steel rods attached to the ceiling.

In the meantime, police from Elephant Butte State Park arrested David Parker Ray and Cynthia Lea Hendy driving down Springfield Road in his red camper—not far from where Vigil had found her refuge. The police housed the two suspects in the Cooper Police Training Center on the edge of the nearby town, Truth or Consequences.

Prior to 1950, the town had been called Hot Springs, New Mexico, but Ralph Edwards, popular host of a radio game show called *Truth or Consequences,* said he would broadcast a segment of the show from any town that changed its name to honor his program. The locals took the bait and ever since then the town has been called Truth or Consequences, New Mexico, or as the locals call it, T or C. The name change officially took place on April 1, 1950.

Control of the David Parker Ray case quickly jumped from local T or C hands into the more experienced hands of the New Mexico State Police (NMSP). Agent Wesley LaCuesta was a five-year veteran of the Criminal Assault and Violent Crimes Investigation Section when he first got the call to help on the case. When he heard the news out of T or C, he left his office in Las Cruces, New Mexico, and hurried north on Interstate 25, arriving in Truth or Consequences at 5:55 P.M.

Within hours he was briefed, and later that Monday night, he started interviewing Cyndy Vigil at the local Sierra Vista County Hospital. His report on the victim, as filed in the early arrest warrant issued for David Parker Ray, is chilling. It reads:

> I observed small cuts on both her legs, bruising on her right arm and bruising and abrasions on both her wrists. I also observed welt marks on her back and small puncture wounds and light bruising on her breasts.
>
> She indicated that on Saturday, March 20, 1999, between 10:00 and 11:00 A.M., she was streetwalking on Central Avenue (Highway 66) in Albuquerque and she was introduced to the two suspects by a local pimp. She met Ray and Hendy in a recreational vehicle owned by Ray. When she stepped inside the RV, Ray showed her a small police badge and told her she was under arrest for solicitation. Hendy then came out of the vehicle restroom and handcuffed her. She was restrained to a fixture in the camper and the suspects stripped her of all her clothing and threatened to shock her if she resisted.

Ms. Vigil stated that she was then taken to an unknown location where she was restrained by her arms and her legs. She said Ray placed dildos into her vagina and rectum simultaneously while Hendy watched on. She described receiving "shock therapy" in which Ray attached electrical connections to her breasts, which would send electrical shocks through her body. Both times, Hendy would wave a small revolver, threatening to shoot her if she tried to escape.

Ms. Vigil recounted how on Sunday, March 21, 1999, Ray and Hendy hung her from the ceiling in one bedroom by her arms and legs. She was then whipped on the back with a leather whip. After the whipping, Ray inserted a large metal dildo into her vagina.

Ms. Vigil also stated that an introductory audiotape recording was played to her, detailing what David Ray was going to do to her. She was also shown photographs of other naked women who had been tied up. Ms. Vigil stated that Ray took photographs of her while she was restrained from the ceiling of one of his rooms.

She referred to this room as "the dirty room."

CHAPTER 2

They say before this thing is over, the Charles Manson family will look like Snow White and the Seven Dwarfs.

—Mary Jo Montgomery, chief clerk, magistrate court (T or C), 6/13/1999

Before David Ray attracted national attention, Truth or Consequences, New Mexico, was just another small, sleepy community. Population 6,000. Most of the residents were "snowbirds," folks who moved there for the spectacular weather (355 days of sunshine a year, according to the *Sierra County Sentinel*). The average age of residents was fifty-eight years old. Six months before Ray put T or C on the map, Andrew Alexander, president of the chamber of commerce, made a few off-the-cuff comments on the local state of mind.

"Before 1998, there was a sentiment that nothing's going to happen around here, which troubled some, but pleased those who wanted it to stay small and quiet," said Alexander. "Now there's a sentiment that something is going to happen, and that troubles people, too, but I think it brings them together."

It took only two days in the spring of 1999 for David Parker Ray to bring the community together.

Local leaders had declared 1998 to be "the Year of the Bible," and by Tuesday night, March 23, many elderly people in the retirement community felt like 1999 was truly going to be called "the Year of the Devil." They were in a state of panic over the allegations that the nearby city of Elephant Butte might be home to a group of crazed sexual sadists. People were up in arms.

The state's "top cop" quickly called a town hall meeting to allow people to express their fear and anger.

Darren White, head of the New Mexico Department of Public Safety, dropped his busy schedule in Albuquerque and hurriedly flew into the tiny Truth or Consequences Municipal Airport. He was picked up by state police and rushed to the meeting. He sat at a small table in front of several hundred worried people and calmly tried to answer as many questions as he knew the answers to (there still had not been charges filed). One eighty-eight-year-old lady asked him what he was going to do about the "evil nightmare" that threatened the peace and quiet of her beloved desert home. White looked back at her, shaken.

"The nightmare is behind bars," he told her. "This is a safe community."

The next day, Wednesday, March 24, David Ray and Cindy Hendy were brought to the magistrate court in T or C to face separate arraignment hearings in front of Magistrate Judge Thomas Pestak. They were both in chains and shackles. Hendy walked into the courtroom in her orange jail jumpsuit; the dour dishwater blonde told the swarming media in a hushed voice, "I'm innocent. . . . I'm afraid to talk." David Ray, his face rough and wrinkled from years of working in the sun, shook his head and spoke softly after a reporter asked him if he "did it."

"It didn't happen that way," he said.

Inside the courtroom, both suspects told Pestak they were too poor to pay for an attorney and each one asked for a public defender. Ray worked, but Hendy told the judge she was trying to get by on only $331 a month from her welfare check. Pestak listened to Socorro, New Mexico, prosecutor Jim Yontz present a list of twenty-five felony charges against each defendant. The charges included kidnapping, criminal sexual penetration (rape with dildos), aggravated assault and criminal conspiracy. If convicted of all charges, Ray and Hendy would each be sentenced to 197 years behind bars. Judge Pestak was concerned that Ray and Hendy might flee, so he set their bail high enough so that neither would try to make a run for it.

"One million dollars each," he told them. "Cash."

There was a true media feeding frenzy when the case broke. The *New York Times* and *People* magazine were on the scene. The *Albuquerque Journal* sent down several reporters. The supermarket tabloid the *Globe* had a reporter up in Everett, Washington, digging up the dirt on Cindy Hendy, and a reporter in T or C looking into David Ray's past. CBS, NBC and ABC all had lead stories on the evening news that week. Television stations from all over New Mexico filled the twenty-two town motels. The Associated Press reporter and cameraman were everywhere, as were the three local T or C weeklies, the *Sentinel*, the *Herald* and the *Desert Journal*.

Local county sheriff Terry Byers watched the media mobs take over the two neighboring towns during those first few days of the investigation: "The first night we only had one television news truck and after Wednesday we had ten trucks here within hours."

Major Bob Barnes of Elephant Butte complained that noisy helicopters were disrupting his traditional afternoon nap. He told a news conference that most of the people in town didn't even lock their doors at night and now Elephant Butte was becoming famous as a haven for white-trash sadists.

"We feel violated," he said.

When the Rio Grande was dammed in 1916 to create Elephant Butte Lake and more irrigation water for the farmers and ranchers of southern New Mexico, thousands of rattlesnakes congregated on an island that later became known as Rattlesnake Island. The island is right across the lake from where David Ray lived on his lease lot property at Hot Springs Landing.

Frances Baird was only seventeen years old when Ray was arrested, and she didn't have any idea how nasty the story would be, but she was the only crime reporter for the *Sentinel*. When the story broke, she already had an inside scoop on what was going on "with that snake in the grass, David Ray."

Her boyfriend, Byron Wilson, twenty-seven, was the park cop who arrested Ray and Hendy on the first afternoon.

During the first week of the investigation, the New Mexico State Police spearheaded the effort to collect evidence from Ray's property, including—what Frances heard described as—shocking videotapes, possible "snuff" videos, and a bunch of audiotapes David had made to try to "freak out" the victims. She also heard that David used to call the cargo trailer his "play box"; that is, until Cindy Hendy talked him into renaming it the "toy box."

It wasn't long before the FBI started snooping around, sensing a blockbuster case. Frances nicknamed the New Mexico State Police "the Indians" and the man in charge of the FBI special agents "the Chief." When Doug Beldon moved down from Albuquerque and set up a field office in T or C to supposedly help the NMSP gather more evidence, Frances used her connections to find out about the expanding case.

One afternoon Frances asked Beldon what was going to happen next.

"Are there any more suspects?" she asked him.

"I do expect more arrests," he told her.

"What about victims?" she asked.

"I don't know," he said, shaking his head. "We think there might be many more."

CHAPTER 3

I went over there to pick up some cake mix . . . and they kept me against my will.

—Angie Montano, late March 1999

On Saturday night, March 27, Angelique Montano, twenty-seven, sat in front of her small television set and watched the unfolding Cyndy Vigil escape story. Angie and Cyndy never met in person, but the two young women had two things in common. Both had worked as hookers on the most dangerous section of Highway 66 (Central Avenue) in Albuquerque, and both had been kidnapped and tortured by David Ray and Cindy Hendy during the first three months of 1999.

Angelique had moved to Truth or Consequences in 1996 in order to turn her life around. Methamphetamines had almost killed her in the big city and she figured a new chance to start all over might be just what she and her infant son, Abel, needed. Life was hard as nails—living off the monthly welfare checks—and she still had trouble resisting the underground supply of drugs in T or C, but at least she was off the street. She desperately wanted to be a good person, like everybody else.

On Sunday, March 28, after watching television all weekend, she walked over to talk to her friend John Branaugh. She told him about how David had kidnapped her on Febraury 17 and then how she had talked him into letting her go on February 21. She told him it all happened back in the winter, right about the time the movie *8 MM* came out. John had heard the story before, but he hadn't believed it the first time around. He'd been watching the news all weekend, too, so this time he listened to every word.

Later that day, Angelique let John take her down to the police station, where she poured out the rest of the story about her five-day ordeal with Ray and Hendy. Both Vigil and Montano told of similar experiences, except Ray never got a chance to take Vigil to the toy box because she stabbed his girlfriend and ran away. Angelique Montano wasn't so lucky,

The next day, the media descended on Angie and made her feel like a celebrity. Locals winced when she went on NBC-TV and told the national audience what the two monsters had done to what she called "my poor little vaginer." Though many of the so-called respectable people in town lacked sympathy for her lifestyle, a guest editorial in the *Sentinel* reminded the citizens that "even the worst of us deserves protection under the law."

Tabloids like the *Globe* recognized the story's power, and Joe Mullins, their man on the beat, courted Angie until he got her to agree to sell her story to the tabloid. Mullins called Craig Lewis, his editor in Florida, and told him about the interview.

Angie had one blue eye (a prosthetic device) and one brown eye, and a face covered by small pocklike scars from a lifetime of drug abuse. She wanted an operation to get a new artificial eye, so both of her eyes would be the same color; Lewis gave Mullins the go-ahead to seal the deal with a special offer from the "deep pockets" of the *Globe*. Joe Mullins was to pay her $700 and promise that the newspaper would pay for her surgery. When Angie heard what they were going to do for her, she was thrilled.

Mullins did an interview and got Angie to give him some old pictures; within a week, the *Globe* was on sale all over America, sporting a front-page headline that read NEW MEXICO VICTIM'S OWN STORY: "I ESCAPED SEX SADISTS' TORTURE CHAMBER."

Angie got a chance to tell her story, with only minor editorial "flourishes" by the touch-up staff of the *Globe:*

> For five days, I was tortured in a chamber of horrors by a monster named David Ray and his evil mistress Cindy Hendy.
>
> The terrible things they did haunt me constantly. It's a nightmare I know I never will escape.
>
> The horror began the day I decided to bake a cake for my boyfriend Frank Zambrano who lives with me and my five-year-old boy, Abel.
>
> I knew Cindy vaguely through a friend and she had offered to give me a cake-mix packet and ingredients for frosting.
>
> I went with her to a white-and-brown recreational vehicle. David, whom I'd never met, was hiding inside. He put a knife to my throat and said I was being abducted.
>
> They drove to their home, a trailer with a small trailer parked nearby—at Elephant Butte. They sat me on a bed and Cindy told me to just relax and everything would be alright.
>
> David left the room and came back with a big knife. I pleaded with him. **"I want to go home, my little boy Abel needs me."**
>
> He slapped me viciously. The blow sent shivers of terror through my whole body. I realized this was not just some weird game. My life was in dan-

ger. I am legally blind from a previous injury but I could see the knife at my throat and Cindy pointing a pistol at me. David ripped my clothes off.

They bound me naked to the bed with chains around my ankles. They also padlocked a metal collar around my neck.

They told me: "Welcome to your worst nightmare. If you've ever woken up screaming in the night, we are the people you were dreaming about."

Then they began a sick introduction to what they were going to do to me. On a TV in front of me, they played a video that showed their torture room and things they had done to others. I was so terrified I could hardly watch, but they were getting a kick out of showing it to me. They left me chained to the bed for three days. David went off to work as usual and Cindy stayed to watch me.

On the third day, David told me "We're going to the Playbox. I want to show you my toys." The way he said "Playbox" gave me the creeps.

They took me to the other trailer where David put me on a table and tied me down, hand and foot.

Looking around, I could see things that looked like medical instruments—pliers, clamps, saws and scalpels. There were also whips and chains and padlocks and other scary-looking restraints.

It looked like some kind of torture chamber that you see in movies.

The sight of all those things for pinching, twisting and cutting flesh paralyzed me with fear. David called those horrible instruments his "friends."

I realized that I had to stay cool or never get out alive. If I tried to fight them, I was sure they'd kill me and dump my body. David had stripped to the waist. Looking into his cold eyes was like seeing the Devil himself.

I was gagged and blindfolded. Suddenly, I felt a

terrible pain as they jammed something into me from behind. The pain paralyzed me. I prayed, **"Dear God, please help me survive this, I don't want to die."**

I could hear David breathing heavily and he and Cindy began inflicting as much pain on me as they could.

Later, they led me back to the bedroom where I was again chained to the bed.

The next day David said to Cindy, "I think Angie would like to pleasure me, wouldn't you little girl?" He made me perform a sex act on him.

They took me back to The Playbox and strapped me to the table, telling me I was going to have electrotherapy. David clipped wires to my breasts and lower body. Cindy watched as he switched on the power. It was like scorching fire surging through my body.

I thought, **"Dear God, he's going to kill me. I'll never see Frank and my little darling Abel again."**

Through my agony I could hear David and Cindy "ooing and aahing" as they watched my torment. "Look at how she moves," he said. "Watch as the current hits her." I tried to scream in my agony, but the gag kept me from making a sound. The torture went on for at least an hour. I thought it would never end.

I was shaking like a leaf by the time they took me back and chained me like a dog to the bed. These evil people had taken my pride and my morals. I was outraged. I knew I had to beat them.

I began saying prayers I remembered from my childhood. **"Hail, Mary, full of grace, pray for us sinners, *now* and at our hour of death."**

"Dear God, Blessed Mother, especially deliver us from evil. Oh yes, Dear Lord, especially from that. Save me from these two torturers."

The prayers made me feel stronger.

On the fifth day, Cindy Hendy went out to do shopping. Left alone, I began thinking about how practiced these two devils were at what they were doing. They had probably done this many times before to countless other women, I thought.

I knew I had to work my street-smarts to survive.

I figured to work on David Ray. While I was chained to the couch naked and weeping, I said to him, **"David, come over here and sit by me. I'm feeling so down. Come hold me, please."**

Sitting next to me, David told me that he liked me and thought I was a nice person. He said: "If I had known how nice you were beforehand, I wouldn't have started all this. Cindy didn't tell me you were so sweet. I think we could have been friends."

I could hardly believe my plan was working. In a sincere tone, I told him it wasn't too late. We could still be friends. And I would never tell anybody about what he'd done.

Somehow, I convinced him to let me go. When Cindy came back, she wasn't happy about it.

She finally went along with him, but I was terrified that they were teasing and at the last minute would take me back into their hell-hole.

I promised to hitch a ride to Albuquerque, over 100 miles away, and not come back. They took me in their car and dropped me off on I-25.

On February 21, 1999, Angelique Montano, wearing the same clothes she was wearing five days earlier, put out her thumb and tried to hitch a ride back to her home in Truth or Consequences. After a couple of hours and without much luck, she managed to flag down an off-duty sheriff from Los Lunas County. She told her whole story to the officer as he drove her back to her boyfriend and young son in T or C. He doubted that she was telling him the truth, and her account went unreported to the Sierra County Sheriff's Office. A month later, after the officer saw the unfolding Ray investigation on TV, he regretted his mistake.

"If I had thought it was one hundred percent legitimate," he told authorities, "I would have taken her to the police station right then and there."

Not everyone between T or C and Elephant Butte believed that Ray and Hendy were guilty. They did have friends. Debbie Fisk collected her weekly disability checks and liked to hang out with Hendy. She'd been over to Ray's trailer on many occasions and knew his daughter, Glenda "Jesse" Ray, and his best buddy, Dennis Roy Yancy. Right after Hendy got arrested, Fisk went over and cleaned out Hendy's trailer. Fisk knew almost everyone from the wrong side of the tracks, as the conservatives in town used to call all the places where the party animals liked to party.

She even knew Angie Montano.

When she read that Angie had fooled the *Globe* into thinking that she was borrowing "cake mix" to bake a cake, Fisk giggled.

"You know—you go over and get seven hundred dollars' worth of cake mix, and something's bound to happen," she told anyone who would listen.

"That's a lot of cocaine."

CHAPTER 4

We found a videotape of another naked woman with a swan tattoo on her right ankle.

—FBI Agent Tony Maxwell, 3/31/1999

By April 1, the mainstream-media types were beginning to lose interest in the "next big story." Both victims were girls who turned tricks to support their drug habits—not exactly the kind of heroes the media yearned for in their desire for more copy. *People* magazine reporter Carlton Stowers complained of being stuck in "this godforsaken country" and was especially critical of Angelique Montano.

"If she can snort it, drink it or smoke it—or do all three at the same time—she'll do it."

One night he was at Rocky's Lounge relaxing and talking to a small group of reporters. Everyone was disappointed that the cops had been unable to unearth any bodies. Stowers told everyone that *People* was sending him back home to Dallas, Texas, and he commented, "This is the first pornographic report I've ever sent in."

* * *

By Monday, March 29, the FBI took over the investigation and immediately sent in three crack teams of eight agents each to help the NMSP collect evidence. Right away they found what they said was a six-minute videotape of David Ray playing doctor and examining a naked young woman who'd been strapped down to a black bench press and made blind and speechless with duct tape. The FBI was hoping she was still alive. In the video, there was only one way the police might be able to identify her.

She had a small swan tattoo on her ankle.

The NMSP immediately took a blowup of the tattoo and pumped it into the National FBI Rapid Start System, hoping a computer search would allow them to match a description of a woman with the same kind of tattoo. It wasn't long before they hit pay dirt. A woman from Arizona had called the FBI right after she saw David Ray on TV and reported that her daughter-in-law had disappeared for three days and nights way back in 1996.

Janet Murphy told the FBI the following story about the twenty-two-year-old girl with the swan tattoo, Kelli Van Cleave.

"In July of 1996, my twenty-year-old son, Patrick, married a young girl from Truth or Consequences he'd only known for six weeks. He was in the navy in San Diego and home on leave when he met her. It was kind of a quick thing when they got married. I wanted him to take it a little bit slower. I just figured she latched on to Patrick because she wanted some financial security.

"Right after they got married, they were staying at my house and he was catering to her all the time. I guess they were having sexual problems, just like a lot of newlywed couples do. They fought one night, and the next morning, Kelli came to me and said, 'Mom, I'm going to go see some friends and I'll be back later.'

"She didn't come back for three days.

"I was really upset and so was Patrick. He reported

her missing and he looked for her night and day. He was really worried that she was hanging out with some really bad people. By the end of the second day, we talked and he decided to divorce her. We thought she just up and left him and was out fooling around with her friends.

"On the third morning, we were out doing yard work when this state vehicle pulls up. David Parker Ray was behind the wheel. Kelli gets out of the truck, and right away I noticed that she looked all messed up—dirty—and that wasn't like Kelli at all, she was a very clean person. It looked like she had a hangover, but I knew for a fact she hardly ever drank. She didn't do drugs, either. Her eyes were wandering. She was barefoot and missing her wedding ring. Her hair was all messed up. She came over and sat on the porch and I tried to talk with her, and she said mostly she couldn't remember.

"Mr. Ray told us he'd found her wandering on the beach down at Hot Springs Cove, and then he smiled and said, 'I thought I'd better bring her home. She was dehydrated, and we stopped at Earl's Diamond gas station and I bought her a cup of coffee.'

"My son came walking out of the house and told Kelli he wanted a divorce, and we told her she couldn't come in the house unless she signed the divorce papers. She left with David Ray and came back two days later and got all her belongings.

"Patrick divorced her at the end of July and he didn't see Kelli until the following April when the two kids talked about the possibility of getting married one more time. She moved in to stay with me for a few days. He didn't trust her and neither did I. After a few days, I asked her to leave my house and I didn't think about her too much until I saw all the TV news about David Ray kidnapping and torturing those other two girls.

"I feel so darn guilty," she told the FBI, sobbing uncontrollably.

"I didn't believe her and now I think that David had her all three of those nights. I don't know what he did to her memory, but I think he probably did some wicked things to her body.

"My son and Kelli Van Cleave had only been married two weeks . . ."

Two weeks later, the New Mexico State Police called Kelli Van Cleave in Craig, Colorado, where she moved in 1998. She confirmed that she had a swan tattoo on her right ankle. Agent Carrie Parbs of the NMSP made arrangements to drive up to Colorado to interview Van Cleave. She told Kelli she would be accompanied by Agent Larry Houpt of the FBI, a specialist in violent crimes as well as, coincidentally, an ordained minister in the Mormon Church.

Kelli Van Cleave, now twenty-five, sat down nervously for her interview with the two investigators. Parbs showed her a picture taken from the video and asked if that was her leg and her tattoo. Kelli shook all over and said, "Yes, that's me." She told the pair she'd been having nightmares for three years and now the memories were slowly coming back. Parbs asked her to start at the beginning.

"I was friends with Roy Yancy," she said. "He's a good friend of David Parker Ray. Roy used to tell me he was in a satanic group for years and he said David Ray had always been the leader. I knew Roy Yancy was very violent. I seen him beat people up, both men and women. Everybody in town was so scared of him—nobody would turn him in. One time Roy told me that he could kill someone and not even blink an eye.

"I'd never met David, but I knew his daughter Glenda Ray. We called her Jesse. I'd known her for three years and I knew a lot of people in Truth or Consequences who got their drugs from her. She was a major-league drug runner—coke, meth, grass—the whole bag. I'd never done drugs before, but I liked to hang out and party with Jesse, Roy and her friends.

"T or C is a real party town.

"The night I got in trouble was July 25, 1996. It was hotter than hell, so I went out barhopping with a bunch of my friends and we ended up out at the Blue Waters Saloon. They drank all day but I only had one beer. I was the designated driver. Later that night, Jesse said she would take me home. She drives a big motorcycle and she's always letting people hitch a ride with her. She said she wanted to drink some coffee first, so we got on her big ole motorcycle and, instead of taking me home, she drove me over to her dad's trailer.

"Inside, I sat down on the couch while Jesse and her dad went into the back room. When they came out, one sat beside me and the other one knelt at my feet. I can't remember which one did what, but I do remember that one held a knife to my throat and the other used duct tape to cover my eyes and my mouth,

"At first I thought they were playin' a joke on me.

"When I realized they were serious, I guess I kinda froze up and I went along with them because I didn't want them to hurt me. They took off my clothes and put a dog collar around my neck. Then they took me out to the toy box.

"I still don't remember too much; I just remember being tied up. And I remember David poking me with a metal dildo—you know, right between the legs.

"I remember going to the bathroom twice in a little potty. I know that David was the only other person in there with me. One time he got mad because I kept licking the tape around my mouth so it wouldn't stick. One time I pleaded with him, 'I want to go home; I want to go home.' Another time he was using those huge rubber spiked dildos on me and it hurt real bad. I told him, 'It hurts, David,' and he quit. Another time he was playing gynecologist and it really hurt, and he quit that time, too.

"He told me that his satanic group had been watching me for a long time because they wanted me as a sex slave, but he finally decided I was too tight between the legs for good sex and eventually he let me go.

"The day he drove me home, I asked Janet Murphy if I could go inside her house and pick up my clothes. She told me she wouldn't let me in the door, not even to get my toothbrush.

"She sent me off with David Ray. He took me to the south end of the lake and my friend 'Damsite Dave' Connolly took care of me. I stayed at his house for a few days."

Carrie Parbs interrupted and asked Van Cleave how it felt to finally tell her side of the story. Kelli paused and looked down at the floor for the longest time. Then she wept softly.

"I feel so guilty," she said. "I can't tell you how dirty I feel."

"You're doing a brave thing," Parbs told her.

"What if I'd come out sooner—maybe the two other girls wouldn't have been kidnapped."

Agent Houpt asked her if she ever told people in T or C any of the details she was now telling them.

"No," she said. "I knew nobody would believe me."

"Why not?" he asked her.

"They all thought I was out there screwing around."

"Your friends told you that?" asked Houpt.

"I guess I've got lousy friends," she told him.

"Not anymore," the FBI man told her. "There's nothing to be afraid of anymore."

"One thing still freaks me out," Van Cleave said.

"What's that?" he asked her.

"I'm afraid of duct tape."

CHAPTER 5

Grabbing a hooker is easier than grabbing a housewife.
—David Parker Ray audiotape, recorded in 1993 and seized by the FBI in 1999

By early April 1999, over one hundred FBI and NMSP agents were swarming all over the David Ray property at 513 Bass Road. Many of them were wearing white jumpsuits and masks and digging in the yard. Others wore surgical gloves and concentrated on what evidence they could find inside the white cargo trailer and the brown-and-white mobile home Ray used as a house.

Eleven days after he was arrested, Ray claimed another victim when Patty Rust killed herself after spending four days inside the toy box making detailed drawings for the Federal Bureau of Investigation.

The day after Rust killed herself, Jim Yontz took a stroll through the toy box. He wondered why the FBI sent a woman into a torture chamber when everybody working the case suspected that other women had been literally "frightened to death" by the tall, skinny mechanic with a reputation for being "good with his hands."

When Yontz walked up to the rear end of the $100,000 handmade chamber of horrors, he first noticed the 7259-TRJ New Mexico license plate. There was an Arizona Highway Patrol Association decal right next to it that said I SUPPORT THE BEST. The trailer was jacked up on wooden blocks and Yontz noticed it didn't have any windows. He walked up the four steps and opened what had previously been a double dead-bolted, steel-reinforced door.

He immediately spotted a can of Folgers coffee. The Charles Manson Family had killed Abigail Folger in 1969 and Yontz wondered if David Ray was paying his respects in some sicko kind of way. Next to the coffee can was a box of Kellogg's corn flakes and a small refrigerator. Hanging on the wall was a roll of paper towels that said HOME-SWEET-HOME.

After that, it got ugly.

On the left wall, Jim noticed a large white sign with big red block letters that identified David Ray's name for his little private hideaway: SATAN'S DEN. Next to the big sign was a smaller white sign with black underlined letters that identified what Yontz was about to see: THE BONDAGE ROOM. Down at the other end of the trailer was a hand-lettered sign that said I AM RATHER BUSY—WOULD YOU PISS OFF!

Standing right next to the Satan's Den sign was a tall tripod with a very expensive RCA Victor camcorder pointing toward a large black leather table/chair rigged up with metal stirrups, electrodes and dozens of red plastic straps. Hanging from the ceiling next to what looked like the gynecology table was an RCA Victor television set, positioned so the female victims could see what Ray was doing to them.

Walking up the left side of the chamber, Yontz saw a coat hanger with a long black robe hanging from it. The robe had a red cape. There was a bussinesslike clipboard hanging next to the robe and Yontz noticed that Ray had what looked like a "roll call" list of victims he'd kidnapped between 1993 and 1997. Yontz knew that was the period of time after his fourth wife, Joannie Lee, divorced him and before the time he met his last live-in lover, Cindy Hendy. He read the list and tried not to let his emotions get in the way. It wasn't easy. Each nameless woman on the list had cowboylike "notch marks" after their date of capture.

KIDNAP DATE	NUMBER OF ASSAULTS	
February 7th, 1994	IIIIIIIIIIIIIIIIIIIIIIIIIII	(27)
April 16th, 1994	IIIIIIIIIIIIIIIIIIIIIIIIIIIIIIIII	(33)
July 3rd, 1994	IIIIIIIIIIIIIIIIIIIIIIIIIIII	(28)
September 9th, 1994	IIIIIIIIIIIIIIIIIIIIIIIIIIIIIIIIIIIIIIIII	(41)
March 6th, 1995	IIIIIIIIIIIIIIIIIIIIIIIIIIIIIIIII	(33)
May 8th, 1995	IIIIIIIIIIIIIIIIIIIIIIIIIIIIIIIIIIIIIIIIIIIIIIIIIIIII	(53)
June 10th, 1995	IIIIIIIIIIIIIIIIIIIIIIIIIIIIIIII	(32)
August 4th, 1995	IIIIIIIIIIIIIIIIIIIIIIIIIIIIIIIIIIIIIIIIII	(42)
September 25th, 1995	IIIIIIIIIIIIIIIIIIIIIIIIIIIIIIIII	(33)
November 15th, 1995	IIIIIIIIIIIIIIIIIIIIIIIIIIIIIIIIIIIIIII	(39)
January 27th, 1996	IIIIIIIIIIIIIIIIIIIIIIIIIIIIIIIIIIIIIIIIIIIIIIIIIII	(51)
March 2nd, 1996	IIIIIIIIIIIIIIIIIIIIIIIIIIIIIIIIIIIIII	(38)
May 7th, 1996	IIIIIIIIIIIIIIIIIIIIIIIIIIIIIIII	(32)
July 3rd, 1996	IIIIIIIIIIIIIIIIIIIIIIIIIIIIIIIIIIIIII	(38)
October 4th, 1996	IIIIIIIIIIIIIIIIIIIIIIIIIIIIIIIIIIIIIIIIIIIIIIII	(48)
March 16th, 1997	IIIIIIIIIIIIIIIIIIIIIIIIIIIIIIIIIIIIIIIIIIIIII	(46)
September 23rd, 1997	IIIIIIIIIIIIIIIIIIIIIIIIIIIIIIIII	(33)

Halfway down the left-hand wall, Yontz walked up to a large cork bulletin board covered with color and black-and-white photographs and black-and-white drawings of women—all being tortured. A sign above the bulletin board seemed to sum up the driving force behind David Ray: THE LURE OF SATANISM.

The photographs showed women in various stages of bondage. Yontz's attention was first drawn to a young redheaded woman, naked, with her hands tied behind her back. She was gagged with a red bandanna and looking the camera right in the eye. Her eyes seemed to be smiling. Another picture showed a woman in obvious pain. Her naked breasts were hog-tied at the base with circles of constricting white rope, making them bulge. Old-fashioned wooden clothespins were attached to each nipple and her face seemed smothered in fear. A third picture showed a faceless woman tied down to a bench press with her legs forced wide apart. Bruises covered her body, especially the inside of her thighs.

Posted next were a series of "drawings" showing the stages in which Ray liked to torture women. One showed a table with a woman arching her back in pain, her wrists and ankles tied together behind her back. A handwritten sign above her body read NEW TABLE FOR CHURCH RITUALS. The drawing below showed how to hog-tie a woman to the "gynecology table," one step at a time. Another drawing showed a woman down on her hands and knees attached to something Ray called his "doggie frame." Still another showed a woman hanging from the ceiling by her ankles and hands with a man below her inserting two dildos into the two openings between her legs. The man playing doctor wore a satanic pentangle around his neck and resembled a much younger version of David Parker Ray, mustache and all.

Stapled next to the photographs and drawings was a detailed warning list prepared by Ray. Yontz copied the wicked list from top to bottom and noticed Ray hadn't forgotten a single detail.

REMEMBER

A WOMAN WILL DO OR SAY ANYTHING TO GET LOOSE

THEY WILL:

KICK	SCRATCH	OFFER MONEY
BITE	YELL	BEG
SCREAM	RUN	OFFER SEX
THREATEN	LIE	WAIT FOR OPPORTUNITY

STANDARD EXCUSES AND SOB STORIES:

MENSTRUATING
PREGNANT
V.D.
AIDS
SICK
KIDS WITH BABYSITTER
HAVE TO WORK
A SICK BABY
A SICK PARENT
CLAUSTROPHOBIA
MISSED BY HUSBAND OR FRIEND
BAD HEART
CAN'T MISS SCHOOL

DON'T LET HER GET TO YOU
IF SHE WAS WORTH TAKING—SHE IS
WORTH KEEPING
AND
SHE MUST BE SUBJECTED TO HYPNOSIS BEFORE
THE WOMAN CAN BE SAFELY RELEASED

NEVER TRUST A CHAINED CAPTIVE

The wall on the right-hand side of the toy box was covered with the tools of his trade: chains, whips, paddles, pulleys, leather belts, saw blades, harnesses, handcuffs, ropes, wires, needles, pins, screw clamps, nipple clamps, breast clamps, breast suction cups, metal bras, sandpaper, metal dildos, wooden dildos, plastic dildos, latex dildos of all sizes, a branding iron, a soldering iron and weighted lead sinkers—there was even an assortment of fishhooks.

Yontz looked up at the ceiling and saw dozens of red straps hanging down, all covered with rows of wooden clothespins.

A large yellow generator sat on the floor under the wall of dangling sex toys. It had a handle on top and was attached to the back of a fifteen-inch flesh-colored motorized dildo pointing forward and designed to look exactly like a man's penis, right down to the crooked and bulging veins. The giant rubber device looked as big as a large sausage and it was so thick no man could ever grip it around the middle with a closed fist. The back of the generator had three switches: BUZZER, LIGHT and PROBE. The entire apparatus looked like it could be picked up and wielded like some kind of jackhammer.

The space between the walls of the cargo trailer was filled with the large gynecological table/chair rigged to slide back and forth on a six-foot tract. It was wired to a voltage meter, with wires that could be attached to a woman's breasts and genitalia. There was also a generator that controlled the position of the black leather table—changing the elevation, foot position, back angle and, if necessary, the tilt of the entire female body tied down by red nylon straps to the D rings that served as wrist and ankle stirrups. A large hooded elbow light was bolted to the end of the table to illuminate the victim's vagina while Ray forced her to watch him rape her live on TV.

Walking down the right side of the chamber, Yontz looked down at the floor and saw a one-foot-tall Barbie doll with long black hair. Miniature chains were attached like shackles and hanging from her ankles, wrists, nipples and neck.

Finally, arriving at the back of the trailer on the right side, Yontz examined Ray's stainless-steel medicine cabinet. It was covered with latex gloves, forceps, rolls of cotton, Spanish K-Y jelly, petroleum jelly, bottles of chloroform, ammonia "poppers" and hypodermic syringes. Three white candles were mounted on top of a model of a human skull and the bleached skull was standing next to a handcarved wooden dildo. To the left was a collection of David Ray's small library of mostly female anatomy and withcraft books. Jim Yontz jotted down some of the titles that caught his eye:

Birth
Family Medical Guide
Emergency Victim Care
Fundamentals of Human Sexuality
Sexual Behavior of the Human Female
The Dark World of Witches
American Psycho

On the very top shelf of the cabinet, he noticed two naked baby dolls, one with a big patch of blond pubic hair and the other with a big patch of black pubic hair. Underneath the cabinet was an aluminum confinement drawer with a six-foot-long cot that slid out like a tray in a morgue and seemed to be the perfect place to store a live female body until Ray decided what to do with her next.

Jim turned and saw a plastic curtain that seemed to close off a small dressing area for the women. Ray had assembled a collection of nightgowns, along with a shelf containing shampoo, body lotion, baby powder, baby oil, mouthwash, perfume and lipstick.

Just before he completed "the grand tour," Jim Yontz looked up and saw another set of torture drawings, even more grotesque than the first set he'd seen on the other side of the trailer. This group was numbered 1 through 13, and after looking at all of them, Yontz found there was one that would forever leave a permanent imprint on his mind. It was labeled THE 12 VOLT MOTORIZED BREAST STRETCHER and he'd seen a photograph of Cyndy Vigil that looked just like the drawing.

David Ray had a drawing of a naked woman strapped down by her hips, belly and chest with a hood over her face. Rubber-lined clamps were attached to her nipples and connected to the machine by nylon cords. Ray had typed instructions telling his followers how to torture the victim:

1. Operate motor with the lever in the "up" position.
2. Attach clamps securely to each nipple.
3. Tighten cord until breasts are stretched to the maximum length.
4. Turn machine "on" and watch nipples for indication of tearing and check clamps for slippage. Continue to operate.
   NOTE: This process is very painful and due to the constant motion, the body will not adjust to the pain. During the operation, the subject will remain in extremely painful distress.

By the time Yontz was ready to leave the toy box, his mind was crowded with disturbing images. He wondered if the four days in the box had triggered lost childhood memories for Patty Rust. There was no way to know, he concluded. One item he saw would make any woman shudder, however. In the very back of the trailer, he had seen a small ceramic ashtray shaped like a woman floating on her back in a pool of turquoise water. Her legs were spread wide and her large black pubic patch seemed to invite any man with a smoke in his hands to put out his burning cigarette right between her legs.

Jim Yontz walked out of the toy box, thankful that his own wife would never have to take a walk through such a horrible place.

A few days later, prosecutor Jim Yontz sat down to listen to one of the six audiotapes the FBI found inside the mobile home; he suddenly caught himself thinking about Patty Rust one more time. True, she had seen what a monster the good-old-boy handyman David Parker Ray could be inside his torture chamber, but at least she had not been forced to listen to the heartless

Ray on the audiotapes he recorded to help indoctrinate his new recruits.

This was Ray at his worst, Yontz thought.

The sound of David Ray's calm voice could make your skin crawl:

> Nikkie was a whore in Phoenix, Arizona.
>
> I had known her two or three years, but I didn't screw around with her then. She had long blond hair, pretty well built, not beautiful, but not bad-looking, either. What really fascinated me about her was that she had these big, humongous tits. I used to watch her working, walking back and forth in front of Canal Motors, watching those big ol' tits bounce, fantasizing about what I would like to do to them.
>
> Seven or eight months after I left that job, I had to go back over to Arizona for a few days. I pulled my trailer and, needless to say, I went and looked Nikkie up. What I had in mind was to keep her chained and locked up in my trailer for about a week and use her for a sex toy, but it didn't work out that way. When I picked her up, her boyfriend knew where she was at. I asked her what she would charge to let me tie her up and spank her before I fucked her. She said a hundred dollars, but I didn't want to spend a hundred bucks, so I just got a blow job and took her back to town.
>
> The bitch gave me the clap.
>
> I didn't think you'd catch the clap with a blow job, but the doctors assured me that you could. Needless to say, I was pissed, but I wasn't in Arizona anymore and there wasn't a whole hell of a lot I could do about it, at least not at that moment.
>
> About six months later, I was in New Mexico and I took some stuff over to Arizona for an auc-

tion. I had my trailer and I looked Nikkie up. It took two days to find her [*snicker*]. That bitch got around! During that two days, I talked to several guys that had been fucking her pretty regular. She had gotten rid of the VD. Her boyfriend wasn't anywhere around when I picked her up that time. I took her back to the trailer and I told her I wanted to do the hundred-dollar deal: tie her up, spank her and fuck her. And she went for it—made it almost too easy for me.

The bondage table and related equipment folds up in concealed compartments, so she didn't have a clue as to what my real motives were. She didn't know exactly what I wanted to do, so I led her through it. She sat on a small cot, I used a rope to tie her ankles together, and then I used two separate ropes to tie her wrists down to her ankles—one rope on each wrist. I had a specific reason for tying her wrists that way, as I will explain later.

She cooperated completely until I brought out a tube-tied breathing gag and a roll of duct tape.

That cunt did not want to be gagged. But I got it in her mouth and put several wraps of duct tape around her head to hold it in place. To be double sure, I wrapped duct tape under her chin and over the top of her head several times so she couldn't open her jaws. She still wasn't too upset, just pissed off because I gagged her. I moved across the trailer, pulled the latches, and let the bondage table down. That bitch took one look at the table and the rack that had been concealed behind it holding whips, harnesses, dildos and other devices related to bondage [*snicker*].

She came unglued!

She really got upset. I sat down beside her and told her in no uncertain terms what I thought of a whore who gave me the clap. About the aggravation, the problems with the girlfriends, the doctor bills, trips to the hospital, and that there was going to be a hell of a lot more retribution than just spanking: payback's a real motherfucker [*snicker*].

She just sat there trying to get loose and shaking her head back and forth—like *No, no, no,* but it was really *Yes, yes, yes.* I picked her up and sat her on the table, pushed her over on the middle of it, and positioned her on her back with her feet and arms pointed up. I held her that way and locked the chain around her neck that was attached to the table. That settled her down a little bit, but not much. A rope from the ceiling ring was tied to her ankles so she couldn't kick. The wrist bindings on the upper corner of the table consist of an adjustable chain that is attached to the corner of the table with a handcuff on the other end. Releasing one rope at a time, I secured her arms up to the upper corners of the table. Her legs were folded back, spread well apart, and also chained to the upper corners. That little whore was bouncing her ass all over the table while I finished strapping her down. I buckled table straps across her upper chest, her rib cage and her belly. Two more table straps were buckled over each side and pulled tight, holding her ass firmly down on the table. Two more straps went across the back of each knee, holding her legs securely down. That position gets uncomfortable as hell for a woman after a while, but it works pretty neat for me.

She was absolutely and totally immobilized. Couldn't move any part of her body at all except her head. Legs folded back and spread, and hips turned up with the asshole and pussy fully exposed. With her knees strapped down to the table on each side of her chest, the legs didn't interfere with access to her tits. They sagged off each side a little bit, but that was okay. God, they must have weighed five pounds apiece. The bitch was top-heavy. She had large fluffy cunt lips on each side of the slightly open pussy.

She was a hooker because she had a hundred-dollar-a-day drug habit; she had already told me that. That was why she agreed to let me spank her for a hundred bucks. She'd go get her drugs so she didn't have to work the rest of the night. I didn't tell her then that she wasn't going to be working for quite a while. She also didn't get the hundred-dollar bill. I'd already taken it out of her sock. Anyway, I picked up the whip and gave her about a dozen good whacks. . . .

By that time, I was horny as hell. I climbed on the table and put just a little bit of Vaseline right around the head of my dick and stuck it in her asshole. Apparently, she didn't get into that too much; it was nice and tight.

After that, I gave her a damn good ass-fucking.

CHAPTER 6

"I really don't have any feelings for her—I really don't miss her much at all."

Cindy Hendy's 22-year-old son, Shane 4/08/1999

Until Cindy Hendy moved to southern New Mexico in 1997, fifty-seven-year-old David Parker Ray had it all his own way. He never got into trouble with the law and whatever he was doing in the toy box was hidden from the outside world. The only people who knew what he was up to were his close-knit group of satanic followers. David Ray had covered his tracks and nobody except his victims, dead or alive, suspected him of any dirty deeds.

Enter thirty-seven-year-old Cynthia Lea Hendy.

Hendy grew up in Washington State and had three children when she fled the law in the spring of 1997 and moved with her then boyfriend, John Youngblood, to Truth or Consequences, New Mexico. She was on the run from convictions for grand theft and drug possession; she had already done jail time and didn't want to ever see the inside of a cell again.

By the end of 1998, in a pattern repeated over and over with the men in her life, she had Youngblood in front of a judge in the seventh judicial district court, accusing him of domestic violence. Her order of protection dated December 17, 1998, stated:

> He was threatening me and my friends with bodily injury, possibly death. john has beaten me before (1 yr. ago), and he also has beaten a friend of mine to near death behind the town museum, in the alley (1 yr. ago). we were living together and he pushed me down on december 14th, 1998, at 1603 Corzine Drive and threatened my life. he also threatened Candy Fairs life on 12/14/98 at 1603 Corzine Drive. he tried head-butting me, too.

Four days later, on December 21, 1998, Hendy changed her mind and wrote the following note to District Judge Thomas Fitch:

> District Judge,
>
> please disregard these charges that i have made in my statements against john youngblood and myself. as they are not true. john youngblood has not threatened me or anyone else. and i am very sorry that i lied and put john and myself in trouble for no reason. i have been in counseling for manik depression and am on medications. and i tend to go off for no reason.
>
> i do—and then i think later.
>
> john has been working hard, and i have been working off and on. but laid off. we love each other. please forgive me for trying to make trouble when there was no trouble to begin with. this will never happen again. i am going to talk with my counseler on this. i have done this before and its going to stop. and i am getting help. I am very sorry that i have put everyone through alot of

paper work, and your time. you certinly did not need this. and John did not need this kind of trouble either. please think this over. and reconsider and drop this so that we don't have to go to court and waste everyones time, money and paperwork.

i drink too much alcohaul—that's why i'm on medications.

very, very sorry.

please believe me, Judge Fitch.

Cynthia L. Hendy

By the time Cindy Hendy flip-flopped on John Youngblood, she already had experienced a close sexual relationship with both Roy Yancy and David Ray. Right after she drifted down to T or C, she fell in with Yancy, but it wasn't long until she threw over the younger man and moved in with David Ray. They were living together at the time Hendy got mixed up with Youngblood in seventh district court. A year earlier, Hendy had already gotten into trouble after fighting with Irwin Arrey, another boyfriend, and Ray had first met her when she was assigned to a work-release program at Elephant Butte Park back in 1997.

Ray might someday live to regret the day they first got to know each other.

Right after Hendy was arrested, a freelance reporter working for the *Globe* interviewed a man and a woman who knew Cindy well. The conversation took place in a dusty bar in the logging town of Everett, Washington. Neither one of them wanted to see their names in print, and after hearing what they had to say the reporter understood why.

The man had known Cindy Hendy for nearly thirty years. It was early in the afternoon of April 6, 1999, and right off the bat the skinny man in the black-and-blue plaid wool shirt told the reporter, "I like free beer—it tastes better!" Then for the next hour he unloaded his memories of the woman he'd known since they were little kids growing up in the same dirt-poor neighborhood right on the edge of Everett.

"When we were little kids, her mom worked down at the American Legion in Everett. She was a bartender, and she would never give the kids a dime. All of us were hungry. We'd be lucky to get a can of tuna fish out of her. We'd go over after school, and Cindy would have to beg like hell till her mother threw out a can of tuna fish just to get rid of us.

"When Cindy was just a little girl, her mom started going out with a guy named Dick. I seen Dick and Cindy's mother get in a fight and all of a sudden Dick hauls off and smashes her in the face—right in front of Cindy. When she was eight, her mom got married to another guy, and a couple of years later, her new stepfather tried to mess with her in bed. Cindy finally told her mom when she was barely eleven years old. The stepdad just told the mom he was drunk and when he crawled in bed with his daughter he must have thought it was his wife. The mom believed her husband and didn't believe Cindy and the two of them finally kicked her out of the house when she was almost twelve. From then on, Cindy was always the black sheep of the family. They called her a 'box of rocks,' and they still do.

"After she left home, she moved in with a guy named Mike—he's a notorious 'cedar pirate' up in Monroe, Washington. He used to drive his old World War One meat wagon down to the lumberyards and go over the fence and toss back blocks of cedar shingles and shakes that he would sell for drug money. Then, a few years later, Cindy lived with another guy named Abe and the two guys together were both notorious coke dealers. Cindy would live with the one who got her the most coke.

"Years later, Cindy and Abe were stealin' aluminum guardrails and tryin' to sell 'em at the metal scrapyards for drug money. They got caught. While they were out on bail, they went out to get an eight ball of cocaine and they ended up sellin' it directly to an undercover cop. Those were the crimes that made Cindy decide to hightail it out of town and run off to New Mexico.

"I started dating her when we were both sixteen. I owned an old beater Chevy, and one afternoon I saw her walkin' down the road and I pulled over and asked her out for the first time. I said, 'Hey, you want to get in my car and go drink beer in the gravel pits?' She looked me over real good and said, 'Sure'

"I remember she liked sex rough and hard. She'd dig in her fingernails and I'd have these big ole scratches on my back and it would take a long time until the claw marks would go away. She liked to have her ass slapped. She liked me to hold her down and tell her I was going to rape her. She always wanted to partner swap. She'd say to me that maybe we should 'rape somebody, maybe a prostitute.' I told her that shit might be fun to think about, but I wasn't gonna do it—ever. I told her flat out, 'I'm not gonna go to jail.'

"She was never ashamed of anything. She'd take her clothes off right in front of other people. She'd stand on the side of the road and take a piss. She really got off on 'doing it' in public.

"What really pissed me off was when she'd have sex with other men. I'd be comin' home from work and I'd see some other guy jumpin' out of the bedroom window. You could never trust her. I had a rich friend, a guy named Frank, and he had a real nice black Corvette. She latched on to him and he moved in a few days later and she stayed with him for about a month and then split.

"She'd even screw old men for money.

"One time we got into a fistfight and she went over to

Marysville and looked up this old man named Walter. He's in his sixties now. They came back with a U-Haul truck and backed it up to the house and hauled everything out. He'd give her money and she'd give him sex. She stayed with him for about a week.

"Another time Cindy was screwin' some 'Chink' doctor for painkillers. She'd trade the pain pills for coke.

"She'd even trade sex for dental work. A long time ago, she went downtown and had some doctor declare her mentally incompetent and she's been collecting SSI welfare money ever since. I swear she hasn't worked a day in her life. She'd spend all her money on booze and drugs and there wouldn't be any left over for her teeth. So when her mouth got sore, she'd go over to this place right outside of town. Every time she went there, the dentist would fill her teeth and she'd give him a big ole blow job."

The woman in the bar sat quietly and listened to the man talk. She'd known Cindy Hendy for twenty years and currently was a born-again Christian, a far cry from her lifestyle when she used to drink all night with Cindy in the downtown bars.

"She and her sister are two of a kind," she said. "Their mother was married six times to six different men, and between the two daughters, they have eight kids by eight different men. She even had sex with her sister one time and another time they were both in a motel room and they had sex with the same man. Cindy had all her kids raised by other people. She's had at least fifty boyfriends since I met her."

The ex-boyfriend interrupts.

"Her whole life revolved around cash registers—*ka-ching, ka-ching, ka-ching!* I had a real nice black Camaro one time. It was fast and I could always outrun the cops. She talked me into signin' the car over to her name, and then she sold my car and told me she never wanted to see me again.

"When we were together, she got pregnant by another guy. She'd always just sit around the house all day tryin' to figure out how to get high. She never paid for anything. One afternoon this guy comes over to clean the carpet and she's so horny she screws the goddamn carpet cleaner! His name was Eddie and seven months later baby Shane was born. He only weighed two pounds when he was born. He was in the hospital for five months. He almost died.

"When Shane was a little boy, Cindy and Eddie just passed him back and forth. One time, when he was seven years old, Cindy overdosed on sleeping pills, and I guess it was pretty scary for Shane. She was out stone-cold on the floor and he was shaking her. Shane's a good boy—he's still got a big heart. That night, he had to call the nine-one-one operator all by himself.

"Shane, he was never given nothin'. He was never given a brand-new bicycle or new clothes—or nothin'. Cindy would go off partyin' and leave him with her mother for days. He started stealing things. When he'd get in trouble and go to jail, Cindy would go into his bedroom and steal all his stuff, like his stereo, and sell it off and buy drugs.

"When he grew up, he turned into a thief, just like his dad. His father has been in and out of prison his whole life. He is illiterate. He can't even read or write his own name. Eddie's on the run from the law again right now—probably for burglary. He's the best thief in Snohomish County and that's what Shane does, too.

"They don't know how to do nothin' but steal.

"One time Shane was robbin' an elementary school and the cops sent in a German shepherd and he was all chewed up. Another time he stole firecrackers and set them off in the front yard and he caught the whole yard on fire. I remember one time he robbed a greenhouse down the street and Cindy was real happy with all the nice shrubs he brought home."

This time the woman interrupted the man.

"I know Cindy fought a lot with her boyfriends. Like cats and dogs. They'd hit each other in the head with lamps, throw television sets or whatever was in their way. Shane told me one time he was hiding under the bed and she kicked him in the head. He also told me that after years of fighting, he thought, she got used to the beatings and he wondered if she even enjoyed it in a strange kind of way.

"He's twenty-two years old now and he just got out of jail for having sex with some little fourteen-year-old girl.

The man in the black-and-blue plaid shirt had a lot more to say about the rest of the family. "Heather is nineteen and she belongs to me and Cindy. She's pregnant and just about ready to give birth to a baby boy. She talks to Cindy more than anyone else. When she was growin' up, though, it was real tough on her. Cindy used to read a lot of true crime and she'd always have these witchcraft books layin' around her trailer. She'd try to pawn 'em off on the kids. She and Heather used to get in these big arguments, and if you pissed her off, she'd get violent with you—she'd jump your shit. Cindy used to throw Heather down, grab her by the hair and beat her. One time I saw Cindy grab her by the hair, throw her down on the front porch and punch her in the face.

"It was over in minutes.

"Cindy's youngest kid is Muffy. She's twelve now and she's the one who really hates her mother. When Cindy got arrested, Muffy only had one thing to say.

" 'Good.'

"Her dad—his name was Doug—was a drug dealer who died when she was a kid. Cindy used to fire up coke a little bit, but Muffy's dad was a real 'banger.' Can you imagine how that kid feels when she realizes that her father died of a drug overdose when she was only four years old?

"She'll never see him again.

"Around Cindy, Muffy had to watch everything she said, or she'd get slapped. Muffy would always leave the room when her mother was around. Cindy would always have guys over and she'd tell Muffy, 'You squeal on me and I'll beat you.' Her number one rule was that Muffy not rat on her.

"One time I went over to Cindy's trailer and I knew that she hadn't been feeding Muffy. There was almost no food in the refrigerator. Cindy was determined that she herself was not going to get over one hundred five pounds. She was real thin and fairly good-looking, and that was all she cared about.

"I'll tell you a weird story about Muffy. Cindy used to live in this blue trailer up by the small town of Snohomish. One time Muffy was walking through the woods and she found one of her 'blankies' laying on the ground. There were four big butcher knives sticking in the ground and one of Muffy's stuffed animals in the middle of the blanket, with a note.

"It said, 'If you come back, I'll kill you.'

"Muffy ran home, hysterical. Cindy claimed she didn't know anything about it and moved out of the trailer the next day.

"Cindy took Muffy to New Mexico with her in 1997, when Muffy was only ten. She broke up with Youngblood and moved in with some guy named Arrey, and at night they would go out and party and leave Muffy locked in the trailer. One other time she ran off and left Muffy with the Mexicans. I think Cindy might have sold Muffy to the Mexicans for sex and that's why Muffy hates her so much. When Cindy met David Ray, she told Muffy not to go near the torture trailer, but I think Muffy knew what was going on in there—and I think it scared the hell out of her.

"Muffy's seen a lot. She doesn't even act like a little girl anymore.

"Cindy always wanted animals as pets, but she never took care of them. She had a five-hundred-dollar German shepherd dog she wouldn't feed and a three-hundred-dollar Persian cat that died. She was never satisfied with a mutt dog or a mutt cat.

"Her biggest problem in life, though, was violence."

At this point in the conversation the man had switched to drinking straight shots of Captain Morgan's rum. His tongue was loose.

"Let *me* tell you about her and violence!" he snorted.

"She liked to drink and she'd be fine until she had three or four drinks. Then she'd black out after that. Some girls have a button once they've had enough alcohol—they just go off. She's still like that to this day—she's a real Jekyll and Hyde. She'll come after you with almost anything—even an ashtray. People have seen Cindy pick up boards and hit guys over the head and knock 'em out. I warned other girls not to fight with her—that girl was one hundred five pounds of pure muscle.

"She can take on a two-hundred-fifty-pound girl and take her out.

"She could get anything she wanted—all she had to do was talk away. But she'd interpret stuff wrong. She thought everybody was sayin' something bad about her and then she would pick fights because she wanted to get rid of somebody.

"One time in a bar she got pretty violent. She was jumping on guys and beating on them. They were throwing her off. Then she started beating on women. She didn't like fuckin' women much; most of her friends were men. She left a lot of blood on the floor that night.

"Cindy is also a real jealous bitch. She was going out with my friend Kris, and one night Cindy was in the living room masturbating and Kris was in the bedroom screwing this big inflatable doll. Cindy finishes up and comes in the bedroom and sees what Kris is doin' and freaks out. She runs in the kitchen and gets this big butcher knife and comes back into the bedroom and attacks the doll, screaming at Kris, 'You love that thing more than you love me!' Not long after that, she tried to poison him with rat poison. A little while later, she busted Kris over the head with a beer bottle and split his whole head wide open.

"I'm positive she doesn't feel bad about anything she's done. She doesn't know right from wrong. All you gotta do is whip out a twenty-dollar bill and she's yours. If you were hard up, you could always go to the store with her. You could always be straight up with her. You'd just have to give her a little 'warm-up' and she'd pull her pants down and then tell you to hurry up. She's still that way, to this day.

"They got her dead to rights down in Truth or Consequences and she's probably going to hang. She's been in trouble all her life and she finally got caught. She played a little game of hopscotch with the law and the law won. I'm tellin' ya—it's the straight-up truth. The girl is a no-good bitch.

"David Ray better be careful, though. She's the dumbest blonde you ever seen, but she'll sell his ass out in a heartbeat.

"She'll turn on him like a vicious dog."

CHAPTER 7

I love reading books about serial killers, and now I'm living with one!

—Cindy Hendy, talking to a close friend, February 1999

At 4:44 P.M., on the afternoon of April 6, Cindy Hendy cut a deal with Assistant DA Jim Yontz and cut all her ties to David Parker Ray.

She had been charged with twenty-five felony counts and was looking at 197 years in prison if convicted, so she figured it was time to save herself. After accepting the plea bargain in return for valuable testimony against Ray and Dennis Roy Yancy, she was only charged with five felony counts and was facing a sentence ranging from a high of fifty-four years to a low of only twelve years.

She pleaded guilty in the Seventh District Court of New Mexico and the court papers indicated she pleaded guilty to two counts of Kidnapping in the First Degree for helping David Ray kidnap Angie Montano and Cyndy Vigil during February and March 1999. Montano was nabbed on February 17 and held until February 21; Vigil was nabbed on March 20 and held until March 22. The walls came crumbling down around Cindy Hendy on the afternoon of March 22 when Vigil stabbed her in the neck and ran down Bass Road buck naked, blowing the lid off the case once and for all.

Hendy also got nailed for two counts of Sexual Penetration (Rape) in the Second Degree for helping Ray illegally enter the bodies of both victims. The court documents specifically note that Hendy pleaded guilty to helping Ray penetrate the anal opening of Angie Montano and the vaginal opening of Cyndy Vigil.

And, last of all, she pleaded guilty to one count of Conspiracy to Commit Kidnapping in the Second Degree. That was the one that probably proved to be the ultimate undoing of Ray and Hendy. In the springtime of 1999, Cindy Hendy was excited about becoming a grandmother for the first time and made plans to sneak home to Everett, Washington, sometime before April 11, when her daughter Heather was due to give birth. David Ray didn't want her to go and told her if she wasn't careful, he'd be "looking for love in all the wrong places," according to Hendy's friend John Ashbaugh. Ray demanded that she help him round up a "little play thing" he could torture while Hendy was back home in Washington State. Hendy agreed and the two drove to Albuquerque on March 20 and found a pimp to introduce them to a hooker along Highway 66. Her name was Cyndy Vigil.

The day after Cindy Hendy was arrested on March 22, she was interviewed by two NMSP officers: Sergeant K. C. Rogers and Agent Wesley LaCuesta. Hendy seemed relaxed during her conversations with the two male cops, even telling K. C. Rogers that she was "out in the kitchen—making potato salad" when she heard Vigil fumbling with the padlock keys in the living room. "We were going on a picnic that afternoon," she told Rogers, "and I wanted everything to be real yummy." She talked openly with LaCuesta about Ray and his friends. When she was assigned public defender Xavier Edward Acosta two days later, he advised her to plead guilty in hopes of getting a break from the newly assigned seventh district court judge in the case, Neil M. Mertz.

"You might only get fifteen to twenty years," he told Hendy.

In the sealed documents filed and signed by Assistant DA James A. Yontz, Cindy Hendy pointed out that she had only known David Ray for eight months, adding, "I've only been doing this a few months, but David has been kidnapping, torturing and killing people for years." She told investigators that "David told me he'd killed at least fourteen people, both men and women, and he buried some of them in ravines and arroyos in eastern New Mexico." The report goes on to state that "one particular location which was pointed out by Hendy was a deserted ravine north of Truth or Consequences."

The police searched the ravine the next day but could not find a body.

She also told police that Ray sank dead bodies in Elephant Butte Lake, and the report states that he told her he did this "by cutting open the stomach of the victim so the victim would not float to the surface." Hendy also pointed out that Ray had told her he disposed of bodies between his residence and a prominent rocky island he could see from his kitchen window. When they first used nighttime search warrants to explore Ray's mobile home, the NMSP found detailed maps of Elephant Butte Lake with several Xs marked offshore from a stony outcrop along the eastern shore called "Kettle Top." They assumed this was the place where Hendy said he "sank the bodies."

The police knew that hundreds of people accidentally drowned—or were murdered—since the Rio Grande was dammed in 1916. If the lake were not forty-four miles long and four miles wide, the FBI and the NMSP might have considered draining it and looking for fresh missing-person DNA in the gigantic boneyard at the bottom of the lake. Time and expense made that an impossibility, however.

Cindy Hendy also acknowledged that she was with Ray when he bragged to friends in T or C that he knew what he would do if he were going to kill someone and dump their body in the big lake. "I'd know how to eliminate evidence," he told the curious group. "The thing to do is cut them down the belly, scoop out their guts, fill the chest cavity with cement weights and then use bailing wire to wrap them up." His idea was to turn them into "human achors" so they would sink to the bottom of the lake and not come bobbing to the surface, bubbling over with gases.

The police report did state that "in at least one of these situations police have been able to verify initial similarities to a body which had previously been discovered in Elephant Butte Lake." The person they were referring to was forty-one-year-old Billy Ray Bowers, a man who had been found wrapped in a blue tarp and floating in the lake back in September 1989. He had been killed by a single gunshot wound to the back of the head. Police also found out from Hendy that David Ray and Billy Bowers had worked together at the Canal Motors used-car lot in Phoenix between 1980 and 1988. Bowers was Ray's boss. Ray had leased his property on the western bluff overlooking Elephant Butte Lake back in 1984 and then quit his job at Canal Motors in 1988 and moved permanently to Hot Springs Landing in 1989, one year after Bowers had been reported missing from his job in Phoenix.

Hendy told the police that Ray killed his former boss because he didn't like him. She couldn't remember why.

Hendy lived with Ray and she had been in the toy

box plenty of times. Early on, Ray told her he "made special audiotapes to play for the victims as an introduction to what he was going to do to them." Hendy said she was there when he played one of the tapes for Cyndy Vigil and Angie Montano. Police had found six tapes dealing with everything from Ray telling girls he was going to use "dildos designed for an elephant" to describing how he made sadomasochistic videotapes to sell to collectors for "$1,000 each." In one of these tapes, Ray tells his victims how he had already kidnapped thirty-seven girls and these "wild urges" had led some psychiatrists to classify him as some sort of "sexual psychopath." Another tape even described how one night a girl bit down on his sexual organ during oral sex and he had to "cut her nipples off and made her swallow 'em." Just like Hendy claimed, all the tapes were designed to instill mortal fear in the mind of the listener.

She also told the police that David would "photograph victims in various stages of bondage and torture," and she went on to add that in the white cargo trailer "David would use makeup on his victims so they would photograph properly—especially if he felt portions of their bodies would not photograph well without makeup." Then she went on to verify that "at least two of the women displayed in photographs along walls had been killed."

Inside Ray's mobile home, agents had found a coffin-like box 7 feet long and 2½ feet square, lined with ½-inch brown carpet and rigged with D rings and black straps for tying people down. The chamber also had ventilation holes for breathing. Hendy told investigators that "David would store live captives in the coffin until he decided what to do with them."

During her interrogation, Hendy also "gave up" Dennis Roy Yancy. She said that Yancy was a hard-core satanic follower of David Ray's and she told them where they could find his name written in red paint on rocks out in the Jordana del Muerto, the sprawling desert east of town. During one lengthy interview, she told K. C. Rogers that "Yancy killed Marie Parker back in 1997 under instructions from David Ray. Roy strangled her to death while David sat nearby taking photographs."

Over 1,500 pieces of evidence had been gathered in the first 2½ weeks. Soon police were expanding the massive investigation, which was rumored to stretch from California to Florida. FBI agents were particularly interested in David Ray's work history and they prowled around, knocking on doors, in the neighboring states of Arizona, Texas and Oklahoma.

By the evening of April 6, FBI supervisory special agent Doug Beldon from Albuquerque was telling the dwindling press corps, "I'm very pleased with the progress of this case. The FBI and the state police are continuing to work hand in hand."

Back in Elephant Butte, overworked prosecutor Jim Yontz was leaning heavily on help from the hordes of FBI agents and the new revelations from his best new eyewitness, Cynthia Lea Hendy. Before he started getting too comfortable with all this new ammunition, Yontz figured he'd better send Hendy up to the Women's Correctional Facility in Grants, New Mexico, for a standard sixty-day psychiatric evaluation.

Just in case.

CHAPTER 8

One pair of black cowboy boots
Green T-shirt
Blue shirt
Green pants
Brown wallet with seven credit cards
White watch
Chap Stick
Two yellow fuses
Brown necklace
Black knife case, no knife

Property taken from David Ray upon his arrest and booking into the Sierra County Detention Center, 3/22/1999

FBI Agent John Schum had been assigned to conduct a lengthy interview with Ray shortly after his arrest. Before talking to Ray in person, Special Agent Schum wanted to take one more walk through the mobile home where David had lived between 1989 and 1999. Schum knew all about the toy box, but he felt like he might get a better feel for the man behind the crimes if he just strolled through the kitchen, living room, study, bedroom and bath where David Ray spent his time eating, sleeping and relaxing like any other normal person.

Schum knew that to David Ray, everything the man did in his everyday life was "normal."

Walking in the front door, the first thing Schum noticed was a copper crucifix hanging on the living-room wall—upside down—with the head of Jesus Christ pointing at the floor. On the opposite wall, there was a large framed painting of two black wolves running through the snow, chasing a white rabbit. On a mantel overlooking the fireplace, there was a picture of Cindy Hendy and her youngest daughter, Muffy, both smiling and looking happy.

Schum walked into the study and picked up a gray metal toolbox on the floor and opened it. Inside, he found a pearl-handled .38 Colt handgun, a small bottle of Hot Damn! Schnapps, a large hunting knife, a tube of Vaseline and a leather whip coiled around a small "fake" New Mexico State Police badge. Schum opened the closet and found a neatly pressed dark green park ranger uniform hanging from a hook right above a small collection of Remington hunting rifles.

He closed the closet door and walked over to Ray's desk, which was piled high with a large assortment of videotapes. There must have been at least a hundred movies stacked on top of, under and beside the desk. In the middle of the desk was the statue of a small white devil's skull with tiny horns protruding from the top of the head and a long tongue sticking out of the twisted, unhappy mouth. It looked like Ray had used the skull as a paperweight. Schum picked it up and fingered through some paperwork on the desk, noticing a list of torture recommendations typed up by Ray. Two tips stuck out in his mind: one that said "use a warm soldering iron up inside her vagina" and another that advised Ray's followers to "pluck pubic hairs out, one at a time, using a small pair of tweezers."

Schum leaned over next to a small bookcase of true-crime books and picked up a maroon binder full of

Ray's "fantasy" sketches and drawings. He thumbed through the sixty pages of pencil drawings of David Ray chasing young girls and doing what was probably just run-of-the-mill acts of sadistic pleasure to Ray's way of thinking: kidnapping, bondage, torture and killings. Schum was a religious man and the drawings nearly made him sick to his stomach. He feared that if these drawings were ever released to the public at large, America would spawn an epidemic of sexual sadists.

When he walked into the bedroom, Schum looked at the head of the bed and noticed a large olive green "dreamcatcher" hanging from a hook in the ceiling over the pillows. There was a small card attached to the web of interlacing threads and two long leather thongs with green plumes attached to the ends. Schum read the card:

> All the bad dreams are
> held in the web and all
> good dreams spiral back
> out to the dreamer. In
> the morning when the
> rays of the Sun fall
> on the Dreamcatcher,
> the bad dreams are
> released to burn up
> in the Sun.

Schum looked down on the floor and spotted a white plastic bucket with the same blue sweatshirt that Cyndy Vigil had been wearing the morning when she met Ray and Hendy on Central Avenue. The white letters on the front of the sweatshirt spelled out B.U.M. The broken green lamp was on the bed and the bloody ice pick was on the floor.

He walked around the end of the bed and into the bathroom and noticed another white bucket turned over on the floor—it had human feces smeared inside. Schum knew Cyndy Vigil was addicted to heroin and he wondered if she had been going through withdrawal during her three days in captivity.

He'd seen enough inside the house, so he took a stroll out to the front yard, where David had parked his white Dodge Ram Charger. He opened the driver's door and saw an emergency red beacon on the floor—the kind of flashing light the police put on the roof of their patrol cars when they're running down a suspect. Schum glanced up on the dash next to the steering wheel and saw a police scanner. David Ray had the perfect setup to play highway patrolman, Schum thought. Spot the victim, pull her car over late at night, and the rest was history.

The next afternoon, March 24, John Schum met with David Parker Ray at the Sierra County Correctional Facility on Date Street in downtown Truth or Consequences. Schum had been "profiling" killers for years and knew they were almost impossible to spot with the "naked eye." Yet, when he first shook hands with Ray, he was a little surprised that David Ray came off as such a polite and soft-spoken gentleman. It didn't take long to get down to business and John Schum just settled back in his chair and let David Ray do most of the talking. Their interview spanned three days and took over nine hours to complete. Unfortunately, David already had a court-appointed attorney and the 300 pages of notes were later ruled illegally obtained by the FBI.

Special Agent Schum asked David to start at the beginning.

"My grandmother's name was Dolly Parker. One afternoon, the year before I was born, her two youngest sons were left at the ranch while my grandpa went to town to get groceries. They lived thirty miles from Mountainair. Alden and David was left there alone.

Alden was fifteen and David was thirteen and they was playin' cowboys and Indians with real guns—there was always guns at the ranch and Alden shot David in the heart and killed him. There was a bullet in the old Winchester and Alden didn't know it.

"Alden put David's body in the old pickup and tried to, tried to take him to town and it run out of gas—so Alden run down a horse and rode to the highway and—and flagged a car and—and tried to get help.

"Of course, David was already dead.

"When she found out what had happened, my grandmother flipped out. I wasn't born yet—it was 1938—but I was born a year later and she decided that I was a reincarnation of her son, of her dead son David, and consequently I'm named David Parker Ray. . . . And that's why she always wanted to raise me.

"There really wasn't much affection in my childhood. I was there physically, but nobody paid any attention to me, you know, it was like . . . like I wasn't really there at all."

"What about the sexual fantasies?" asked Schum.

"This thing is literally tearing me apart," David Ray told John Schum. "For forty years my life has been a private hell."

Special Agent Schum asked David how he got interested in sex.

"When I was a little kid, my mother and father pawned me and my sister Peggy off on Dolly, my mother's mother, who lived on a farm up in the hills near Mountainair, New Mexico. There wasn't anything to do up there. My dad was a drunk and a drifter and every six months he would drop by and bring me a big pile of *True Detective* magazines, and when I was about ten years old, I started to have these fantastic dreams about raping and killing young girls. In the dreams I always used a broken beer bottle.

"I hated my grandmother. She didn't care about us.

By the time I was twelve years old, I was making my own bombs and setting off explosives all over the woods. My granny didn't have a clue—she was a real fruitcake! I blew up a lot of tree stumps when I was a kid.

"By the time I was fifteen, I had a private dungeon under a big piñon pine tree—I had a hangman's noose and a collection of broken beer bottles I planned to use on girls someday. When I got lonesome, I used to fuck a hole I dug in the ground.

"I was real shy when I was a child. I still am. I wouldn't even look at a girl—I always kept my eyes down. I didn't have my first date until I was eighteen years old. It was kinda funny what happened that night. We were parked by the Rio Grande in her car and she said she wanted me to drive home. I asked her for the keys and she dropped them down the front of her blouse and told me to come and get them.

"The next year I got married for the first time and I swear to God I was almost a virgin when I got married.

"I got married in 1959 and joined the army about a year later and went to Korea. My wife got pregnant in 1960 and we had a son. I came home on an emergency leave in 1961 to get a divorce. My wife was leavin' the baby alone while she went out to party. By the time I got back to the United States, my son was being cared for by the Department of Public Welfare and I asked them to give me custody. They did, and my mother, Opel, and my stepfather, Cecil, raised my son until I got out of the army.

"I got married again in 1962 when I was only twenty-two years old. Ninety days later, I went back to court and got another divorce. We just didn't click.

"In 1966 I married a woman named Glenda Burdine. We were married for almost fifteen years. We had a daughter, Glenda Jean, in 1967. Work was hard to find, so we divided our time between New Mexico, Texas and Oklahoma. I was twenty-six when we got married and I wanted to have a skill so I could make a living. I was going to aircraft mechanics school in Tulsa and we didn't have much money. One day, out of the clear blue sky, my wife decided she was going to bring home the bacon for us by . . . becoming a whore. I didn't like it at all, but it sure paid the bills. I still thought about the fantasy sometimes and she let me tie her up a couple of times, but that was it. I had this dungeon downstairs in our house and most of the time she didn't have the slightest idea what I was up to. By the late 1970s, I was designing custom-made torture equipment and selling the stuff in *Screw* magazine.

"I left her in 1981 when I found her in my bed with another man. It was her day off, so I knew it didn't have anything to do with money. I walked out the next day with Joannie Lee, her sister-in-law.

"We drove to California and for the next year we lived in Grass Valley, up in the Sierra Nevada Mountains. We grew marijuana up in the hills for a year and lived out of our trailer, and then one day we just decided to leave. We wanted to get regular jobs. We drove down to the turnoff at Death Valley—the spot where the road forks one way to Las Vegas and the other way to Phoenix. We flipped a coin and I won, so we went to Phoenix.

"I got a job as a mechanic at Canal Motors, a used-car dealership in Phoenix. We got married in 1983 and I changed my name back to my mother's maiden name, Parker. We were David and Joanie Lee Parker. I still had the fantasy, and about every six or eight months, I would get the urge. I can't tell you what it felt like working around all that temptation—anytime of day you could see them—hookers—four or five of them walking by, night and day. I started hiring girls to help relieve the pressure of my fantasy. I'd hire a hooker to do the dirty deed and pay her three hundred dollars an hour.

"I'd whip them, but I'd never break the skin—never.

We had a code word we would use when it got too rough. When it got too painful for one of them, all they had to do was say the code word out loud."

"And what was that word?" asked Special Agent Schum.

"Raspberry," answered Ray.

"That's all?" asked Schum.

"Yeah, raspberry, that's all.

"There was no way Joannie Lee would take part in the fantasy. She knew what I liked, but she wouldn't let me use her. She was jealous of the fantasy. We kind of drifted apart. Over the years she just got more and more crazy. She was having epilepsy attacks and she started drinking real heavy, and one time she held a pistol up to my head. I couldn't take it anymore. Finally I had to send her home to her mother in Pennsylvania. That was 1994, and after she left, I changed my name back to David Ray.

"For the next three years, it was just me and the fantasy.

"I'm past the point where therapists can help me. One year I had six different shrinks. I tried to change, but it didn't do no good. Anyway, it didn't seem like some of 'em was too bright in the head. They didn't understand my problem, I guess you could say.

"By 1994 I was getting the urge every two or three months. After that, it really got worse, especially after I started taking Viagra. I even started taking other pills to suppress my sex drive. Nothing worked. I have this master sketch notebook of drawings—some of them are real frightening. The sketches kind of track the progress of the fantasy. If the FBI would like, I'll give you the drawings. Maybe you could help other people with the same problem. If I can help other people, I'd be glad to—it's a curse that destroys your life."

Agent Schum thanked Ray for the offer.

"I also read a lot of true-crime books," added David.

"They kinda fuel the fantasy. I've been collecting books on serial killers for the last fifteen years. I've read all twelve of the Ted Bundy books and, of course, I really like Stephen King. I also like Dean Koontz. I read a book by Christine McGuire called *Perfect Victim* in 1989, and after that, I changed the way I did things. The killer in the book used to put a woman's head inside a box so she couldn't see what was going on around her and that really turned me on. I've got a library of about seventy-five true-crime books and the FBI can have those, too."

Again, John Schum thanked David Ray for his generosity.

"I was real lonely before I met Cindy Hendy. She moved here in 1997 and I met her after she got into trouble for fighting with one of her boyfriends—I think his last name was Arrey. Judge Fitch sentenced her to do community service work at Elephant Butte State Park, where I work. The first day I met her, she told me in a real matter-of-fact voice, 'I don't like women, and I don't like men much, either.'

"It didn't take long until I fell madly in love with her—even right now, I love her dearly.

"I did not discuss this thing from my past with Cindy. . . . I'm a very private person and I'm very ashamed of this hang-up. Slowly I manipulated her to my fantasy. She allowed me to do anything to her body, even though she didn't like it. I softened my fantasies for her because I didn't want to alienate her. Once I showed her my album of drawings and it scared her."

Special Agent Schum and David Ray did their dance for several more hours. Schum used the same mellow, easygoing approach that worked so well for him so many other times when he was facing down a difficult and intelligent criminal. At one point Ray reminded Schum that he knew Schum was a profiler and he realized Schum was just doing his job. Finally, when it looked safe, Ray gave Schum his best shot. And Agent

Schum listened with professional respect for what he thought David was trying to say.

"I am potentially dangerous," said Ray. "I'm like a time bomb—and one way or the other, the problem stops here. I'm fantasizing about ten- and eleven-year-old girls, so if it takes a sterilization, that's what I'll do, you know. I'm serious about that. I like to cause pain, but I don't like to physically, actually hurt a girl. I'm old and I'm tired and there's not going to be any more incidents.

"I get the urge every two or three months now," said Ray. "This thing is ruining my life. I've been having the fantasy since I was ten years old, and gradually it has gotten worse and worse. The fantasy is a curse for everyone around me, but somehow I'm going to beat it, one way or the other."

CHAPTER 9

Roy's not a violent person at all. He can't even spank my kid, much less murder anybody.

—Christina Yancy, before visiting her husband, Roy, in the Truth or Consequences Jail, 4/11/1999

On April 9, 1999, agents from the FBI and the New Mexico State Police arrested twenty-seven-year-old Dennis Roy Yancy, a close friend of David Ray's, Jesse Ray's and Cindy Hendy's. He was arrested at the Black Range Restaurant in T or C, where he had just started a job as a fry cook only ninety minutes before police hauled him away. Doug Beldon, tight-lipped agent in charge of the FBI investigation, issued a brief press release on the arrest of the third suspect in the David Parker Ray case.

"We arrested Dennis Roy Yancy, charging him with the July '97 kidnapping and murder of Marie Parker."

Jackie Williams, owner of the Black Range Restaurant and Motel, was there when the police rushed in and handcuffed Yancy. "He was a clean, good-looking guy," she said. "I thought he was going to be a good cook. He made real good biscuits. He was staying in room eighteen of the motel and the FBI agents investigating him were staying just three doors down in room fifteen. It was crazy! I think he knew they were hot on his heels. Roy was staying with his wife and her little girl and, I swear, he was constantly on the phone, tying up our only phone line in the office. When they arrested him, he went quietly."

On Saturday, April 10, Roy Yancy took the police out to an isolated stretch of Highway 195, north of T or C and west of Elephant Butte Lake. They were hoping to dig up the body of Marie Parker. The rolling hills were covered with creosote bushes and stretched for miles in all directions. After digging all day, the authorities came up empty-handed. By this time, Yancy had not pleaded guilty, but he was completely cooperating with the police. On the drive back to town, Roy turned to a police investigator from the NMSP and gave his version of why they didn't find Marie.

"David must have moved the body," he said.

State policeman K. C. Rogers questioned Yancy later that afternoon. They talked for hours and finally Rogers asked him to write it all down. For a moment, Yancy balked, but then signed a confession.

Afterward, K.C. Rogers didn't have too many nice words for Dennis Roy Yancy.

"Poor bastard—he was a loser with women. David Parker Ray was offering him free sex and he just couldn't turn it down."

On Sunday, April 11, Yancy was sitting in his cell at the Sierra County Detention Center when he got a visit from his pregnant wife, Christina. Yancy didn't know she had gotten pregnant by another man and he used her as a sounding board to vent his feelings about what went down back in 1997 on the night he killed Marie Parker. After he talked to his wife, she walked outside and disclosed the conversation to a very surprised reporter for the Associated Press, Chris Roberts.

"Roy said he and another person went to the Blue

Waters Saloon on July fifth to conduct a drug deal for Marie. Once outside, the other person held a gun on Marie and told her to get in the back of a pickup truck. They left and went over to David Ray's place and someone else held a gun on Marie while David took pictures of Roy killing her. He thinks the police have pictures of him killing Marie. He strangled her, I guess."

Dennis Roy Yancy married Christina in 1997, thereby having the distinction of marrying one woman and killing another, all in the same year. Even though he was a murderer, Christina stood by her man, telling the AP that Roy was manipulated into it. "He didn't want to kill her is what he said.

"I'm worried he's going to get the death penalty," she told the press.

Little chance of that happening in New Mexico. Although the neighboring states of Texas and Oklahoma routinely execute murderers (Texas once executed eight men in one month and a short time later Oklahoma tied that record), New Mexico was more like old Mexico, where nobody dies for killing another human being. Since the U.S. Supreme Court brought back the death penalty in 1976, New Mexico had never executed a single murderer. In fact, the last execution to take place in 1960—not that murder and mayhem take a holiday in the Southwest. The rate of violent crime in New Mexico is notoriously high.

Dennis Roy Yancy was already beginning to feel the pressure of life in a small-town jail, where everyone knows everyone else. David Ray was already making friends and Christina told the AP that after just two days in jail, Roy had already gotten a note passed along by another inmate. It said: "Rats die in jail."

The week after Dennis Roy Yancy was arrested, prosecutor Jim Yontz charged Yancy with five felony counts: kidnapping, first-degree murder, conspiracy to commit kidnapping, conspiracy to commit murder and, finally, tampering with evidence—which explained why he was on the phone twenty-four hours a day at the Black Range Motel. Yontz asked that Yancy be held without bail and the Sierra County Magistrate Court agreed with the assistant DA. If convicted, Yancy was facing life in prison plus 46½ years. Jim Yontz made it clear to Roy Yancy that if he was going to get a reduced sentence, he had to cooperate in the continuing investigation of his "violent coach," David Ray.

Two years before he met Ray, Dennis Roy Yancy had already been a well-known fixture on the scene in Truth or Consequences. He'd gone to Hot Springs High School and by the time he was sixteen he'd been arrested for the first time on a burglary charge. In the fall of 1987, he and two other men broke into the house of a local schoolteacher and stole a stereo and a computer, dumping the computer in Mud Canyon, south of town. He was arrested just a few days before Halloween, 1987, and many residents of T or C didn't think it was any big surprise that he was in big trouble with the law.

Dennis—as he was known to the locals at the time—and a small group of friends were in a satanic cult and that very fall they'd been terrorizing the community. They had been turning over gravestones and then spray-painting them with satanic graffiti, killing small pets, even going so far as threatening to kill small children. In 1987 city officials in T or C actually canceled all Halloween festivities in town and parents locked their doors and kept their children at home, some fearing for their children's lives.

The *Sentinel* went so far as to hire an undercover reporter to infiltrate the gang and report on their evil ways. The reporter got sucked into the group and refused to expose his new friends. One of those friends was Dennis Yancy. The reporter was fired by the *Sentinel*, but not before five-year-old Frances Baird's grandfather wrote a blistering editorial condeming the activities of

Dennis Roy Yancy and his ilk. Mr. Baird's column from October 21, 1987, takes dead aim at Yancy and his buddies—without ever mentioning them by name:

> I know that by revealing what I am about to write about it will probably result in vandalism to our property. It is time that the local school leaders know that there is a SATANIC MOVEMENT in our local system that is attempting to enroll followers. The recent vandalism of the high school was painted over quickly, but not before students could see that SOME OF THOSE CHARACTERS WERE SYMBOLS OF THE SATANIC CULT.
>
> We must get rid of this social vermin and prevent the conversion of any more of our young people.
>
> It should not be allowed to grow.

While Yancy was flirting with the devil, David Parker was in Phoenix, arguing daily with his boss, Billy Ray Bowers. The two men did not like each other, but they were forced to work side by side every day trying to repair and sell used cars. In the fall of 1988, a year after Yancy had his brush with the law, Bowers disappeared from work one day. It was September 22, 1988, and his family immediately offered a $5,000 reward for information leading to his safe return.

A year later, on September 28, 1989, a fisherman found the body of a dead man floating off McCrea Canyon, along the eastern shore of Elephant Butte Lake. The unidentified body had been wrapped in a blue tarp and roped to two heavy boat anchors—weighing eleven pounds apiece. He had a single bullet hole in his head and $49.47 in his pockets, but no identification. Police put out an all points bulletin to neighboring states, but they were unable to identify the five-foot ten-inch white male in his late thirties or early forties.

For ten years the body remained unidentified. It wasn't until Cindy Hendy told the police that David Ray had told her he killed Billy Ray Bowers that the authorities checked dental records and ID'd the "other" man from Canal Motors.

On April 16, they called his oldest son and Michael Bowers traveled over a thousand miles from his home in Kansas City to come to T or C to retrieve the body of his long-lost father. On April 17, he was taken out to the town cemetery and police led him to his father's grave site, the last resting place of Billy Ray Bowers for the previous ten years. Michael looked down at the undisturbed headstone and read the simple inscription: "MR. JOHN DOE" SEPTEMBER 28, 1989.

Ten long years later, in the spring of 1999, twenty-two-year-old Marie Parker was probably in the ground, too, but nobody knew where she was buried. She'd been missing since July 5, 1997.

A week before the police found her abandoned car in the parking lot of the Blue Waters Saloon, she and her two little girls, four and five, had been kicked out of their apartment for not paying the rent. They were living in a pup tent on the western shores of Elephant Butte Lake. She was camping at Hot Springs Cove, just north of David Ray's trailer. In fact, she had borrowed the tent from Ray, and when her campsite got too messy for him, the fastidious Ray had come down and chewed her out.

"I've got a good reputation in the community," he told her. "I don't want it ruined."

By this time in her life, Marie Parker was a junkie, unable to stay away from the easy supply of "meth" and "coke" in Truth or Consequences. Parker had been trying to kick her drug habit for years, but according to her friends, she just wasn't strong enough to say no. Her main drug dealer was David Ray's daughter, Glenda Jean "Jesse" Ray.

Two nights before she vanished, Marie Parker had gotten into a loud argument with Jesse Ray at the Kettle Top Cafe, right across the street from the Blue Waters Saloon. According to the former owner of the café, Roy Yancy was there, too. The whole time he was there, Marie was very nervous. She had dated Yancy years before, but now she thought he was sort of "strange" and she always felt uncomfortable around Jesse.

"Jesse had the 'hots' for Marie, and Marie didn't want to have sex with her. At the time Jesse rode a big motorcycle and she had a nickname in T or C. They called her 'the dyke on the bike.' "

The next night, Marie Parker was at Raymond's Lounge at the intersection of North Date and Marie Street in T or C when Roy Yancy walked in. Parker didn't want to have anything to do with him. After they broke up, she had not remained friends with him. Her friend Julie Lawrence saw the fear in her eyes that night.

"Marie tried to avoid him as much as possible," said Lawrence. "She was very afraid of Roy and wanted to leave immediately."

The night she vanished was a hot July 5 and she was in the Blue Waters Saloon with four of her friends. The last person she spoke to was Clay Hein. Just before midnight, Jesse Ray offered to give her a ride somewhere; Marie was hesitant but said yes. She came up to Clay to tell him what was going on. He never forgot what she said: "I've got to go home and check on my daughters."

"That was the last time any of us saw her," said Hein. "She never came back."

Drugs had been an off-and-on problem for years for Marie Parker. At one time she was engaged to Larry Brock of Center Point, Texas. He wanted to marry her, but he also wanted her to change friends. "I couldn't live with the fact that she was running around with druggies," he said. "I gave her a ring and a few days later she took it to a pawnshop in Truth or Consequences. The ring was nice—it was all I could afford, but it was still a half-carat gold ring. She sold it for two hundred dollars."

The last night Marie had a warm bed to sleep in was July 1, 1997. She was staying in an apartment with her kids and her half brother, Tom McCauley. They couldn't afford the rent. Years later, when McCauley read in the *Sentinel* that Dennis Roy Yancy had admitted to killing his sister, he was visibly shaken. "It angers me to hear about these people in T or C, these so-called friends. I don't understand how they could do such a thing. My sister was a wonderful person who shared with the poor, often giving food and shelter to homeless people. I want people to know what a good person she was. She never once did anything to deserve this. Nobody deserves anything like this."

The last morning Marie Parker showed up at work, she was working at the Fast Stop Convenience Store on South Date Street in Truth or Consequences. Her good friend Sonya Hall still works as a cashier at the store and thinks about Marie every week. She still feels sorry for her, and especially for her children.

"She wasn't ever right in the head," said Hall. "Things were always happening to her. One time one of her daughters was missing and Marie was just out of her mind. She was going nuts. I said, 'Marie, have you checked your van?' She told me no and so I checked it myself and, sure enough, there was the kid—Sierra was playing on the floor in the back. I think the little girl was only three years old at the time.

"If you knew Marie, she wasn't a degenerate at all—she was just mentally ill, the poor thing. She was frantic all the time. I don't think most of the time she was in her right mind."

CHAPTER 10

In all my years working as a reporter in downtown Los Angeles, I never saw anything this frightening.

—Betsy Phillips, reporter for the the *Herald,* in T or C, 8/08/1999

Jim Yontz took over as lead prosecutor the day after his forty-seventh birthday, and from the beginning the big, burly cop-turned-prosecutor felt he had a lot to prove. He was always the strong guy who tried to go out and save the weak people of the world, and in one moment his whole world had come crumbling down all around him.

In the summer of 1998, Yontz was head of the Narcotics Bureau operating out of Albuquerque. He was struggling to come to grips with his mother slowly dying from cancer. He was a married man, and just after midnight on August 15, undercover police picked him up with a prostitute on Central Avenue, on the eastern outskirts of Albuquerque. The cops spotted his pickup truck parked in an alley just west of Wyoming Boulevard and Highway 66, and when they pulled up behind and asked Yontz to get out, he was very upset because he knew the whole situation looked bad. He even started to cry when they asked him what he was doing with "a known hooker." He claimed he was driving through a high-crime area along Highway 66 when he saw a woman walking alone. He stopped and offered her a ride. He denied he gave her money for sex. The officers found no evidence of money changing hands and let him go, but they reported the incident to their boss.

Word got back to the Albuquerque district attorney and he suspended Yontz, pending an investigation. Five days later, James A. Yontz resigned under pressure, strongly denying that he'd done anything wrong. At the time he told the AP: "I often stop to help people out. I don't drink. I don't smoke. I don't do drugs. I lead a very dull life. I only stopped to help a woman I feared might be a crime victim. I just didn't do anything wrong. I only tried to help somebody."

A year later, he found himself assigned to an assistant DA job out in the small town of Socorro, New Mexico; as luck would have it, he was in charge of the biggest crime case in New Mexico history. In his own quiet, straightforward way, he expected to convict David Ray and his cohorts and save his good reputation that he developed over twenty-six years in law enforcement—seventeen years as a prosecutor.

He got his first public chance to corral the bad guys at a preliminary hearing scheduled for David Parker Ray on April 15 and 16 at the Sierra County Courthouse in T or C. Yontz normally worked out of the bigger Socorro Courthouse, but this time he was crammed into a little chamber that barely held sixty spectators behind the two small wooden tables facing the judge's bench and the witness table only a few feet away.

That Thursday and Friday, Jim Yontz went up against two men with good legal credentials. Men he expected to face over and over during the rest of 1999: Jeff Rein, the soft-spoken, handsome thirty-six-year-old defense attorney for David Ray, and Judge Neil P. Mertz, the chain-smoking fifty-three-year-old father of two grown children who ran his court with a tight fist and was now firmly in charge of all criminal trials in what the press had dubbed the "New Mexico Sex/Torture Case."

On the first day David Ray walked into court with his head down and his shoulders slumped. As soon as Mertz outlawed all cameras in the courtroom, Ray perked up and seemed to manage an occasional "smirk," at least according to Frances Baird, ace reporter for the Sierra County *Sentinel.* Frances was a tall, leggy blonde with horn-rimmed glasses and had been born into a newspaper family. According to her mother, Frances always had "ink in her blood." Myrna Baird, publisher of the *Sentinel,* did not like the idea of her teenage daughter sitting there right next to David Ray and listening to witnesses talk about an old man with a dirty mind and filthy habits. But there was no way Frances was going to miss the story of the century in the tiny town where she had spent all of her days.

April 15 and 16 brought three of the major players in the Sex/Torture Case together under the watchful eye of an ambitious and experienced-beyond-her-years reporter.

It didn't take Jim Yontz long to call his first witness on the morning of April 15. Angelique Montano, twenty-seven, looked haggard and confused as she took the witness stand. She didn't want her one blue eye and one brown eye to be noticed, so she tried not to make eye contact with anyone. Her voice quaking, she told the story of how she ended up spending five days with Ray and Hendy between February 17 and 21, 1999. She told the truth, except for the part about the cake mix. At least Yontz hoped she was telling the truth.

"I'd been livin' in Elephant Butte for about two and

a half years, and the day it happened, I went to David's to pick up some cake mix. Cindy Hendy gave me the mix so I could make my boyfriend a birthday cake on February seventeenth. Me and Cindy were inside the house when David went outside and came back with a tool box and pulled a dagger out. I thought he was kidding until he punched me in the face.

"They took off my clothes and right away they put on handcuffs, shackles and a metal collar around my neck. They chained me to a bed in the den and Hendy gave me some kind of orange pill.

"I was there two days and nothing happened until the third day when David got off work and finished dinner. He took me out to a trailer he and Hendy called the toy box, tied me down, blindfolded me and then put electrodes on my breasts and vagina and shocked me with a stun gun. Then they brought me back inside the mobile home and chained me to a bed while they watched a Stephen King movie.

"They made me have sex with them on the fourth day, and on the fifth day I tried to be friendly to Ray so he would let me go home. It worked, and they drove me out to I-25 on Saturday and I hitched a ride back to town. I'm surprised I made it out of there. I didn't know if I was going to see my kid again."

The next witness was the off-duty cop who just happened to be driving down I-25 when he saw Montano walking next to the freeway.

"I stop for all women. I seen her waving down traffic and ten minutes after she got in my car, she says, 'If I tell you something, you're not going to believe it.' She didn't know I was a cop when she told me the story. I thought she might have been making something up just to get a ride. If I had thought it was one hundred percent legitimate, I would have taken her to the police right then and there."

Angie Montano and Cyndy Vigil had never talked

until April 15, yet they were bound like twin sisters by the fact that they were both tortured at the lakeside mobile home of David Ray and Cindy Hendy in the first three months of 1999. The big difference was that Montano was taken to the toy box, whereas the younger Vigil managed to escape before David had a chance to take her outside.

After Montano stepped down from the witness stand, Cyndy Vigil, twenty-two, stood up and walked forward and took her seat at the witness stand. She had been kidnapped and kept from March 20 until March 22, but unlike Angie, people did believe her story. Yontz told her right after the escape that she was the true hero of the story—if she hadn't stabbed Hendy in the neck and run away, David Ray would still be doing business. Clutching a rosary and listening to her grandmother Bertha whisper support from the front row, Cyndy Vigil unloaded her story in front of the steely eyes of Judge Mertz.

"I met Ray and Hendy on the corner of Central and Washington in Albuquerque on Saturday morning, March twentieth. He acted like he was a john and said he wanted to pay me for oral sex, so I got into his RV. All of a sudden, he shows me a badge with a little star and he tells me I'm under arrest for soliciting sex. Then Hendy comes out of the bathroom and tries to handcuff me. I thought something was weird, so I tried to get away—to just run. I screamed. They grabbed me and handcuffed me to some kind of a 'screw thing' in the trailer and then David drove away.

"After a while they stopped, took off all my clothes and put a metal collar around my neck and shackles on my feet. At one point they put a leather mask over my head that had a zipper for a mouth and no eyeholes."

At this point in the hearing, Yontz showed Cyndy Vigil the metal neck collar and asked her if it looked like the one she was wearing when she escaped. Vigil grabbed it with both hands, looked at it for a moment, then dropped it on the wooden witness stand and started to cry. She buried her face in her hands and turned away from the packed courtroom of spectators. She was trying to hide the horror written all over her face. Cathy McClean, the court cerk, gave her a hug and then Vigil turned to David Ray, who was sitting only three feet away. She tried to stare him down; then she shouted at the top of her lungs: "How could you do this to me? You sorry bastard! YOU BASTARD!"

Judge Mertz, looking red in the face, cleared the tiny courtroom, and after Vigil got some minor medical help, everyone was slowly ushered back into the proceedings. Mertz, in the meantime, moved David Ray and his attorney Jeff Rein to the other side of the courtroom, as far away from Vigil as possible. In a calmer voice Vigil continued telling her story.

"When we got to his house, I didn't know where I was. They took me inside and chained me to a bed. They forced me to have sex with them, and then David poured hot gravy on my belly and had a dog, a German shepherd, come in from outside and lick it off. . . ."

Frances Baird looked around the hushed courtroom and it looked to her like everyone was going to throw up, especially the women. During a brief lull, David Ray caught her watching him and smiled and gave her a big wink. Gulping, she looked down at her notebook and kept trying to take notes on Vigil's testimony. Her hands were shaking the whole time.

"After they chained me to the bed," Vigil continued, "I went to sleep to try to forget about where I was. The next day was Sunday and they put clips on my breasts that were connected to wires that went through a pulley system with lead weights at the end. While I was hooked up to the pulley system, Ray shocked me with a cattle prod to make me squirm. When I tried to wiggle free, it pulled my breasts out away from my body. I have small breasts and one time they looked like they had been pulled out at least a foot away from my chest. It hurt so bad. . . . I was screaming.

"That night they used my neck collar to hang me from this thing in the ceiling and then they would whip me with leather straps and put these big, huge dildos in my body.

"On Monday morning David Ray went to work and I saw my chance to escape. Cindy Hendy was out of the room for a second and I moved my feet to reach a coffee table holding the keys to the padlock. Just after I grabbed the keys, Hendy walked in the room and ran over and started pulling my hair. I unlocked the padlock and pulled the chain out of the I bolt on the wall. Then Hendy grabs this big green glass lamp and hits me over the top of the head, trying to knock me out. So I looked on the floor and there was this ice pick and I grabbed it and stabbed her in the back of the neck. Then I ran out the front door and started to run as fast as I could go. All I was wearing was a dog collar around my neck."

At this point Cyndy Vigil broke down and wept.

"I ran and ran and ran. It seemed like I ran forever. I seen some door open in some trailer—some lady was in some trailer and I just grabbed her and told her to help me."

On Friday, April 15, Jim Yontz called one more witness, John Briscoe, a state trooper who had been inside both the house and the toy box. Briscoe read off a long list of David's sex toys: chairs with stirrups, a coffin with a fan, dildos, rings, clips, chains, eyebolts and hooks, duct tape, dog collars, ankle-and-knee spreaders—the list seemed to go on and on. He added information about the books and drawings and photographs of missing victims and even showed pictures of the "voodoo dolls." He finished his testimony by reading from a list of "do's and don'ts" created by Ray for other people who were helping him handle his captives, including little suggestions like "don't cut her any slack," "play with her sex organs," "rape her," "whip her and use electro shock" and on and on and on.

Judge Mertz bound David Ray over for a jury trial.

As Frances Baird left the courthouse, she remembered the first thing that struck her when she heard about the inside of Ray's house. "He didn't have a Bible," she remembered thinking. She'd never heard of anyone who didn't have a Bible in their house. On her way to her car, she overheard Cyndy Vigil's grandmother talking to Angie Montano's mother, comparing notes on what had happened to the two young women they loved. Bertha Vigil told the younger woman how horrible it still was for her granddaughter.

"Even when she's awake, she's still having nightmares."

Baird introduced herself to Jim Yontz in the parking lot and he told her anytime she needed information about the case just to give him a call at home. They discussed Neil Mertz and Baird told Yontz she'd known the judge since she was a little girl. She told the prosecutor she thought Ray was the "ultimate sicko" and she knew Judge Mertz would do a good job of managing the upcoming big trial.

"I love Judge Mertz like a father," she said, smiling.

She waved good-bye to Yontz and hurried home to the offices of the *Sentinel*, run by her mother. She had a deadline to meet.

The next week, her story ran on the front page under big headlines: STORIES OF TORTURE TOLD DURING HEARING. Truth or Consequences had three weekly newspapers, selling a combined total of 10,000 copies a week, but there was no doubt in Frances Baird's mind where most people would go to get the best scoop on true crime: the *Sierra County Sentinel*.

Down in the left-hand corner of the front page, the *Sentinel* always printed a little prayer box called "Quiet Moments." On April 21, 1999, Frances Baird dominated the top of the front page of the newspaper, but to the many senior citizens who made T or C and Elephant Butte Lake their home away from home, the inspirational message at the bottom of the page was the first thing they read when they picked up their Wednesday afternoon paper. It was always uplifting:

Dear Heavenly Father,
How good it is that instead
of treating us as we justly
deserve,
You are there,
waiting to forgive our
wrongs.

CHAPTER 11

I like to read true crime—if it's true.
—Letter from Glenda Jean "Jesse" Ray, 8/15/1999

Like a lot of the drifters moving in and out of Truth or Consequences, Glenda Jean Ray always seemed to be somewhere else when things got ugly. Right after Marie Parker was killed in the summer of 1997, she and Roy Yancy left town and migrated to their favorite hangout, Galveston, Texas. They lived in a hotel for a year, and after things had cooled down, they came back to Truth or Consequences in the fall of 1998.

Glenda had returned to Galveston when her dad got arrested on the afternoon of March 22, 1999. Her friend "Big Debbie" Fisk called and persuaded her to return to T or C, and the next day, Glenda wrote to another friend that she was going to come back and defend her dad and "separate fact from fiction." She drove home nonstop and moved into her dad's trailer on Bass Road the next day.

It wasn't long until the FBI subjected her to two intensive interrogations about her past history with her father.

Jim Yontz wanted to find out what her connection was to her father, so he asked Special Agent Wesley Weller of the FBI to interview Glenda right after she returned from Galveston.

Weller sat down with an extremely nervous Jesse, who stumbled over her words again and again during the three-hour interview.

"I grew up in Temple, Texas," she told him. "My dad worked as a mechanic on the Santa Fe Railroad for about three years between 1977 and 1980. He was gone a lot when I was growing up. Everybody in the family knew about my dad's fetish. They always have, you know. I learned right away to keep my mouth shut. It's just something you don't talk about. He's always had this stuff, like padded leather straps, you know—and it's hard to hide stuff like that from kids—they're so curious, you know.

"Dad's always been the golden boy, Grandma's favorite."

Weller had read all the notes from Special Agent Schum's nine-hour interview with David Parker Ray. While Jesse was telling him how her father was the smartest guy in the family, he chuckled to himself, remembering what David had said about growing up with his granny outside of Mountainair, New Mexico, known in the 1940s and 1950s as "the Pinto Bean Capital of America." Weller recalled there was no one watching the bored little David while he spent his free time toying around with explosives. Asked to describe how he was raised as a small boy, Ray only had one opinion of his grandmother: "She was a real fruitcake."

On Monday morning, April 26, Jim Yontz issued orders and the long arm of the law finally caught up with Glenda Jean "Jesse" Ray. Police came and arrested thirty-one-year-old Jesse Ray, charging her alongside her father with teaming up to kidnap and torture Kelli Van Cleave back in the summer of 1996.

Jesse was a good pool player and a popular local drug dealer. She usually could be found hanging out with her friends at Raymond's Lounge, a rock-and-roll biker bar on the main drag running through T or C. She dealt coke, marijuana and the cheap drug that was sweeping the nation, "meth"—known to people on the streets as "the poor man's cocaine." Jesse was the mother of a seven-year-old daughter, Kayla, who was growing up in Louisiana and living with her granny. Kayla was being raised by Jesse's mother, the former Glenda Lois Ray, who was now remarried and going by the name of Glenda Blood.

According to long-standing rumors in town, Jesse's daughter was fathered by David Parker Ray shortly after Jesse moved up from Texas in 1992 to live with him. "The kid is his," states ex-druggie Gail Astbury, Jesse's pal. "That's the reason Jesse's so sick all the time," added Astbury. According to another friend, Jo McClean, Jesse was always there for her father when he reached out to her. "It seemed like whenever she went away, he'd get sick and ask her to come back to him. And whenever she came back, she'd get a bleeding ulcer and get real sick herself." It was a well-known fact that Jesse had serious ulcer problems ever since she moved to T or C when she was twenty-four years old. Twice, she had to be airlifted out of town to get treatment.

"I have ten to eleven ulcer attacks a year," she once told Astbury.

Prosecutor Yontz had Jesse charged with a dozen felony counts, and during the arraignment, bail was set at $1,000,000—cash. She was charged with the same identical twelve counts as her father: kidnapping, six counts of criminal sexual penetration, criminal sexual contact, assault and three counts of conspiracy. Yontz was also having Jesse investigated in the September

1995 disappearance of Jill Troia, twenty-two, who was last seen the night she vanished chugging beers with Jesse Ray in a gay bar along a Central Avenue sleazy motel strip in Albuquerque. Although the locals in T or C also heard rumors that Roy Yancy had implicated her in the death of Marie Parker, she was not charged in the Parker case.

During her second interview with the FBI, she'd opened up a little bit more to Special Agent Weller and told him that her relationship to David Ray was not good.

"My relationship with my father is strained—very much so," she told him.

In jail she told a very different story when she was visited by Gail Astbury. During their conversations she told Astbury she "idolized" her dad and angrily denied that he had ever had sex with her and fathered her child. She also denied any involvement in the three-day disappearance of Kelli Van Cleave.

People who knew Jesse Ray had a mixed bag of reactions to her arrest. Her stepbrother, Ron, was surprised and told the press that "it really caught me off guard." Michael Kitts, who had known Jesse for years, said, "She rarely held a job for long," adding that "she drove a cab for a while and I think she worked in a pizza joint once.

"She's quiet and reserved," he added. "Kind of laid-back, like her dad. She's not the kind of person to be noticed in a big crowd. She's off to the side in the corner, smoking a cigarette and drinking a beer. She can be charming, but I've seen her really get angry."

For ten years Jesse lived in Albuquerque with her lover, a woman named Teri Hafenbrack. At one point they actually got married. Before Jesse got arrested, Teri had nothing but kind words for her ex-girlfriend. "Jesse's a kind and caring individual. I've known her for eighteen years and I don't think she's involved with anything that her father may have done—not at all."

After the police put Jesse behind bars, the *Albu-*

querque Journal did a criminal background check on her and the picture of her domestic life—with and without Hafenbrack—showed a much darker side. Police reported that during that same ten years she'd gone by at least three first-name aliases (Linda, Brenda and Sissy), and in 1992 her partner, Hafenbrack, reported her to the police and filed a domestic-violence complaint against her. Hafenbrack told the cops Ray "pushed her." In 1993 Hafenbrack filed another complaint, telling investigating officers that Ray "hit her" and "took my car without permission." In neither case did Teri Hafenbrack file charges against Jesse.

By 1995 Hafenbrack had a new lover, Tammy Younglove. One hot August night, Jesse Ray came by to visit her ex-wife and got into another disturbance with Teri's new girlfriend. Ray and Younglove got in a heated argument after Younglove asked Jesse to leave the house. Ray became very agitated and pulled a can of pepper spray out of her purse and sprayed Younglove in the face. Again, no charges were filed.

Jim Yontz spent the next two weeks preparing for Jesse's preliminary hearing on May 11, in front of Judge Pestak in the Sierra County Magistrate's Court in T or C. Pestak always seemed more reasonable than the hard-ass Mertz, so Yontz looked forward to making a strong case against Glenda Jean Ray. Her felony charges mirrored her father's first twelve charges and Yontz knew what he had to do. His main job was to show that David and Jesse Ray had true evil intent when they kidnapped Van Cleave on the night of July 25, 1996. He also wanted to establish that Jesse was the likely female partner David mentioned in his kinky introduction-to-torture audiotape. So Yontz planned to play about fifteen minutes of one of the six tapes in court so the judge could get a good feeling for what a sickening duo the state of New Mexico was trying to put behind bars.

On Tuesday, May 11, Kelli Van Cleave was the first to testify. She told how Jesse had drugged her at the Blue Waters Saloon and taken her back to David's, where the two of them tied her up. She told how David Ray spent three days penetrating her with one particular dildo he called "the devil's dick."

"The details have been slipping back into my mind for years," she told the judge. "I remember him telling me he was in some kind of satanic group, and the people in his group had been watching me—and wanting me as a sex toy, kind of a sex slave."

Frances Baird sat in the courtroom taking notes for the *Sentinel,* and when the words "sex slave" came up, she got the chills. Another rumor around town was that Ray and Hendy had targeted the ten-year-old daughter of Pamela Hinkle because they wanted to kidnap a child and keep it as a long-term sex slave. They supposedly put out a "hit" on the girl's mother and planned to kill her sometime in 1998 or 1999.

On July 27, 1998, Hinkle went to court in T or C to get a restraining order against her husband, Duane Hinkle. They had been married for only two weeks in the summer of 1998 and she claimed that on one occasion he had already tried to kill her. In her court papers filed in the seventh district court, she wrote: "My husband Duane tried to kill me. He picked me up by the neck and slammed me all over the walls. He was on top of me and choked me. I did not touch him or argue with him."

She got a restraining order, and then on January 7, 1999, she reported to the police that Duane was prowling around her apartment.

The next week she heard from friends that Ray and Hendy were going to kidnap her youngest child. A few days later, she found out Duane was a good buddy of David Parker Ray's, and on the 27th, after a divorce hearing in front of Judge Edmund Kase, she was drunk and driving her brown Dodge van when she tried to run

Duane down in a parking lot. The next day, she packed up her bags and moved her two children out of town—all in one day.

Frances Baird snapped out of it and listened to Yontz bring on Janet Murphy, who testified that when David Ray brought back Kelli Van Cleave, she was drugged up and dirty and couldn't remember hardly anything. Yontz pointed out to Pestak that three days earlier, Jesse waited at the Blue Waters Saloon until almost everyone else had left and then offered Kelli a ride home on her motorcycle. Instead of doing her friend a favor, David's daughter took the new bride to her dad's trailer so he could use her for his own fun and games. Jesse was just as guilty as her dad, Yontz added.

"She procured the victim for Daddy," he told Pestak.

Next up was the audiotape. Billy Blackburn was the public defender representing Jesse and he vehemently objected, claiming that there was no proof David Ray played the tape for Kelli. Judge Pestak disagreed and allowed Trooper John Briscoe to play the cassette for the hushed courtroom. Frances Baird got ready to take notes a mile a minute. Right away she recognized David Parker Ray's gravelly cowboy voice and his first three words out of his mouth shocked Frances more than she was willing to admit:

> Hello there, bitch. [*David greeted his next unknown victim.*] You're chained, handcuffed, scared and disoriented. Listen to this tape. It was created July 23, 1993, as an advisory tape for female captives based on my several years of experience.
>
> You are here against your will. You probably think you're going to be raped. You're right about that—you will be raped thoroughly and repeatedly. . . . My female companion and I are very selective. . . . We'll snatch anything clean, young and well-built. . . . We're basically like predators.

We're always looking. I don't want to kill unless it's absolutely necessary.

If I killed every victim I ever kidnapped, there'd be bodies all over the country.

When the tape was over, most reporters present knew they couldn't file the specifics of such a vile report in a family newspaper. Baird wanted to put every last word in the *Sentinel,* but she knew her mother would not allow it.

Jim Yontz wrapped up his arguments in favor of binding Glenda "Jesse" Ray over for a jury trial and it didn't take Judge Pestak long to agree. Pestak said Jesse would go to trial within six months.

On the way out of the courtroom, Baird ran into Yontz and he told her to expect another big bombshell from the FBI in the next few days. Baird kidded him about not announcing news before it happens. Then she giggled and added: "If it hasn't happened, I don't want to hear about it."

Two days later, on May 13, she heard about it.

Federal Bureau of Investigation SSA Doug Beldon of Albuquerque held a press conference and flabbergasted almost everyone within earshot when he confirmed another rumor circulating about Jesse Ray and her dad. Thirteen years earlier, she had turned him in to the FBI.

"In June 1986, Jesse Ray volunteered information to the FBI in New Mexico concerning her father," Beldon said. "She alleged that David Parker Ray was abducting and torturing women and selling them to buyers in Mexico. For over one year thereafter, the FBI in New Mexico conducted an investigation in an attempt to substantiate the allegations. The investigation was conducted under the jurisdiction in the FBI's White Slave Traffic Act. No victims were identified, and none came forward," Beldon said.

Jesse's friends were dead sure why she turned her dad in to the FBI back in 1986. He'd always told her he was "untouchable," and by the time she was nineteen years old, she was beginning to believe him. According to one close friend, "That was her last try to get out from under her dad's influence. It was the last time she said to him, 'No, Dad, what you're doing is wrong.' I blame the FBI," said the friend. "They did nothing. After that, she didn't even try."

What her friends did not know was that Jesse Ray had told the FBI something completely different during a second 1999 interview that was conducted with her prior to the news about the 1986 story going public. Jesse's version of events was quite at odds from what everyone assumed after hearing that she'd try to hang David high and dry with the Feds back in 1986.

She told the FBI it was all about selling pot, not kidnapped sex slaves.

"We lived up near Fence Lake, New Mexico, and in 1984 to '85 we were growing marijuana and selling it to the local 'stoners.' Us kids did all the physical labor. We had this little greenhouse and we'd let the grass plants get real big before we took 'em outside to plant 'em in our yard. We had to, because the rabbits were so bad out there—they'd eat 'em before we could pick 'em!

"We sold 'em in the fall of 1985, and my dad—he tried to cheat me out of my share of the money and I was real mad at him. So I turned him in to the FBI," Jesse said.

"Simple as that."

CHAPTER 12

"Bill King's son is a locksmith—he opened up the toy box and right away he saw jars on the kitchen counter. He turned to an FBI agent standing outside the trailer door and said, 'Oh my God—they're human body parts!'"

Rick Hart, T or C photographer,
November 4, 1999

Juggling the prosecution of four perverts was a full-time job for Jim Yontz, and by the end of April, he was working almost every weekend. Yontz had recently remarried and his new wife, Karen, had been a street cop in Los Angeles. She knew what he was up against and tried to help him take time away from the grim reality of the David Parker Ray case. On May 1 she got up early and brewed a pot of strong coffee. He went out to his barn to spend a few minutes training his new palomino horse—a chance to work off some steam before taking the freeway drive to work. An hour later, he arrived at his out-of-the-way office in Socorro.

He walked in and said "Hello, Bernie" to a black-bear hide that covered the top of the table next to his desk. He'd shot the bear years ago on a bow-hunting trip up in Alberta, Canada. Bernie was eating blueberries at the time. His head and body were now covered with eight boxes of paperwork on the Ray case.

Yontz sorted through the mess and found the audiotape he wanted to review. It wasn't the tape he'd played for Judge Pestak, but it was the tape he sure as hell wanted to play for Judge Mertz on October 4, when the David Parker Ray case finally got under way. It was the most powerful of all six tapes Ray made back in 1993, a year after Jesse moved in and a year before Joannie Lee moved out. More than anything else, it showed David was ruthless and single-minded in his predatory efforts to exert his will on women and girls. The tape started with the same disclaimer as most of the others: "This audiotape contains very graphic material for adults only. It was designed and created to be used for entertainment purposes."

Then the tape really got down to business:

> Hello there, bitch! Are you comfortable right now? I doubt it. Wrists and ankles chained, gagged, probably blindfolded. You are disoriented and scared, too, I would imagine. . . . Perfectly normal under the circumstances. For a little while at least, you need to get your shit together and listen to this tape. It is very relevant to your situation. I'm going to tell you in detail why you have been kidnapped, what's going to happen to you and how long you'll be here.
>
> I don't know the details of your capture, because this tape is being created July 23, 1993, as a this-is-what's-going-to-happen-to-you tape for my captives. The information I'm going to give you is based on my experiences dealing with captives over a period of several years. If at a future date, there are any major changes in our procedures, the tape will be upgraded. Now, you are obviously here against your will. Totally helpless. Don't know where you're at. Don't know what's going to happen to you. You're scared or pissed off. I'm

sure that you've already tried to get your wrists and ankles loose, and know you can't. Now you're waiting to see what's going to happen next. You probably think you're going to be raped, and you're fucking sure right about that.

Our primary interest is in what you've got between your legs. You'll be raped thoroughly and repeatedly in every hole you've got, because basically, you've been snatched and brought here for us to train and use as a sex slave. Sound kind of far-out? Well, I suppose it is to the uninitiated, but we do it all the time. It's gonna take a lot of adjustment on your part, and you're not going to like it a fucking bit, but I don't give a rat's ass about that. It's not like you're gonna have any choice about the matter. You've been taken by force, and you're going to be kept and used by force.

What all this amounts to is that you're going to be kept naked and chained up like an animal to be used and abused anytime we want to, any way that we want to. And you might as well start getting used to it, because you're going to be kept here and used, until such time as we get tired of fucking around with you, and we will eventually, in a month or two, or three.

It's no big deal; my lady friend and I have been keeping sex slaves for years. We both have kinky hang-ups involving rape, dungeon games, et cetera. We found that it is extremely convenient to keep one or two female captives available constantly to satisfy our particular needs. We are very selective when we snatch a girl for use for these purposes. It goes without saying that you have a fine body, and you're probably young, maybe very young. Because for our purposes, we prefer to snatch girls in their early to midteens, sexually developed, but still small body, scared shitless, easy to handle and easy to train. And they usually have tight little pussies and assholes. They make perfect slaves.

Anytime we go on a hunting trip, if we can't find a little teenager, we usually start hitting the gay bars, looking for a well-built, big-titted lesbian. I thoroughly enjoy raping and screwing around with lesbians, and there's not as much danger of them carrying a sexually transmitted disease, and I don't like using condoms. Also, even though they're a little older, unless they've been playing with dildos a lot, they still have tight holes between their legs, like the younger girls. If we can't find a lesbian that we want, we snatch anything that is young, clean and well built. We seldom come back empty-handed, because there's plenty of bitches out there to choose from. And with a little practice in deception, most of them is very easy to get with little risks.

At this point it makes little difference what category you fall into. You're here, and we're going to make the most of it. You're going to be kept in a hidden slave room. It is relatively soundproof, escapeproof, and is completely stocked with devices and equipment to satisfy our particular fetishes and deviations. There may or may not be another girl in the room. Occasionally, for variety, we like to keep two slaves at the same time. In any case, as the new girl, you will definitely be getting the most attention for a while. Now, as I said earlier, you're going to be kept like an animal. I guess I've been doing this too long. I've been raping bitches ever since I was old enough to jerk off and tie a little girl's hands behind her back. As far as I'm concerned, you're a pretty piece of meat to be used and exploited.

I don't give a flying fuck about your mind or how you feel about the situation.

You may be married, have a kid or two, boyfriend, girlfriend, a job, car payments—fuck it! I don't give a big rat's ass about any of that, and I don't want to hear about it. It's something you're going to have to deal with after you're turned loose. I make it a point never to like a slave, and I fucking sure don't have any respect for you. Here your status is no more than one of the dogs or one of the animals out in the barn. Your only value to us is the fact that you have an attractive, usable body. And like the rest of our animals, you will be fed and watered, kept in good physical condition, kept reasonably clean and allowed to use the toilets when necessary. In return, you're going to be used hard. Especially during the first few days while you're new and fresh.

You're going to be kept chained in a variety of different positions, usually with your legs or knees forced wide apart. Your pussy and asshole is going to get a real workout, especially your asshole because I'm into anal sex. Also, both of those holes are going to be subjected to a lot of use, with some rather large dildos among other things. And it goes without saying that there's going to be a lot of oral sex. On numerous occasions you're going to be forced to suck cock and eat pussy until your jaws ache and your tongue is sore. You may not like it but you're fucking sure going to do it.

And that's the easy part. Our fetishes and hang-ups include stringent bondage, dungeon games, a little sadism, nothing serious, but uncomfortable and sometimes painful. Just a few little hang-ups that we like to use when we're getting off on a bitch [*laughs*]. If you're a young teenybopper, and ignorant about fetishes and deviations, you're about to get an enlightening crash course on sex ed. Who knows, you may like some of it. It happens occasionally.

Now, I've already told you that you're going to be here a month or two, maybe three, if you keep us turned on. If it's up to my lady, we'd keep you indefinitely. She says it's just as much fun and less risky. But personally, I like variety, a fresh pussy now and then to play with. We take four or five girls each year, depending on our urges and sometimes accidental encounters. Basically, I guess we are like predators; we're always looking. Occasionally some sweet little thing will be broke down on the side of the road, walking, bicycling, jogging. Anytime an opportunity like that presents itself, and it's not risky, we'll grab her. . . .

Yontz turned off the tape recorder and gazed out the window of his cramped office. He remembered a picture from the newspapers back in 1994—a beautiful blond girl listed as missing and presumed dead. She was nineteen years old and her name was Tara Calico. She was last seen pedaling her bicycle down a road south of Belen, the town where David was born. She just seemed to have vanished off the face of the earth that hot summer afternoon, never to be seen alive again. They never found her body. Someone remembered seeing a white van shortly before Tara was kidnapped, but nobody got a license plate number. David Parker Ray owned a white Dodge Ram (license 705 GLN) utility vehicle and he had a red flashing police light hidden under the front seat that the police assumed he used when he wanted to pull someone over. Yontz knew there was only a faint chance of pinning the Tara Calico murder on David Ray, but he was going to try like hell.

He leaned over and pulled the blinds down over his window to the outside world and turned the tape recorder back on in his darkened office. He couldn't get Tara Calico out of his mind. And a second later, he couldn't get David Ray out, either.

Variety is definitely the spice of life. Now, I'm sure you're a great little piece of ass, and you're going to be a lot of fun to play with, but I will get tired of you eventually. If I killed every bitch that we kidnapped, there'd be bodies strung all over the country. And besides, I don't like killing a girl unless it's absolutely necessary, so I've devised a safe, alternate method of disposal.

I had plenty of bitches to practice on over the years, so I pretty well got it down pat, and I enjoy doing it. I get off on mind games. After we get completely through with you, you're gonna be drugged up real heavy with a combination of sodium Pentothal and phenobarbital. They are both hypnotic drugs that will make you extremely susceptible to hypnosis, autohypnosis and hypnotic suggestions. You're gonna be kept drugged a couple of days while I play with your mind. By the time I get through brainwashing you, you're not gonna remember a fucking thing about this little adventure. You won't remember this place, us or what has happened to you. There won't be any DNA evidence because you'll be bathed, and both holes between your legs will be thoroughly flushed out. You'll be dressed, sedated and turned loose on some country road. Bruised, sore all over, but nothing that won't heal up in a week or two. The thought of being brainwashed may not be appealing to you, but we've been doing it a long time, and it works and it's the lesser of two evils. I'm sure that you would prefer that in lieu of being strangled or having your throat cut.

There may or may not be a missing-persons report, but nobody is going to be looking for you. There are not going to be any knights in shining armor coming to rescue you. As for escaping, I'm sure you'll try to figure out a way—that's human nature—but it's not hardly worth talking about here. It wouldn't be prudent on our part to have you running around in the woods screaming "Rape." It would be embarrassing, to say the least. Consequently, you're gonna be kept in an environment that's even more secure than a prison cell. A steel padlock is going to be placed around your neck. It has a long, heavy chain that is padlocked to a ring on the floor. The collar will never be removed until you are turned loose. It's a permanent fixture.

The hidden playroom where you are going to be kept has steel walls, floors and ceiling. It is soundproof and has a steel door with two keyed locks. The hinges are welded on and there are two dead bolts on the outside. The room is totally escapeproof, even with tools. If you are in the room alone, your wrists will be chained. There is a closed-circuit TV system wired to the main TV in the living room, so we can check on you every once in a while—or just sit and watch you for the fun of it.

Electronics is a wonderful thing. Expensive—but hell—everything in the playroom is expensive and well worth it. If everyone knew how much fun it was to keep a sex slave, half the women in America would be chained up in somebody's basement.

Okay, let's talk about your training, the rules and the punishment. Here you are a slave, and discipline is extremely strict. You're gonna be given a set of rules. As soon as each rule is told to you, it will become law. This is what will happen if you fuck up. We use a couple of different methods of punishment. A whip is an excellent training aid, so is the electro-shock machine. Anytime you get out of line, one or both will be used on your body. And I assure you, it will not be pleasant. After the first day, we won't cut you any slack at all.

Now, let's start this off right. You're a slave. I'm your master and the lady is your mistress. You will be totally docile. You will be very quiet, and you'll speak only when spoken to. Never initiate conversation. Keep your mouth shut. Do exactly what is told to you, nothing else. Obey my commands—anything less will get you beaten. If I tell you I want to be sucked off, you say, "Yes, Master," and open your mouth. Each time when I get ready to come, I'm going to push my penis down your throat, and keep it there until I get through squirting. I'm not going to choke you, but you need to learn to hold your breath and to swallow every bit of sperm. If I see one drop leaking out of your mouth, I'm going to punish you. It's the same with your mistress. Learn how to use your tongue. If during oral sex or any other time you should bite one of us, I'm going to cut you a little bit. Your teeth are serious weapons. I have been bitten and I've cut off nipples, so don't fuck around.

If your mistress comes into the room and tells you to get down on the floor, you say, "Yes, Mistress." If she tells you to pull your knees up, you say, "Yes, Mistress." If she tells you to spread your knees, you say, "Yes, Mistress," and spread them wide apart and hold them there, so she can play with your pussy.

Don't kick, struggle, or resist in any way. If you do, you're gonna be in a world of hurts. For repeated rule violations, the punishments are eventually going to become harsh and even brutal, and you won't have nobody to blame but yourself.

Now, let's discuss talking. You cannot talk. I believe that rule gets more bitches into trouble than anything else, because they can't keep their damn mouths shut. They always want to whine, beg, plead, try to talk me into turning them loose. I used to listen to it. I don't anymore.

I enjoy blessed silence.

Around here, your mouth is for sucking, not talking.

The only time I ever want to hear you initiate speech is if you have to use the rest room. If you have to pee, say, "Pee, Master" or "Pee, Mistress." You definitely need to tell us, because if you make a mess, you're going to be punished and you'll have to clean it up.

Now, I've got to tell you, there is another side to the coin. Once in a while we get a bitch who is rebellious and won't mind. That doesn't work here. I'm sure that you realize you are on thin ice. If you should hurt either one of us, you could be in very serious trouble. I'm sure you want to survive this experience, but you are expendable. It's no big deal to go out and grab a replacement. It may sound harsh and cold, but if you give us too much trouble, I won't have any qualms at all about slashing your throat. I don't like killing girls, but occasionally bad things happen.

I would really hate to have to dump that pretty little body off in a canyon somewhere to rot.

Everything we do to a girl is designed to cause pain, not injury. No matter how painful it is, nothing we plan to do to your body will cause any permanent damage. I'm not lying to you. You're gonna be whipped lightly, for pleasure. Your're gonna be shocked lightly, for pleasure.

Most of the other nasty little things we're going to do, for the most part, will be done to your breasts, nipples and between your legs. The lady is fortunate; she can get off anytime. She just likes to be a little sadistic with the slave once in a while.

In my case, I could not get off with a girl unless I hurt her first. That is basically the reason I'm into rape and slavery. And that's the reason you're going to be subjected to a certain amount of pain. Mostly, what we do to a captive is stick needles in her breasts and through her nipples, through her cunt lips, through her clit—and I'm also into stretching certain things. Clamps with long nylon cords will be put in your cunt lips, so your pussy can be kept pulled open, and they're also going to be attached to your nipples. The nylon cords will be put through ceiling rings and pulled very tight to stretch your tits. Occasionally, your clit will also be clamped and stretched. And we're going to be using dildos. The dildos are going to be used a lot, more than anything else, and consequently, what you're going to have the most trouble with. Many of them are very long, vary large in diameter, and very painful while they're being forced in. I like to use them in both holes and your mistress will use them in your pussy.

As far as needles go, they'll always be sterilized. The clamps are going to hurt like a motherfucker, but they won't cause any permanent injury. They don't even break the skin.

As far as dildos go, both of those holes between your legs will stretch a hell of a lot. Your pussy is designed for a baby to come out of, and we won't be using anything bigger than that. The really large ones will not be used in your butt.

Every once in a while, we get a screamer. Some bitch that just wants to scream all the time. And that always gets on my nerves. We live in an isolated area, so screaming is usally not a problem—but it irritates the fuck out of me. If you do it habitually, I will keep a ball gag in your mouth all the time—I'll never take it out.

Pretty soon I'm going to be asking you a bunch of questions. I have prepared a questionnaire that I will fill out with each new captive. Some of the questions are going to be embarrassing, but you should answer them truthfully. I don't want to catch you in a lie. You will be naked and you'll be strapped down to the gynecology table so you can't wiggle or squirm around. I like to keep a girl that way while she's answering questions. Before you start answering questions, two small electrical clamps will be put on your nipples. Each time a question is asked, you will respond properly. Think about what you're going to say before you say it, because we're not in a hurry. Each time you fuck up, I'm gonna press a little button and send a few thousand volts of electricity through your nipples. I'm not going to hold it down to torture you, but each time you screw up, it's going to get a little bit worse.

After you finish answering the questions, I'm going to examine you. All girls are different. I want to become very familiar with your sex organs and the size of your holes. Later that first day, you're going to be raped several times, but that's no big deal. The second day, after you get totally familiar with the rules and procedures, we're going to get down to the nitty-gritty. Things will not be very pleasant for you, but you might as well get used to it, because it's going to be like that for a while.

Well, I believe I've told you about everything that I can. Be smart and be a survivor. Don't ever scream. Don't talk without permission. Be very quiet. Be docile and, by all means, show proper respect.

Have a nice day.

Slowly Jim Yontz got out of his chair and pulled the plug out of the wall so he wouldn't have to hear the drone of David Ray's voice coming out of the tape recorder anymore. He walked over and pulled up the blinds so he could let in the slanting rays of some of that famous late-afternoon New Mexico sunshine. Yontz knew that nothing was ever a sure thing when one prosecutes extreme evil, but he felt that if any jury ever heard this tape, David Parker Ray would be a "dead duck."

He left his office and walked out to his state-owned vehicle, opened the trunk and tossed in the tape. He slammed the trunk hood down extra hard and spoke out loud to no one in particular.

"Have a nice day, David," he said.

CHAPTER 13

"This guy is the worst sadistic serial killer in the history of the FBI."

FBI Special Agent John Schum, July 6, 2000

Right after the case broke, the FBI sent out one of their special East Coast profilers to gather evidence on David Ray and determine if he was a "sexual sadist." The National Center for Analysis of Violent Crime (NCFAVC) in Quantico, Virginia, sent Mary Ellen O'Toole, a twenty-two-year veteran of law enforcement, and she immediately met with Jim Yontz and started poring over the evidence in the case. A combined federal-state task force of one hundred agents had unearthed over 1,500 pieces of evidence, and law enforcement officers from the NMSP and the FBI were carrying on investigations in ten states, so O'Toole had her work cut out for her.

After weeks of touring the toy box and watching videotapes and listening to audiotapes, O'Toole had no doubt that Ray was a classic sadist. According to records made public on May 13, Ray fit the profile of an offender who probably started pursuing his fantasies with willing participants and over time escalated into forcing himself on completely unwilling victims. O'Toole felt Ray met almost all the criteria for the most brutal of all murderers.

"His sadistic fantasies probably started in childhood," she told Yontz.

"The fantasy usually involved having complete control over a woman, and he always got sexually aroused watching the victim suffer. By the time he was in his early twenties, he began acting out on the strong sexual urges that overwhelmed him every few weeks. Some men are bothered by their fantasies, but usually it's just a matter of time until this type of man is caught—they usually increase the levels of violence until the victims are injured or killed. Unfortunately, in this case it took nearly forty years.

"And once these predators start forcing themselves on unwilling women, they continue to repeat the same brutalizing rituals over and over until they are caught.

"Sexual sadists are the most violent of all the violent criminals. Most criminals change and improve their MO over time, but not a sadist—they risk identification because the only way to become sexually aroused is for them to repeat the same ritual in each crime. It's a very dangerous lifestyle and it takes a very bright criminal to pull it off. The victim must suffer right in front of the sadist for him to 'get off,' and usually the acts gets worse over time. The thrill for Ray is to see the pain, terror and humiliation reflected directly back to his watching eye.

"He has to have complete control over the victim. Normally, he must dominate the victim by forcing them to crawl or by keeping them in a cage. He also has to restrain the victim and he can do that in quite a number of ways: blindfolding, paddling, spanking, whipping, pinching, beating, burning, electrical shocks, rape, cutting, stabbing, strangulation, torture, mutilation or just plain, outright killing.

"Sexual sadism is chronic. David organized his whole life around the fantasy. He became a master manipulator.

"He has probably written a journal of his tortures and he may have collected 'keepsakes'—anything from jewelry to human body parts—to help him relive his experiences. He probably hoarded and stashed these items in secret places, possibly around his house, somewhere in his yard. Places where only David would know the location of the hiding place."

Yontz told O'Toole they had reliable reports from one of Ray's neighbors that he used to go out in his yard after dark and replant the trees and shrubs—digging until the wee hours of the morning. O'Toole said it would be best if they authorized another massive search around all the structures at 513 Bass Road.

The next day, Lieutenant Greg Richardson from the New Mexico State Police led investigators into David's yard with a huge earthmoving backhoe. Police also used a new type of ground-penetrating radar that could find objects down to thirty feet below the surface of the sandy soil. And police brought back the cadaver-sniffing German shepherds to hunt for bodies.

"We felt it was necessary to get another search warrant to look for new evidence," Richardson told the assembled press. "We felt this could help with the four people already charged, as well as help us identify any other victims."

Three days later, Frances Baird cornered Richardson and pressed him on the progress on the search for keepsakes.

"All we found was a lot of dirt," he admitted.

Yontz felt Mary Ellen O'Toole was the missing link he needed to nail both David and Jesse Ray during a fall trial, so lack of progress finding physical evidence didn't bother him too much. So far, none of the fourteen bodies Hendy mentioned had been found—and the state had no direct evidence linking David Ray to the murder of his ex-boss Billy Ray Bowers. And Marie Parker's body had not been found, either. Frances Baird told Jim Yontz that an unnamed FBI agent had told her that seven more locals would be arrested soon, but Yontz told her he didn't see any evidence tying anyone else to the case. As far as he was concerned, convicting David and three of his followers was enough work for one assistant DA.

Right after Jesse Ray was arrested, the *New York Times* ran its last article on the case. *USA Today* did the same. At one time it looked like David Ray was heading for the front page of every paper in the country, but Craig Lewis of the *Globe* knew better. He was the first to drop the story, telling his New Mexico reporter: "Don't bother me unless they find bodies."

That May, there was other news coming out of southern New Mexico, and Jim Yontz was happy some of it was good. It made him forget about the mounting pressure to find hard facts to win a conviction. Many locals wished they could string David Ray up from an old-fashioned hanging tree, as their ancestors once did before the plodding legal system stole the thunder from the men who administered the quick and sure justice of the Wild West.

Five years earlier, 122 wild horses had died of thirst during a drought at the White Sands Missile Range, just south of T or C. In the spring of 1999, animal-rights advocates rounded up the last three dozen mustangs and were getting ready to ship them north to greener pastures in South Dakota. Yontz read the *Sentinel* and chuckled when he read what the leader of the International Society for the Protection of Mustangs had to say about the ponies and their new home.

"It's a happy ending for these horses," said spokesman Karen Sussman. "These horses are going to heaven, and I mean heaven."

Jim Yontz figured David Ray was going to hell and it was just a matter of time until someone found a body or two. It looked liked draining Elephant Butte Lake might be the only way to find some of the bodies to prove in a court of law that David Ray was the cruel and evil genius whom everyone feared. Yontz looked at his map of the forty-four-mile-long lake and imagined all the places dead corpses might be hiding—Black Bluff Canyon, Flying Eagle Canyon, Ash Canyon, Lost Canyon, Willow Canyon, Catfish Camp. Elephant Butte Lake was huge and had fingers of water everywhere. Yontz even imagined bodies washing up on Rattlesnake Island, Horse Island or the big extinct volcanic cinder-cone the lake was named after—the Elephant Butte itself.

Yontz was an avid fisherman and knew the lake was filled with extremely large bass, crappie, sunfish and pike. But he figured most of the bodies had sunk by now to the bottom of the reservoir and been washed down to the south end of the lake, where they were being slowly nibbled away by the huge seven- to eight-foot-long, 120-pound channel catfish lurking around at the base of the dirt dam—catfish that always ate the human eyeballs first.

As far as the great desolate Valley of Death was concerned, Yontz knew David Ray had endless possibilities of where to stash bodies. Silver and gold mining had been popular around the turn of the century and there were hundreds of deep mines that nobody had searched for years and years. And between the turkey vultures and the natural caves dotting the endless desert landscape, Yontz figured they might never find a single body. He wasn't worried, though, because he had enough hard evidence and testimony to nail David Ray—the videotape of Ray fondling Kelli Van Cleave, six horrific audiotapes and now the increasingly right-on-the-money testimony of Mary Ellen O'Toole.

There were other troubling developments, though. As Yontz followed the news, he noticed an alarming trend. People were moving out of Truth or Consequences. They didn't want to have anything to do with the now infamous town. On April Fools' Day, 1950, the good people of Hot Springs gave up the image of the hot springs where Geronimo used to bathe and named their town after a quiz show. Now some people wanted to hide from the David Ray spotlight and rename the town Hot Springs, New Mexico.

Every year since 1950, game-show host Ralph Edwards himself had come to town for the annual mid-May "Fiesta Days" celebration. He'd squint in the noonday sun and wave to the residents from his float in the T or C parade. Then he'd show up at the lake for the big community BBQ. With the news so bad in 1999, not even Edwards was going to show up.

And Jim Yontz noticed Edwards wasn't the only one not showing his face in Truth or Consequences or out at Elephant Butte Lake. Cyndy Vigil and Angelique Montano were both in Albuquerque. Cyndy was in jail on heroin possession charges and Angie had run away from T or C (and her son) to become a prostitute all over again back on Highway 66. Kelli Van Cleave had remarried and moved to Craig, Colorado. Her ex-husband, Patrick, was back in San Diego and his mother, Janet Murphy, was now living in Phoenix. Billy Ray Bowers was now buried in Kansas City and Marie Parker's mother, Kate, had taken the two girls to Albuquerque, trying to escape what she and many others called the evil in the little desert "motel town." All the other players were either dead or in jail, Yontz noted to himself.

By the end of May, the only shocking and appalling news leaking out of T or C concerned a "diorama"

David Ray kept in his house showing small "dolls" posed in different positions of torture and bondage—old news for a town where a lot of single people reportedly enjoyed group sex. The sensation-starved locals were beginning to think the FBI profile of David Ray was just a bunch of mumbo-jumbo.

They suspected things were a lot worse—a whole lot worse.

Driving home late one night, Jim Yontz popped in a tape that made the locals sound like prophets. On this cassette David Ray talked about making and selling videos using live victims, all the time speaking into the microphone while trying to deal with the screams of a live captive in the other room.

> I make very special adult videos. The videos sell for about a thousand dollars each and they are only sold to a very select group of collectors of sadistic erotica. I've learned over the years that there's a hell of a lot of people out there with some awful weird fantasies. I rather enjoy the work; the money's great. Our customers want a lot of wide-angle and close-up camera shots of the breasts, nipples and sex organs being abused with a variety of instruments in a variety of ways. The action has to be real; it can't be faked. We need to actually kidnap a woman for the action scenes.
>
> Sometimes the movies are shot in the woods, sometimes in a boat or in the desert. Other times we shoot you in a dungeon-type room in our house. The shooting of the action scenes usually takes three or four days. We videotape a dozen or so rapes, several whippings, and several hours of abuse with a woman chained in a variety of differ-

ent positions. And, if I may say so myself, we put out some pretty damn good movies.

There is a bright side to this. Before I turn you loose, I'm going to give you a hundred dollars for your trouble. Thirty to forty percent of the movie will be where the camera zooms in for a close-up between your legs. So all you have to do is show us what you've probably already shown some other poor sucker who had to pay a lot more than a hundred bucks to catch a glimpse of the promised land. The pink hole.

Fuck flicks are a dime a dozen. You can buy them all over the place for eighty-nine dollars and ninety-five cents. Our group of clients want to see a woman actually raped, whipped and tortured. They like to see a woman wiggle, squirm, bite the chains and sweat a lot. And if you don't sweat enough, we'll put baby oil on your body to simulate it. We strive to please; that's our claim to fame. I prefer to use the word "abuse" because I don't think we actually torture a woman in our films.

Let's go into a few types of abuse. We use damn big dildos on your two holes and they look wicked as hell. We're careful and we use them with restraint. That's necessary to create the illusion of reality. If our procedures didn't cause pain, we wouldn't have to kidnap a live woman to make these movies.

Since these movies are into bondage, it's necessary that we tie up your tits. We attach long nylon cords to each nipple and we put on a few drops of Super Glue to bond the cord to the skin. A woman's breasts are very elastic and they can be stretched upward like two slender cones. You're going to squeal like a stuck pig while I'm doing it, but it won't bother me at all.

You'll also be whipped, about twenty lashes during each session. The whip has to be used hard enough to leave some good welts for the camera. I don't want to get you all bloody, so the whip strokes will be concentrated on your thighs, your butt, sex organs, belly and tits. Even if you're gagged, the microphones will pick up the sounds. The whip is a great tool for effect.

It never ceases to amaze me how barbaric some people can be. Our customers want to see you getting hurt. We use some gigantic dildos. To create some special effects, we pull the skin around your vagina back and then thrust in a dildo four to six inches wide at the base. On the viewing screen it looks pretty terrible. It looks like we're tearing you apart, and that's what we want the viewer to think. Our customers think that's exactly what we do to a girl when we make these movies. But that's not the way it works at all. . . .

[*Voices can be heard in the background.*]

You may be tempted to strike out, kick, bite, try to scratch me. I wouldn't do that if I were you.

[*Still lots of screaming, sighing and crying in the background.*]

Can't you all keep that bitch quiet in there? Put a gag on her or something. Fuck, I'm trying to make a tape out here. Close that damn play room door. Anything!

[*The background screaming ceases.*]

Shit, that's better. Fuck, that bitch has got a set of lungs on her. My friend was forcing the devil's dick up her ass and she didn't like it for shit, that's for sure.

Now, where were we?

Just be careful what you do with your hands and feet. If you piss me off, things are gonna get a hell of a lot rougher. A woman scratched me in the face one time, and I cut her clit off. Another thing I might tell you right now is that . . .

[*Starts talking to someone in the background.*]

What? What do you all want?

[*Loud noises in the background.*]

All right, damn it, wait a minute and let me turn this damn machine off here [*pause*].

Well, I'm back [*laughs*]. Shit, they're like a bunch of little kids in there with a new toy. They just wanted me to show them how to use the electroshock machine. That little cunt in there is chained down and she can't be over fifteen or sixteen years old. My friends sure are giving her a working over. Damn . . . I guess I should have made this tape when it was a little bit quieter. But you know how it goes . . . the excitement of the moment and all that shit.

Anyhow, what I was about to tell you a while ago was that there is absolutely no way in hell that you're going to be turned loose until I'm done with you. Hell, I even picked up one little old bitch, seventeen or eighteen years old, that told me she had a two-week-old baby at home. And I didn't doubt it for a minute. Her pubic hair was just starting to grow back where it had been shaved off. Her pussy lips were still swollen and puffy, but the really novel thing was her tits. After I had her for a few hours, her nipples started leaking milk constantly. Made a hell of a mess. Even with all her excuses, I still didn't turn her loose, and I'm sure as hell not going to turn you loose.

[*Loud screaming and cries can be heard in the background.*]

Damn! That's carrying right through the walls. I don't know what they are doing to her, but it must be good. Hang on a minute, I better look in there and make sure they're not killing the little whore.

[*Three voices are heard in the background: a male's, a female's and David Ray's. Their words are hard to make out.*]

Yeah, I'm back [*laughs*]. She's okay. One of the girls was touching a lit cigarette to her nipples. But I told her not to do it anymore. I don't particularly like that. Not because of the pain, because we're in the business of pain . . . but because cigarette burns kinda messes up a woman's appearance.

And that doesn't turn me on.

CHAPTER 14

"He'd watch a bumblebee go after a wasp and he'd describe how the bee hunted."

Barbara Dickson, talking about her son Dan when he was a curious eight year-old boy.
August 11, 1999

In the spring of 1999, Dan Dickson, thirty-three, was working as the airport manager at the small airfield just outside of Truth or Consequences. He wore jeans and a cowboy hat to work, and he played fiddle in a small country-western band that occasionally did a gig at the local Pine Knot Tavern. He also had his own cattle brand for a small herd of longhorns he owned, and he liked to think that his aim with a gun was as straight as his talk. Dan always told friends he never went into the vast desert surrounding T or C without carrying his six-shooter, just in case he ran into one of the thousands of rattlesnakes hiding under the sagebrush covering the Jordana del Muerto.

Usually, traffic in and out of the Sierra County Airport was light, and as the director of aviation services, he handled a small number of private planes owned by the very rich, who rightfully thought southern New Mexico was God's gift to splendid scenery—like Ted

Turner, owner of Cable News Network (CNN). According to the *Sentinel,* Turner owned nearly a third of Sierra County. Many of the other superwealthy landowners used to fly in to spend a few days at million-dollar homes perched on a ridge above the lake, a development called Champagne Hills.

By April 1, 1999, Dan Dickson was overwhelmed by the constant noise of helicopters and government planes flying FBI agents in and out of town to investigate David Parker Ray.

"When the FBI first got to town, they were wandering around combing the desert and going on one wild-goose chase after another," said Dickson. "One night I was in Raymond's Lounge talking to a friend of mine who is a treasure hunter. His name is Rex and he's always been convinced there was Aztec gold hidden in some of the thousands of mines and caves in this area. He told me that just the day before he'd been down in a cave looking for treasures when he seen two burlap bags full of animal bones. He thought they might be victims of David. He said he didn't want the publicity, so he asked me if I'd talk to the FBI. I'd already been hired by the NMSP OMI [Office of Medical Information] to help out in the Ray case, so I pulled a few strings and the next day Rex and me went out to the cave and I crawled three hundred feet down on my belly, and later that night, we met with Greg Spain, from the state police Special Investigations Undercover Unit. He contacted the FBI for us.

"Two days later, I took the FBI out to this cave near the Caballo Mountains, south of town. At the entrance of the cave, right inside, there was this big white quartz cross that looked real spooky. Treasure hunters have pursued gold up in them hills for years. The Feds hired professional spelunkers from Carlsbad Caverns National Park and those guys squeezed seventeen hundred feet down that shaft to a pool of water, an underground lake.

"All they found was a bag of coyote bones—some locals must have killed the coyotes. Out here, you cut the ears off a dead coyote and they pay you a bounty of ten dollars apiece. The FBI figured Ray and his followers must have mutilated the coyotes as part of some satanic ritual, because not five hundred feet from the entrance of the cave, they found a site covered with red and black candles and the names of some of David's friends etched on the rocks. The place had Dennis Roy Yancy's name all over it.

"The campsite was marked on a map back at David Ray's house. It had the specific caves marked and later we found out David had a spelunking certificate from the state of California. Lots of other guys have poked around in these caves up in the Turtleback Mountains. There was one guy named 'Old Willie' back in the 1930s—he spent a lot of time crawling around underground. He used to melt down his gold and pour it into the skeletons of cholla cactus to hide it from thieves. His name even appeared in a book titled *Seven Tons of Gold.* He died a millionaire, with a bullet hole in the back of his head.

"You know, you never heard nuthin' about David Ray in this town until that girl, Vigil, escaped. Now everybody thinks they knew him. I remember David and all his low-life friends. I can even put Roy Yancy with David Ray back in the early 1990s. I know when they met and when David took young Yancy under his wing. Same thing with Jesse and Cindy Hendy, too. I remember 'em all. A few years ago, they used to hang out at Raymond's Lounge. I owned that bar between 1990 and 1995, and after I sold it, I worked there as a bartender until 1998. I used to see 'em come in there and pass the time every day.

"David wasn't a drinker, but he'd sit there and buy drinks for his buddies. He'd sit there with some skanky gal, usually some girl like Cindy Hendy, and later with Hendy herself. I remember one time Cindy Hendy was flirting with both men and women. While she was fooling around with both sexes, David Ray would sit back in the corner and fund the entire operation. I figured maybe she was doin' the fishin' and he was payin' for the trip!

"David never did drink; he'd just sit there and watch the other people. He never really said a whole lot. He didn't like to talk, but when he did, he was also quite witty. That surprised me. He used to come in just wearing jeans, a T-shirt and that green-type uniform jacket he wore out at Elephant Butte Park, where he worked taking care of the vehicles.

"That's where he met Hendy. She was in jail and they let her out on a work-release program. I think she got in a big fistfight with a guy named Arrey, one of her many boyfriends she picked up after moving here in 1997. Elephant Butte Park is always full of trash and they'd take prisoners out on free work release to clean up around the grounds and I guess Hendy and old David fell for each other right away.

"I guess goin' to jail was great for her. . . .

"I never did like Hendy. I hear some photographer in town has pictures of her half naked with David and Yancy. Pictures he wants to sell, pictures taken six months before they all got arrested. Hell—Cindy Hendy is ugly enough with her clothes on! Cindy is real trashy—dirty clothes, filthy mouth. One time she was drunk and she got real mad at me because I wouldn't give her free cigarettes. She jumped all over me, informin' me her boyfriend was a cop—hell, he was just a nine-dollar-an-hour mechanic wearin' a Smokey the Bear uniform, for Christ's sake!

"I guess as long as she was drunk, she was happy.

"Jesse used to come to Raymond's all the time. She'd ride her bike up to the bar and come in to hang out with other women. Quite often she'd come in with threesomes—all women. I think she's a tomboy. I know even now, in jail, she's got this attitude that everything will blow over—that she and her dad will get off scot-free.

"Yancy, though, I knew him the best. He and his buddies used to come into Raymond's way back in 1991, back before he was old enough to be in a bar. Yancy, Frank Jackson, Sidd Dodds and Jesse Ray—the whole group was into doin' poetry. They were all into writing poems. Kinda silly, like they was trying to be flower children from the 1960s. They'd say, 'Let me read you a poem'—and then try to hustle me for a few free beers. If Roy was walkin' into a bar and he saw a rip in the bar stool, he'd write a poem about it. If he saw a bug, he'd write a poem about it. If he saw a girl he wanted, he'd write a poem about how to 'get' her.

"Roy wore baggy clothes and always smelled like he needed a bath. He was always bummin' around trying to pick up free cigarettes. Roy Yancy never had anything of his own. He'd sleep on your couch until you threw him out; then he'd go home to his mom and dad—until they kicked him out. Then he'd stay on someone else's couch. He'd be in town for a few months; then you wouldn't see him for quite a while. I don't think he ever had a vehicle, except for his old broken-down bicycle.

"Roy wanted to be everybody's sweetheart. He'd talk real nice when I was tending the bar, but if I wouldn't give him a free beer, he'd get real angry.

"That's what happens when you live in a town with a lot of nuts—they're all strange. People come to T or C and nobody asks about their past. People were saying how surprised they were that all these terrible things happened here. I can't think of a better place for this to happen—nobody in Truth or Consequences asks questions when new people show up.

"There's a mental hospital up north in Las Vegas, New Mexico, and I hear when they let out the nuts they give 'em a one-way bus ticket to T or C. Even the nuts living here swear that's the goddamn truth. One night I was in Raymond's and I heard this one gal named Judy, a strawberry blonde, talking to five different people—and she was the only one in the bar. The next morning, I saw her out on the street corner, hollerin' at cars driving by.

"And the police, they aren't much better. The police department has always been kind of a joke to the people who live here—they're a chickenshit police department. They're corrupt. They go out and corral people and then say, 'This one's my friend, so I'll let him go, and this one's not, so I won't let him go.' The city pays 'em about six dollars an hour, so I guess you get what you pay for. Terry Byers, the police chief, is paranoid as hell. When Byers took over the police department, he locked the doors—that's right, from the inside—twenty-four hours a day. I guess he's afraid of the crooks.

"Of course, after the Kelly Clark case, I don't blame him. She was a local cop who got killed in the line of duty. Byers sent this convicted murderer up to the prison in Gallup with just one policewoman driving the patrol car, and the killer jumped her while she was driving, shot her in the head with her own gun, killed her and got away for a few hours before he was caught. If Byers had put another man or woman in the patrol car, Kelly Clark would be alive today. People in T or C are never going to forgive Terry Byers for that fuckup.

"Some local newspaper reporter asked him how many people in the police department supported him and he got tears in his eyes and said, 'Only about one out of eleven.' "

Dan Dickson worked at the airport full-time and moonlighted as a cop for the NMSP Criminal Investigation Unit. During the Ray case, he was involved in several special operations.

"It was the third week in April and there I was down

in this cave in the middle of the night, looking for a body bag. I get a call on my cell phone from the airport. I had to leave right away because this plane wants to take off in the middle of the night. Not any plane, mind you. A twelve-million-dollar Citation Two, owned by the Full Gospel Tabernacle Church. It was real fancy, even had little solid-gold statues of Jesus hidden away in secret cubbyholes in the passenger section. They had just flown some preacher into town for a three-day conference on sin and redemption. (Actually, he was evangelist Ed Rimer, author of several books, including the ever-popular *The Reverend Lucifer D. Satan, and Doctrines of Devils.*) Now, all of a sudden, they want to leave—a few minutes after midnight! They flew in the same day, telling me they were going to stay for three days. They had limousines there to pick up the dignitaries and, all of a sudden, eleven hours later they're cruising down the runway, heading back to Nashville, Tennessee.

The most outrageous story Dickson had to tell about the Ray case concerned something he overheard at the airport right after the FBI arrived in town. He was sitting there at his desk and Doug Beldon, in charge of the whole federal DPR operation in New Mexico, was talking on the phone to another special agent back in Washington, D.C. Dickson couldn't help but overhear what Beldon was saying about one particularly gruesome videotape. He swears to this day about what he heard.

"I overheard the head FBI agent, Beldon, talking on the phone to his boss back in Washington, D.C. It was about one of the videos they found in the toy box and it was a real bad scene. Beldon said Ray and Hendy were using a cattle prod on a naked woman, all tied down. You could see smoke coming out of her vagina, Beldon said. She goes limp and then you see blood comin' out of her mouth—they have alligator clips attached to her nipples. She is screamin' and jerkin' around and there are burn marks on her thighs. Ray and Hendy are taking turns with this gal. At the end, she dies. The last thing I heard Beldon say to the other operative was something about the FBI agents on the scene.

"These guys all said you could see the girl die—it just blew their minds."

Then, in the next breath, Dan Dickson offers up his explanation as to why the so-called "snuff" video may never see the light of day.

"They can't use it in court," he points out, "because it might be a fake."

CHAPTER 15

I've lived here all my life, and I don't agree that my town is a Mecca for white trash.

—Frances Baird, 7/04/1999
(her eighteenth birthday)

By the end of June, a lull had settled over the residents around Truth or Consequences. Most people felt like the case was stagnating because the police had been unable to find even one body.

Then, on June 30, at approximately 10:30 A.M., a Texas fisherman pulled his boat into a small cove right below Champagne Hills on the east shoreline of Elephant Butte Lake. What he saw in the shallow water, about three feet deep, shocked him.

"Just looking at it made you feel strange," said sixty-one-year-old Ralph Tutor. Frances Baird later called it a "bag of goo."

It was a waterlogged gunnysack containing about eighty pounds of animal flesh. The burlap sack seemed to have been split open along its seam. The sack had a frayed rope tied around each end and one length of the rope was longer than the other.

"The bag had been split, and this material was coming out of it," said Tutor. "I didn't like the looks of it—it just did not look right and I said to myself, 'Well, I can't drive off and leave this just floating in the lake.' I had heard about the David Parker Ray case and I knew there might have been some dead bodies in the lake."

Tutor turned the evidence over to the sheriff's office and prosecutor Jim Yontz immediately sent it off to the NMSP Office of Medical Investigations in Albuquerque. He wanted to find out as soon as possible if it was human flesh and if human DNA tests might link it to any of the fourteen people Hendy claimed Ray had murdered.

In the meantime, he drew up his battle plan for the upcoming trial set to begin on October 4. He knew Neil Mertz was a stickler for preventing any higher court from overturning his decisions and Yontz made careful plans to avoid any legal pitfalls. He wanted to save time, so he decided to call all three of the living victims (Vigil, Montano and Van Cleave) to testify against both Rays—David and Jesse. Yontz filed his complicated "joinder" motions early in July and settled down in his cubbyhole office in Socorro to pore over every document he could find tracing the work history of David Parker Ray, going back at least forty years.

Back in T or C, the locals were disgusted by the whole mess. Right after David Ray was arrested, Jo McClean had told several big-city newspaper reporters she thought David was "normal, normal, normal," but by the beginning of summer, the mood in town had dramatically shifted. David was well known for throwing summer BBQ parties out on David Ray Jr.'s sailboat and it wasn't long before people started making morbid jokes about how he was probably serving up "human hamburgers" to his guests on those sizzling-hot afternoons. On July 3, 1999, city officials of Elephant Butte (New Mexico's "Newest City") tried to celebrate their one-year anniversary as an incorporated city, but there wasn't much to cheer about with all the talk of dead bodies lining the bottom of Elephant Butte Lake. Sheriff Terry Byers summed up the local attitude when he said, "People won't eat the fish coming out of the lake anymore—they think the fish have been feeding on David's victims.

"And some of the people in town knew those victims."

Other people in town knew the criminal suspects, too, and it wasn't long before locals started to open up and spill their guts on the main players in the drama. Two men who chimed in right away were John Branaugh, forty-eight, and Richart Hart, forty-six. Both men had been hired by the FBI as informants and they took their new jobs seriously. Branaugh used to hang out with Cindy Hendy when she was dating David Ray, and Hart used to take nude pictures of people around town, including one shot taken six months before their arrests, showing a half-naked Hendy in the arms of Ray—with Yancy feeling her up. Hart also had the distinction of going to jail on a DUI traffic ticket in July 1999, almost making him a cell mate of "the Godfather of Sadism," what some local jokesters were calling David.

Jean Branaugh married "Johnny," as she called him, in August 1997, just a few months after Hendy came to town. Cindy Hendy stood up for them at the wedding. There was a photograph of John and Jean and Cindy and John Youngblood at the outdoor wedding, with everyone smiling. The marriage only lasted two months, and a year later, in 1998, John Branaugh became close friends with Cindy Hendy. They talked almost every day after the Christmas holiday season, and after the story broke on March 22, 1999, Jean Branaugh told friends: "Johnny went white in the face when he saw it on the television."

John Branaugh was a combat veteran of the Vietnam War who left Kansas in 1996 and moved to New Mexico so he could get a fresh start on his life. Years before, he had been a heroin addict and it almost killed him. During the war he was exposed to Agent Orange and he was still suffering from the side effects. He was on permanent disability and did not work due to the fact that he suffered from post-traumatic stress disorder brought on by the war. Meanwhile, he became addicted to painkillers, and that is how he became friends with Cindy Hendy.

"She used to come over all the time and hustle painkillers," he told the police when he was first interviewed. "She was constantly at my house—drunk.

"She's a coke whore, too," Branaugh added. "She wasn't right in the mind. It was the alcohol and the drugs. She didn't know how to be straight—and if she was, she wasn't fit to be around."

After he contacted the NMSP, the FBI hired him as a special investigator and drained him dry of information about the pair of killers.

"She used to come back to my bedroom and talk my ear off," Branaugh told the Feds. "She'd come into the bedroom and I'd have myself propped up on a headboard and she'd be sittin' on the end of the bed, talkin' away. She told me they were going to kidnap Angie. She'd come over here and run all this stuff down to me before they did it.

"She told me she and David were planning to get married this summer. One time David told her he put six women in that lake, and I believe that's true. He'd use them to make those porno tapes and I think he was sellin' those videotapes overseas.

"I know Hendy was tortured by him, and I know Cindy liked the pain, too. One time she pulled up her shirt and showed me these big purple suction-cup marks on her tits. Another time she pulled down her pants and showed me these big red handprints on her butt from spanking—and she was proud of it, too.

"She's a sex addict—she even went so far as to have the inside and outside lips of her vagina removed by a doctor so rough sex would feel better.

"Hendy was into little girls—all she did was sit around and read those little-girl sex magazines. She and David were going to kidnap Hinkle's little ten-year-old daughter—I heard her talk about it. They wanted her as a love slave.

"Right around the time of the last kidnapping, Hendy's oldest daughter, Heather, was about ready to have a baby up in Everett, Washington. Cindy wanted to go up there for the birth of her first grandchild. David didn't want her to go. Even though she promised to call him morning and night, that wasn't enough, so they went up and grabbed that Vigil girl—she was sort of a replacement sex toy for David.

"I remember when Cindy first showed up in town. She was living down by the river [the Rio Grande] in a little pup tent, walking around with a fluffy white cat on a leash. She was living with John Youngblood. Pretty soon they started fighting. Her and Youngblood would fight like cats and dogs. They'd have fistfights. I know a couple of times Youngblood beat the shit out of her. Other times she would scratch herself up and tell the law he did it—and they'd put John in jail. He was in jail three or four times. Hendy always told me it was Youngblood's fault. I know that wasn't always the truth, though, because one other time she said she hit herself in the face with a teapot to make herself look more banged up.

"She fucked cops, too. In this town the police can be real dirty. One time she told me she'd never get picked up by the police in T or C because she'd slept with half the guys on the force. I don't know if that's true—hell, with her you never know what's true and what's false.

John Youngblood told me she used to lie all the time—but I don't think he always told the truth, either.

"My ex-wife came to hate her. She thought Hendy was trading me blow jobs for pain pills, but I'll swear on a stack of Bibles and my mother's grave that I never slept with Cindy. After Jean and me got divorced, she used to bring up this one thing about Hendy always coming over to our house.

" 'Just when you hadn't seen her for a while,' Jean would always say, 'she shows up, like a bad penny. Cindy Hendy was the worst thing that ever happened to David Ray.'

"Me, I thought it was the other way around.

"I have to admit, though, Hendy did like pain. And I think she liked the thought of handing it out, too. She used to read all those serial-killer books and living with David put her right in the middle of one of those books. One night we were talking about murder and she told me something that really fucked with my head. We were talking about David's victims and she just came right out and put it on the table. About where she was coming from, I mean.

" 'I'd like to take the breath out of one,' she said.

"The only reason they let Angie Montano go was because they knew her so well. Angie also had some bad-dude friends. I hear she's back up in Albuquerque now. You know, that woman never had a chance in this life. I talked to Angie one time and she told me she'd been on the street selling her body since she was nine years old.

"Cindy told me she got kicked out when she was only eleven."

Richard "Rick" Hart always wanted to make his living taking photographs. The only problem was, in a small town like T or C, you only make so much money taking pictures of grandpas and their grandsons at the county fair. Hart preferred a little more kinky way of selling pictures, although he was quick to point out to strangers the not-so-obvious facts about his artwork.

"I don't want to be known as a cheesy photographer," he said.

He is proud of the eccentric tastes he brought to town when he moved there in 1996. During the summer of 1998, he was out with friends on Elephant Butte Lake when he motored down by the Dam Site Tavern, right next to the big rock, and got "mooned by four very attractive married women in another boat." There was also a full moon hovering over the nearby cliffs, so he pulled out his camera and took a photograph of the women bending over and baring their round white bottoms on "this gorgeous moonlit night." Back in his lab that night, he pulled the print out of the developing fluid and decided to call it by its rightful name: *Five Moons over Elephant Butte Lake.*

"People in this town just can't wait to see their names in print," he told a friend one day. "A lot of 'em can't wait to hear what they have to say next. I'm not like that at all.

"I'm a Christian. I've worked on an oil rig at eleven degrees below zero and I've been a bounty hunter. Right now, I don't work, but I've got a lot of irons in the fire. Mostly, I just take photographs. The Lord blessed me with a skill, and if you look carefully at my pictures, you'll notice they are crystal clear—they're almost art. They show character."

Right after all four perps got arrested in the spring of 1999, Rick Hart knew he'd been in the right kind of business all along. As luck would have it, he had pictures of three out of the four perps—David, Cindy and Roy—in compromising positions. Pictures taken way before all the hoopla over the rape and murder business.

"In the summer of 1998, I went to a local wedding. Dianne and Roy Lamb had a traditional wedding at a Mormon church in town, and afterward they had a wedding party at the Lambs' house. We went over to Cindy Hendy's trailer—she lived right next door to the Lambs. She told me she wanted to pose for me. I do nude photos and I'd been after her for months. That night I was kind of confused as to why she all of a sudden decided to let me photograph her without her clothes on. Every time I'd tried to take her picture before, she'd always given me the same excuse.

"'I'm eight pounds too fat,' she'd say.

"That night she was just the right weight. Right after we got into her trailer she was joined by her friends Roy Yancy and David Ray. At the time I think Roy was her boyfriend. People used to say that Roy was her 'boy toy.' David sat on the couch and opened his legs wide while Hendy took off her top, pulled her pants down and sat on the couch between his legs. She leaned back into this old man's arms while Roy Yancy started to kiss and suck on her breasts and run the middle finger on his left hand in and out of her vagina. David was just sitting there with a little grin on his face, his reading glasses folded up in his shirt pocket. I just started shooting away from every angle.

"The next day, I took more pictures of Cindy. I have a picture of Hendy wearing an open leather vest with nothing on underneath. You can see the shooting-star tattoo on her left breast. She's holding a white kitten. It's quite a nice photograph—it shows her character.

"I really don't do sick, perverted stuff. I have a lot of women who pose for me. It's real common for women to 'flash me' all the time when I'm in town. Politicians drop off their wives to be photographed—they know what kind of pictures I take—they're professional portraits."

After interviewing Rick Hart in the spring of 1999,

the FBI hired him as a special undercover agent. He told all his friends he even had a code name, but he wouldn't tell anyone what it was. In his initial interview with the Feds, he admitted that the night he took his notorious pictures of Ray, Hendy and Yancy, he had it all wrong.

"I perceived David Parker Ray as the victim," he said. "Cindy and Roy were using his money that night. He sat there in the trailer, quiet and reserved—he didn't use any bad language. When Cindy Hendy laid down in David's lap, I saw the two younger players as abusive of the old man's lonely good nature. I knew Cindy Hendy from around town and I knew she had a mean streak to her. Roy . . . everyone knew he was a real nutty person. I knew that recently David had been carting them all around; they didn't have a vehicle; they were staying at his house for free. I figured Cindy was telling Yancy, 'We can roll him,' and Roy was probably going along for the rides."

Hart paused while recalling his story for the FBI. "I didn't have a clue," he said.

CHAPTER 16

David did excellent repair work: welding, that kind of thing. He was really great with tools.

—Doug Beldon, lead FBI agent, August 1999

Violent crime in New Mexico is a way of life for many people caught in the class warfare between the dirt poor and the filthy rich. One small town in northern New Mexico recently experienced ten homicides in one month—May 1995—right after the snows melted and generations of pent-up family rage exploded in everyone's face. Many people in New Mexico hate the cops, and Jim Yontz had prosecuted enough cop killers to know that someday he wanted to get away from all the crazies. When he moved to Socorro in 1998, he told his wife he wanted to slow down.

"I just want to prosecute a few burglaries and some good old-fashioned cattle-rustling cases," he told her. "Nothing more, nothing less."

Nobody knows what the future holds, and one day after his forty-seventh birthday, Yontz was thrown pell-mell into the flash flood of the David Parker Ray case. Before David Ray, he thought he'd seen it all. By early

August 1999, he was getting the feeling that he hadn't seen anything yet. As he spent seven days a week in his dimly lit office, poring over file after file of David Ray's lengthy work history, all he could come up with was a big, fat zero. Ray had never even been arrested—not once—in his entire life; he appeared to be a model citizen. Right after the arrest, Glen Parks, a young volunteer at the park, described Ray as the "neatest, cleanest, politest person you could ever want to meet," and Yontz figured that was part of the cover-up Ray designed to make sure nobody ever nosed around asking questions about the man behind the mask. The FBI said Ray had patterned his entire life after "the fantasy," so Yontz spent hours trying to figure out how this gentle guy found the time to go out and torture and kill so many women.

While the crime lab up in Albuquerque tried to find out if the bag of flesh was human, Jim Yontz spent night and day trying to figure out what made David Ray less than human. As he fit the fuzzy pieces of the puzzle together, Yontz found himself looking for the little holes in Ray's seemingly normal life—clues that would show a New Mexico jury how this man hid himself from the outside world for a lifetime. Yontz wanted to be able to show the jurors how Ray organized his private "shadow life" around the three things that turned him on: kidnapping, torture and murder.

The clues unfolded from his jagged work history and his long list of failed relationships with women.

David Ray was born along the shores of the Rio Grande River in 1939, right at the end of the Great Depression and right before the beginning of World War II. He was born on the cusp of history—to the Parker family and the Ray family, the only son of his mother, Opel. He was born between the freeway and the river in Belen, New Mexico, and ten years later his parents divorced and his mother farmed him out to her mother, who lived on a small ranch in the low foothills near Abo Pass, just west of Mountainair.

Ray got his first taste of the world of gunpowder in these hills east of Belen, and it wasn't long until he was working with his hands, fixing things. This was the time when he started to have fantasies about fucking girls with Coke and beer bottles and those gnarled dreams would define the rest of his life. It was just a matter of time until he had a chance to look into the eyes of a real girl and see what he saw in those dreams of his youth: raw, uncontrollable fear.

After he graduated from Mountainair High School in 1957, Ray joined the army and was sent to Korea. He had a natural-born ability to fix almost anything he got his hands on and it wasn't long before his skills landed him a job as an expert repairman, mending wristwatches, binoculars and telescopes. He made friends easily and enjoyed being around other young men who were always out prowling for women far away from home. Plus, he learned a valuable lesson that quite often comes back to haunt a country that prepares men for war overseas—he learned that when he got back home, he would always know how to hurt other people.

Jim Yontz read and reread hundreds of pages of notes, looking for something in Ray's love life that might give a hint of things to come. David Ray was married three times before he was thirty years old, not uncommon for men who married in the 1960s. The first marriage ended after one year and the second marriage ended after three months.

"Not much here, other than bad luck with women," Yontz grumbled to himself.

Ray left the army in 1963 and came to Albuquerque to work as a truck driver for the Springer Corporation—the same company that employed his own stepfather. His parents were raising his son at the time while the single David Ray was out looking for women.

Yontz noticed Ray named his first son after himself—David Ray Jr. Yontz had tried in Albuquerque to interview the quiet thirty-nine-year-old air force master sergeant, and the son refused to utter a word about his biological father. Jim quickly cross-referenced a comment he heard from Rick Hart in late July, right after Hart did thirty days in the Sierra County Correctional Facility. Rick had been picked up while drinking and driving, and later that night, he found himself in the cell right next to David Ray Senior. Pretty soon, the two men got into a late-night conversation about fathers and sons. Hart asked David if he and his son were close, and David chuckled at the thought.

"My son and I don't have much in common," he told Hart. "He's a fundamentalist Christian and he doesn't like to 'party.' "

Yontz chuckled to himself at the thought of the man behind the $100,000 handcrafted "Satan's Den" producing a born-again Christian offspring.

In 1966 Ray married Glenda Burdine and the family moved to Tulsa, Oklahoma. Burdine had a two year-old son, Ron, so now David had two young sons. When Ron was interviewed by the Associated Press after his stepfather was arrested, he told the reporter that he had "a pretty mellow dad" and he'd never seen David Ray lose his temper.

"He never raised his voice or his hand," Ron said. "Mom always did the discipline."

In 1968 David and Glenda had a child of their own and Ray became a father to his only daughter—Glenda Jean Ray. At the time David was struggling to make ends meet. He had three young children to feed, so he decided to learn a skilled trade and enrolled in aircraft mechanics school by day. At night he worked at a Tulsa gas station. It was during this time that Glenda apparently stayed home during the day and decided to try to pay some of the bills by becoming a prostitue while her children were napping. More bad luck with women, Yontz noted.

In the early 1970s Ray moved his young family to Victoria, Texas, where he worked as a truck driver by day and moonlighted at night as a volunteer firefighter. Then in 1975 they moved back to rural Oklahoma, where Ray bought a small gas station out in the middle of nowhere and pumped gas for two years. A pattern was emerging, Yontz concluded. The guy could never keep a job for very long and he kept moving again and again. Always looking for the next best thing.

In 1977 Ray moved his family to Temple, Texas, where he worked as a railroad repairman for the Santa Fe Railroad. This job gave him the freedom he'd been looking for for quite some time, Yontz thought. The pattern was beginning to take a definite shape. Ray traveled all across the huge Texas landscape and had ample opportunity to scout women. He kept getting jobs where the female prospects were fresh and untapped, and then all he had to do was cut and run when things got boring. Or the law too close.

After he caught Glenda in bed with another man, for love instead of money, he ran off with his sister-in-law, Joannie Lee. It was 1981 and they drove to Grass Valley, California, and Yontz figured that was where Ray got interested in supplementing his income by growing marijuana. He moved to Phoenix in 1982 and started working as a car mechanic for Canal Motors. On the weekends he would drive up to Fence Lake, New Mexico, where he set up a small marijuana farm run by his children in 1983, 1984 and 1985.

Not far from the little-known Highway 666, running north and south right outside of the Jicarilla Apache Reservation, in northwestern New Mexico. Bad-luck highway, Yontz thought.

He also spent time on the weekends at Elephant Butte Lake, where he moved full-time in 1989. Yontz skipped ahead to the time a few years later when Ray got a job as a truck and heavy-machinery mechanic working out of Elephant Butte State Park, from 1994 to 1999. This gave David the opportunity to travel throughout the five state parks in southern New Mexico, even scouting for victims clear down at Pancho Villa State Park, right on the sparsely populated border with Mexico. During those five years, Yontz figured, he was free to roam a huge slice of desolate, thorny cactus and creosote desert where very few people could keep track of his goings-on.

"No one looking over his shoulder," Yontz wrote on a small notepad. "Just the way he liked it."

Jim Yontz had interviewed two men who knew Ray well from his job as resident mechanic at the Elephant Butte State Park garage, and reading over their combined comments on his personality added up to a profile of a real sneaky-type guy, just like Yontz had suspected.

A master manipulator.

The guy with the most inside dope on Ray was Byron Wilson, thirty-seven, who also just happened to be Frances Baird's boyfriend in the summer of 1999. No wonder her articles were so accurate, Yontz once noted. Byron was a state park cop at Elephant Butte and he had worked with Ray for five years before he and three other cops had to arrest David Ray late in the day on March 22, 1999.

"When I arrested Ray, he was goin' the other way in a motor home," Wilson told Yontz. "He was headin' back to get her, that Cyndy Vigil gal. Couldn't have been more than two blocks away. I pulled him and Hendy over in David's big red RV. It was a felony stop, so I told him to drop the keys out the window on the driver's side. 'Come out and walk backwards,' I says to him. He looks out the window, smiles and says, 'Byron, this is me—David—this isn't necessary.' I say, 'Shut up and put your hands out the window.' He gets out and he's wearing his park ranger uniform—green pants, tan shirt and green coat. I put him facedown in the gravel and handcuffed him. Cindy Hendy was bloody on the back of her neck, so I put on my rubber gloves and frisked her—then I told her to get down on her face, too."

Wilson went on to give his general impression of Ray.

"David was always skinny as a rail. He worked in the sun all his life and smoked heavy. Always had a cigarette in his hand. He was a quiet guy—I never did see him pissed-off mad.

"He got along real well with another guy out at the toolshed, a guy named Martinez. He had a lot of respect for John. Always followed him around, trying to learn how John fixed the big ole John Deere tractors. It always seemed like the rest of the time it was hard to get David to work, though. He never came to work early, never was askin' for extra things to do. He was always messin' around, doin' paperwork. It seemed like he was always goofin' off.

"The year after he started workin' here, he got some big award from the state parks outfit—someone told me it was for about a thousand dollars for helping out in some kind of a cost-savings program. I guess he got himself cleaned up pretty good for the awards ceremony. He got a certificate of 'special achievement,' with his name typed in gold letters and all. It all sounded like bullshit to me.

"A few years later, he got caught for theft here at Elephant Butte Park. He stole a transmission-cooler out of a heavy-duty truck and they punished him by giving him thirty days off without pay. That's pretty damn serious down here—it was their way of being nice and not firing him.

"He worked at five state parks and was out of town regular. He always made sure he was back in town for the big summer holiday weekends. Around here, the population of Elephant Butte goes up from fifteen hundred to over one hundred thousand on Memorial Day, the Fourth of July and Labor Day weekends. On the big three-day weekends, he was always volunteerin' to go out and shut down parties. He had this big white Dodge Ram and except for the fact that it didn't have decals, you wouldn't know it wasn't from the park—it looked just like ours. Late at night he was always pretendin' to be some kind of cop, instead of a plain ole mechanic.

"Around the park he would always talk about his daughter's girlfriends. He'd always talk about these girls going out with him on his son's sailboat—don't know if I ever saw one out there with him or not. To me, he always seemed like the old pervert who was screwin' his daughter's friends.

"He thought he was the big stud, but all he was doin' was just pickin' up on his daughter's dyke girlfriends."

Byron Wilson spent many mornings drinking coffee with David Ray and the guys, in the toolshed or down the road at the Diamond Gas Station coffee shop. There was always one topic that seemed to come up over and over when Ray was just sitting around shooting the breeze with his fellow employees. Byron remembered that Ray would get a certain twisted smile when the conversation turned to sex. When the subject came up, David Ray's eyes would sparkle.

Jim Yontz flipped back through his notes to find out what John Martinez had told investigators about the older man he worked with side by side for nearly five years. Yontz knew Ray had multiple sides to his personality, so it was no big surprise that Martinez painted an entirely different picture of Ray at work.

"People are either born here or they come here for the sunshine," Martinez told Jim Yontz. "Me—I was born here. I knew David real well. I seen him all the time. Old David, he'd never hurt a fly. The day before he got arrested, he was driving out near Engle, in the Valley of Death, and he ran over a baby Gambel's quail. He killed it and it made him real sad. He felt so bad about running over that little chick—heck, he must have mentioned it to me four or five times later that afternoon."

During the interview, Martinez kept shaking his head.

"Dave—he was the best damn mechanic I ever seen."

As Yontz shuffled through more paperwork, he realized there was a gap in David Ray's work history. He got the Elephant Butte job in 1994, the same year his fourth wife left him, but Yontz needed to know what he'd done between 1991 and 1994, during the time Jesse Ray was living with him. The information about those three years was murky, but Yontz finally located one piece of paperwork that answered all his questions.

It was an advertisement in the local T or C Yellow Pages.

David had rented a garage in T or C and was running his own automotive repair service. "For stranded motorists," the ad said. "Dave's Emergency Roadside Service."

Yontz tried to imagine what it must have been like for the old man and his "clients." All the poor woman had to do was call his number and he'd be there with his van. He'd help her repair her broken-down car somewhere down by the lake or out in the middle of the desert—or on some freeway ramp. Maybe he'd even tow her pile of junk back to town. And if the poor unfortunate woman just happened to call on a night when he had the "urge"—well then, he'd be forced to tow her back to his place.

The listing in the Truth or Consequences phone book looked innocent enough. It was a cheap advertisement, in small letters, designed not to bring too much attention to itself. But its implications were dark.

CHAPTER 17

I thought Satan lived in this town for a while.
—Jean Branaugh, August 1999

By August 1 many women in Truth or Consequences wondered if they, too, had been kidnapped, raped and drugged by David Ray and his followers. To be single and female was to be cursed in T or C, and some women wondered if they were the "walking wounded" who couldn't even remember what had been done to their bodies. Frances Baird had talked to many women who had unsettling stories to tell. Some were still afraid for their lives. Most were making plans to leave T or C.

Linda, thirty-eight, was working as a maid in a local motel when David Ray got arrested. Years before she moved to T or C, she'd worked as a firefighter in another state and she knew how to deal with men who tried to talk their way into her underpants. Right after she showed up in town, she got a job working as a groundskeeper at Elephant Butte State Park. One day David Ray stopped her out by the lake at a remote spot and suggested maybe they could try some kinky sex.

Nothing too rough, nothing she couldn't handle, he told her. She kept looking at the ground and shook her head. He persisted, saying, "Give me a couple of days and I'll turn you around." Linda gave him a dirty look and didn't waste any more time, telling him to "fuck off." She never spoke to him again, and he never bothered her anymore.

Roberta, thirty-four, was working as a bartender at the Dam Site Tavern when Jesse Ray was arrested. She told Frances she knew a woman—she would not give out a name—who had been close friends with Jesse for a short period of time. "After her and Jesse became friends," she told Frances, "Jess asked her if she wanted to try whips and chains and stuff like that and my friend just said no—so Jess left her alone."

Betty, thirty-three, was out of work in April and May 1998. She had recently divorced her husband in order to live as a lesbian, something she'd wanted to do for quite a long time. In June she started to hang out at Raymond's Lounge. She met Jesse there and the two women quickly became a cozy item. For a short while Betty thought they might be in love. She spent several nights with her new lover out at David Ray's trailer, where she and Jesse would sometimes stay up all night making love on the carpet of Ray's living-room floor. It wasn't until after the mass arrests in 1999 that Betty discovered that David Ray had a secret camera mounted behind a hole in the wall of the living room so he could watch his daughter having sex while he sat in front of his television screen back in his bedroom. Betty quivered all over at the thought.

"I still can't believe how close I probably came to getting killed," she told Frances.

Wanda, forty-two, used to date David Ray for a short time. She wouldn't talk to the media, but Frances was able to get a few comments out of her former employer Jackie Williams, owner of the Black Range Restaurant and Motel.

"Wanda Bickle worked for me as a waitress for a short time. Poor thing, she wasn't in her right mind most of the time. Her nineteen-year-old daughter got stoned on something or the other and strangled Wanda's three-year-old granddaughter to death with an electrical cord. Wanda hasn't been right since then. She did tell me, however, that during the brief time she and David dated, he was nothing but a complete gentleman."

On August 11, 1999, prowlers broke into Jackie's Black Range Restaurant by throwing a rock through a large plate-glass window in front of the cash resgister. There was no money in the till, so they overturned the cash register and poured sugar over all the tabletops. Jackie Williams came to work that morning and after she filed a report with the slow-moving T or C police department, she gave one hungry customer standing outside a piece of her mind.

"This is a dirty little town," she lamented. "My husband and I moved to this town two years ago in order to find a quiet little place where we could enjoy our last few years together. We had no idea there were going to be methamphetamine addicts running all over town. I just opened up my restaurant and motel and started hiring the locals.

"I've hired some real 'doozies.' It's hard to hire someone here who doesn't have something criminal in their background.

"Before all the drug dealers took over America, you used to be able to buy a cheap little place, cook up some bacon and eggs and put out a welcome sign—now I don't know. I've had crack heads and coke heads refuse to pay for their room rent at the Black Range Motel, and we had to evict them by using force. After we kicked them out, all hell would break loose. I've had people break the windows of my car, throw eggs at me, try to light my car on fire. Boy, oh boy, what a town. . . .

"When this place takes a dislike to you, watch out."

Two weeks later, Jackie Williams, sixty-three, had a

massive heart attack and closed down the Black Range Restaurant and Motel for good. She and her husband made immediate plans to leave T or C.

The week after Labor Day weekend, Frances Baird was in the Los Arcos Steak House having a salad and a Coke when she ran into J.J., twenty-three, a local waitress. They struck up a conversation.

"You knew Jesse Ray and David Ray, didn't you?" Baird asked.

"I think Jess was rounding up victims for her dad," J.J. speculated. "Jesse was like a man. She'd dress like a man in those blue jeans and that black leather vest. I heard that when she shot pool, she tried to put all the men in the dirt. The first time I saw her driving that big Honda Gold Wing motorcycle, I just thought she was an ugly guy."

"Did you ever go out to David's house?" asked Baird.

"No, but you know how people like to party here. Their idea of a good time is to get a couple of hundred people together and break out a few cheap kegs of beer. I can't prove it by my own experience, but I think group sex is pretty common in Truth or Consequences. I've heard stories about people who like to have five to ten naked couples in a room—and then anything goes. I think people were going over to David's and having some kind of a weekly sex orgy."

"I agree with you," Baird said. "Just before he first published the *Sentinel*, my dad still preached at his own church. The first month he was in T or C, people at church told him unless he agreed to wife swapping, people might not buy his newspaper. That was twenty-five years ago."

"I guess he didn't listen to them," joked J.J.

"Nope, and I think we still have the best newspaper in town," Baird answered, laughing. "Best coverage of crime, that's for sure."

* * *

By September 28, Jim Yontz was starting to feel like the Lone Ranger. His boss, DA Ron Lopez, didn't want to have anything to do with prosecuting David Ray and dumped the whole mess in Yontz's hands. The crime lab in Albuquerque had declared the bag of flesh to be human, but they couldn't even determine if the tissue was male or female, let alone identify any of the women from the stack of unidentified driver's licenses found in Ray's home. Chances for Yontz to make a quick kill were fading and now Judge Mertz had just postponed the October 4 trial for at least another six months. It felt like things were starting to come apart at the seams.

Yontz had already suffered two serious setbacks.

Back on July 2, Judge Mertz had refused to disqualify himself from the case, so Yontz had decided to give him a nudge. He had filed an appeal with the New Mexico Supreme Court to try and have them remove Mertz from trying the case. Yontz feared that Mertz would force him to have two separate trials for David and Jesse Ray. But his deeper fears centered around the possibility that Mertz would crush his speedy prosecution case by forcing the state to prosecute David Ray on three separate occasions—one time for each living victim: Cyndy Vigil, Angie Montano and Kelli Van Cleave. On August 12, the supreme court agreed to hear the appeal concerning Mertz.

On August 25, the supreme court dealt Yontz his first big blow. It declared that Mertz would try all four defendants in the David Ray case.

Then, on September 22, Judge Mertz had dealt Jim Yontz his second big blow. He declared that David Parker Ray and Glenda "Jesse" Ray would be tried separately, thereby creating what Yontz did not want to admit to himself: a nightmare for one man to handle. Yontz was stunned by his predicament and one day when Lopez wandered into his office and asked him how things were going, he shook his head and told the truth in his typical matter-of-fact way.

"It looks like prosecuting David Ray is going to be a lifetime job," he said.

And now the trial had been put off until at least the spring, making it impossible to try David and Jesse anywhere in Sierra County, in either Socorro or Truth or Consequences. On October 4, Jeff Rein, representing David, and Billy Blackburn, representing Jesse, filed a motion with Mertz to change the venue and move the two trials out of town. For once, Jim Yontz found himself agreeing with the other side and the three men worked together to find a list of small, out-of-the-way towns where they all thought the Rays might get a fair trial. Mertz told them to have their recommendations back on his desk by October 11. He would rule on new locations before Thanksgiving, he told them.

The next setback to Yontz was his mounting frustration over trying to deal with Cindy Hendy. She had fired her old attorney, Xavier Acosta, back in August, and by October 15 she had a new public defender, Carmen Garza, working for her. Yontz did not like the sound of things. Word on the street was that Hendy had been sending love letters to Ray and he had been writing her back on a weekly basis. Looking up her file, Yontz noticed that David Ray had told one investigator that when they got pulled over and arrested in March, the last thing he said to her was "Do whatever you have to do to stay out of jail." And now it looked like she had taken his advice—and then, as usual, changed her mind.

On November 5, Cindy Hendy filed motions to change her plea from guilty to innocent. She wanted a trial of her own.

Now Jim Yontz had one more major headache to

work out. In seventeen years of prosecuting felons, he only knew of two cases where defendants had successfully changed their pleas from guilty to innocent, and he damn sure wasn't going to let Cindy Hendy add her name to that short list. He immediately filed motions to prevent her from flip-flopping. The bad news was that he could no longer rely on her to testify against her former boyfriend and he also was prevented from entering all the charges she had made against him: specifically, that he had murdered fourteen people. So it was beginning to look like he was going to have to convict Ray without the mention of a single dead body.

He didn't panic. He knew he could do it, sooner or later.

On November 19, Judge Mertz decided where he was going to move the jury trials for David and Jesse Ray. David Ray would be tried in Tierra Amarilla on March 28, 2000, and Jesse Ray would be tried in Gallup on July 10, 2000. Both locations were fine by Yontz. He could go trout fishing up in the mountains of northern New Mexico in March and bird hunting out in the western plains of New Mexico in July.

Just before Thanksgiving, he got a call from Frances Baird. She told him she'd been interviewing girls around town who narrowly escaped the jaws of David Ray's trap and she asked him if he had any other witnesses he was still trying to locate.

"Yeah, Candy Frairs," he told her. "She took off right after David got arrested. I think she went up to the Mescalero Apache Reservation and I think she's hanging out on the edge of that little town called Riudoso, but I can't find her."

"I never heard of her," said Baird.

"She was in the torture chamber with David and she took everything he had to offer without complaining.

She saw the whole operation from the inside out. She even wrote David some little notes telling him how much she liked it. I don't think he understood what made her tick. He couldn't fathom a woman liking it that rough."

"So you think he liked her?" asked Frances.

"No, Ray doesn't know how to like a woman—but I think he respected her. He couldn't make her cry, and compared to all the other women who broke down hysterically, I think he felt Candy was some kind of superwoman."

"Was she?" asked Frances.

"I doubt it," said Yontz, "but I sure as heck would like to talk to her."

CHAPTER 18

"I don't give sympathy to nobody. I survive in this town, that's it."

Gail Astbury, T or C resident, 12/31/1999

Every fall the residents of T or C celebrate Geronimo Days, a two-day celebration of the Wild West history of southern New Mexico. In 1999 bluegrass bands, six-shooter contests, fiddlin' contests, chili feeds, cowboy poetry and plenty of "palefaces" and Apache Indians managed to take the town's mind off David Parker Ray.

Meanwhile, the so-called town "white trash" huddled together down on Austin Street, one block off Date, and spent their time dealing drugs and sex in the decaying steam baths that once gave the city its name. The police made one drug sweep in November that rounded up over twenty people, including David Ray's old flame, Wanda Bickle. She was arrested for trying to sell a "teener," a sixteenth of an ounce of homemade methamphetamine, to an undercover cop. Her bond was set at $10,000.

The people living on the fringe of life in T or C hadn't contributed much to the public debate over David Ray and his friends, but in private they had plenty to say. They met at one-night-stand motels like the Dude and the Ace and the Honey-Doo Inn. They gathered in run-down steam baths and sweat houses with names like Geronimo Hot Springs and started to tell their stories. Many of them started life on the wrong side of the tracks, but their point of view wasn't always so crazy as the establishment liked to think. Some of them had cleaned up their act and just not bothered to tell anybody from the other side of the railroad tracks.

Gail Astbury, thirty-seven, was one of those people.

A tiny woman who always bragged, "I can kick anybody's butt," she was also a devoted mother and loyal friend. Her dirty little secret was that she was still a fugitive from justice over an outstanding aggravated assault charge in Florida from 1990. She'd been hanging out in T or C long enough to change gears and straighten out most of her life from the days back in Florida when she was a hooker with a $200-a-day drug habit.

"I'm kind of a bitch," she told a reporter from Reuters. "I don't give sympathy to nobody. I survive in this town, that's it. I don't do drugs anymore—I only do pain pills. I stay away from heroin—you can tell a junkie, just look at their arms—my arms, they're virgins. My sister is a heroin addict. I don't beat my kids—I'd rather cuss at my kids than beat 'em. Sometimes I hurt people with my mouth when I talk too much, but that's because I'm brutally honest. I tell the truth and other people make up shit.

"I still have a few bad habits. Last year on Valentine's Day, I popped my husband in the face and broke his nose. He called the cops and they took him to jail. The next day, I bonded him out of jail, but later that day, he told me he still loved me! Right now, my only sin is drinking a little too much. I drink every day, but I wouldn't say I'm an alcoholic. I only drink cheap beer—like, say, Milwaukee's Best!

"Some days I live up to my reputation. When the David Ray case first broke, I was having breakfast in the Hill Top Cafe when I heard Debbie Fisk tell a reporter, 'I saw Hendy hit someone with a frying pan.' I knew that Hendy had slept with Fisk's husband, so I cranked up my voice real loud and said what was on my mind.

" 'Debbie's got this ass that's as big as the front of my car and I know for a fact that she's a nosy bitch. Her mouth is as big as her ass.'

"I've lived in Truth or Consequences for the last five years and I consider it home. There might be people here who dabble in Satanism, but they're not smart enough to pull it off. We do have dirty cops here and that's why so many people are so afraid. But none of us is going anywhere—we all plan to stay right here.

"For nine years I've been hiding from the law, but I don't feel like I'm hiding in T or C. This is my town. Anyway, those charges from Florida are all bullshit. They're as old as dirt. Some girl, she dropped off one rock of cocaine in my car—so I got after her a little. Slugged her right in the face. Anyway, if they come after me, I'm gonna make 'em fuck their asses off in order to get me back to Florida. I hate that place.

"I really want to believe that Jesse is innocent. Jesse is a friend of mine. I used to ride around on the back of Jesse's motorcycle. A lot of people who saw me whiz by thought I was queer, too, and it always made me mad as hell. I talked to Jesse once about David being the father to her kid and 'Yes, Yes,' she told me it was true. She said that was why she was always staying in town rather than out at his house. Another time she denied it. From what I understand now, she lied to me about her father not being the father of her child and sometimes I feel, like, if she'd lie to me, she'd lie to anybody.

"Basically, though, I think she's a good, intelligent person. I talk like a sailor—she doesn't even cuss. I want her to be Jesse again, not a scumbag—her father is a scumbag. Jesse is a pushover for animals. One time she got mad at me for hittin' a rattlesnake with a rake—it was in my front yard. She told me I should have trapped and relocated it.

"Lately she's been telling everyone that her father has never been anything other than an inspiration for her. I'd say that right now she's got him on a pedestal. She told me she had nothing but respect for him.

"Last month my sister, Jeannie, was in jail with David. Everyone has respect for him in jail. When his sister, Peggy, brought him a bag of serial-killer books, he would read 'em, write his name on 'em and send 'em down to the girls. When he gets money, he buys all the girls candy bars. Three Musketeers. Jeannie says the girls wait a couple of days and then moan out through their bars, 'Daaaaavid—I need chocolate.'

"He's got the guards all won over—they call him 'Mr. Ray' or 'Big Dave.' I don't know, though. Half the guards who work there are always high on meth. When the jailers come flying through there, the inmates can tell who the 'tweekers' are.

"David is so frail—I could kick his butt. I can't imagine him ever overpowering anyone, but I do remember Jesse telling me strange stories about Fence Lake. Shit, I think some of this stuff has been going on for years. Jesse told me there was a dungeon in his basement up at the pot farm.

"I also remember when Jesse used to work on my car, there were places on David's property where my kids couldn't go. I also remember being inside his bedroom one time and I noticed big hooks up on the wall. At the time I didn't pay very much attention because people always told me he was a fisherman. Plus, I was probably stoned that night. I know that sounds stupid. Now that I think back on it, this whole thing pisses me off.

"I remember another time when a guy I knew real well went to Ray's property to deliver a boat late at night. He heard a girl cryin' for help inside the cargo trailer and he got real scared and turned around and drove home. He didn't tell anybody until the story broke, and when he told me, I got real mad at him. I told him I only weighed a hundred pounds, but I would have helped her. Then I told him to get out of my house.

" 'I don't know you!' I yelled at him. 'Go away!'

"I know the guy who sold the gynecological table to David. His name is Peter Douglas—we used to call him 'Peter Pan.' He's an asshole. One time I seen him let his dog start screwin' his own left leg, right in front of my kids. They were little tykes then. Later that night, I told my son he was a pervert. I don't have any doubts that he'd try to hump my kid himself if he could get away with it.

"When Cindy Hendy first moved to town, she got to me. She made me feel sorry for her. She showed up with that big motherfucker John Youngblood, and the next time I saw her, her face was beat to shit. It didn't take me long to change my opinion of her, though. One night Mike, my ex-husband, was in town. He'd just got out of prison in Florida after serving nine years on a grand-theft auto charge. We hooked up with Cindy Hendy and went over and scored some pain pills from John Branaugh. That night I listened to Hendy talk and I knew she was a liar. She told some bullshit story about how she and Youngblood went to a party up in Everett, Washington, and there was some kind of orgy going on. She claimed the people there were passing around some dead guy's bloody intestine and everyone was hanging this big sausage around their necks—it was a dumb story.

"Plus, she's a no-good mother.

"I heard the other day that now she wants to change her plea from guilty to innocent. That makes me want to laugh my ass off. She outfoxed herself, that dumb bitch.

"Dennis Roy Yancy—I don't know about that guy.

Most of the time he just seemed like a happy-go-lucky kid. He's so small—only about five foot eight inches tall—I don't know how he could hurt anyone. But a lot of my friends think he's a real mean guy. There's a nasty rumor around town that really scares the shit out of me. A few years ago, a local guy, a guy named Lee, was murdered. Someone shoved a doorknob up his ass and then crammed nuts and bolts down his throat. I hear the last person they seen at his house on the night he disappeared was Roy Yancy.

"I never know who to trust in this town. Take those crazy assholes over at the Full Gospel Tabernacle Church. Those people are nuts. They're known as the Demon Church. They cast spells on people and they speak in tongues. One time I was in Raymond's Lounge when I saw one of the preachers from the church sitting around with a group of drunks. It was last summer and there was this reporter in town trying to dig up dirt on the case. Cynthia Culpepper got up from the table and staggered over to the bar to talk to the reporter. A couple of minutes later, this Pastor Leroy walks up, looking real worried, and takes Cynthia by the arm and leads her back to the table of drunks.

"And that guy Leroy is in charge of the video production for the whole church. When you want videotapes, he's the guy you talk to. That Pastor Leroy—he's no good.

"And that girl Vigil—I heard she was into black-tar heroin. Someone told me she was paid eight hundred dollars to come down here, and when the drugs ran out—she ran away.

"Angie Montano—I know her. She's a real cuckoo bird. She's a total piece of shit—worth nothing. Nothing.

"Her son, Abel, comes over here to my house to visit my kids and I always check his pockets—when he walks in and when he walks out. Abel is a nice little boy, but I don't trust him. You should see his face. He's got a nasty scar on his cheek where a German shepherd bit him one time when his mother was high on meth and not payin' any attention to him. I hear he's livin' with Montano's boyfriend now that she's back on Central Avenue shootin' up.

"Everybody in this town does drugs. You don't get anywhere in this town for working. I collect welfare—so does everybody else. People have too much time on their hands—there are a lot of people screwing around, too—mostly threesomes. But drugs are what make Truth or Consequences tick. Most people run their drug business out of their houses. That's all this town is . . . drugs, and more drugs.

"This is the worst meth town I've ever been in. . . . Methamphetamines are so easy to brew. Any idiot can make meth. You can whip it up in a kitchen blender. All you need is a little drain cleaner, lighter fluid and a lithium battery. People here call it the poor man's cocaine. It hits you faster and lasts much longer. I used to use it—that's why my face is all scratched up. I hear Angie clawed her eye out—dumb bitch. She should have kicked the habit like I did. I don't have any sympathy for people who don't get straight. T or C has a lot of tweekers. Me, I got a bumper sticker that tells everyone where I'm coming from. It doesn't beat around the bush.

"It says 'TWEEKERS really suck!'

"My younger sister, Jeannie, shoots needles. She's been a heroin user since she was thirteen. She's thirty-three years old now. She's in a lot of trouble right now. She just got out of jail for forgery and the other day we got in a big argument. David Ray gave her dominoes in jail and she stole them. I told her to give them back. We got in another big argument last week and she threatened to come out here and burn my trailer down. So I whacked her with one of those little T or C phone books and she hit me in the knee and hurt her left hand. Served her right!"

On November 12, 1999, the *Desert Journal* ran an interview with Jeannie Astbury in which she claimed that Roy Yancy raped her at David Ray's mobile home. The masthead for the *Journal* read IN HOT PURSUIT OF THE TRUTH, but Jim Yontz always called it "the Deserted Journal" because it had the smallest number of readers of the three weeklies in T or C. In the lengthy article, Jeannie claimed that the rape took place in a room with bright white lights everywhere. She said she couldn't remember too many details, but she did remember looking into Yancy's face as he lay on top of her.

> I never expected anything like this to happen from Roy. I could expect this kind of thing from others. Roy was always so polite and didn't do drugs. I knew he was married but I didn't know his wife. I just never saw eyes like that. It was the eyes that freaked me out more than anything else.
>
> His eyes were very bright, bright, bright—very green, green, green—like evil.
>
> I was really, really scared, but I'm a tough chick. I felt like I died a little bit that night. I don't feel right mentally, now. I was pretty strong for quite a few weeks, but I didn't beat it. My sister said she had never seen me like that in my entire life. I couldn't function for a while. I want to remember everything that happened to me but I can't. I want to remember where the room was and why I was gone for seven whole hours, but I can't. I just feel like something terrible happened. I know it deep in my soul.
>
> I think Roy was an evil person that night.

CHAPTER 19

"Your body is the property of the Church of Satan."
—David Parker Ray's voice on an audiotape he recorded on July 6, 1993.

Frances Baird was five years old when the town of Truth or Consequences was terrorized by Dennis Roy Yancy and two of his high-school buddies. It was late October 1987 and down at the worried offices of the *Sierra County Sentinel*, Myrna Baird decided to run an urgent message on the front page of the newspaper. She had already sent an undercover reporter to infiltrate the small satanic group, but he joined forces with the other side and she had to fire him. Still, Myrna knew that cats had been strangled and historical gravestones overturned and people were frightened. Another reporter from the *Sentinel* had already found resistance in the form of white witchcraft graffiti painted on rocks outside of town, so it was time for an official reaction. So she ran the following public announcement in the October 21 edition of the paper.

PUBLIC HELP SOUGHT

In an effort to prevent property damage and
personal injury, the Sierra County Sheriff,
the T or C Police Department
and the Socorro District Attorney's Office
have formed a Joint Task Force.
A telephone Hot-Line has been set up.
Any individuals having information regarding animal
cruelty, property damage, grave tampering,
drug or alcohol abuse,
trespassing at cemeteries, or any suspicious activity,
are asked to call [number given] from 4:00 P.M. to
10:00 P.M. through Halloween night.
The caller need not identify themselves.

Frances had a dim memory of those years. The woman she would later call her mother (and her trusted mentor) was actually her grandmother Myrna Baird, the owner of the *Sentinel.* She had only recently adopted Frances from her biological mother back in Nebraska. What went wrong between Myrna and her own daughter was a mystery to Frances and that whole period of time was very confusing for Frances. She did, however, remember Halloween, 1987.

As the December 6 trial date for Dennis Roy Yancy drew closer, Frances Baird called Jim Yontz at work to get an update on the possibility of a jury trial. They started talking about the year Halloween was canceled in T or C and Baird told him what it felt like to be a little kid that fall.

"I couldn't even go trick-or-treating," she said, still sad recalling the long-ago memory.

"Yeah," said Yontz. "Dennis was already off to a bad start by the time he was sixteen years old, and two years later, after meeting David Ray, he probably went off the deep end. David pushed him over the edge—all Dennis needed was a violent coach."

"If Dennis is convicted, how many years do you think Mertz will give him?" asked Baird.

"That's tricky. Last summer I talked to Yancy's public defender, Gary Mitchell, and we worked out a deal where Dennis would plead guilty to second-degree murder instead of first-degree murder. I'll find out in the next couple of days if we still have a deal. I've got real mixed feelings about Dennis, though. He's told us he kidnapped Marie and later killed her, but he claims that during their four days and nights together, he didn't torture her. I don't know if I believe him, but we don't have a body to examine."

"You're kinda stuck, aren't you?"

"You bet," said Yontz. "In the state of New Mexico, you can't prosecute someone without a body—and without any evidence. We don't have anything other than Dennis admitting to us that he did the dirty deed."

"What about that article in the *Journal* about Jeannie Astbury?" asked Baird.

"No way," said Yontz. "I couldn't use her because the *Deserted Journal* had her memory hypnotically refreshed. Juries don't like that kind of testimony."

"So all you've got is Yancy's confession?" asked Baird.

"Not exactly," admitted Yontz. "We've got another David Parker Ray audiotape that goes on and on about his nasty little group of Satanists and what they did to women, but I don't think Mertz will ever allow us to play it. Dennis's name is never mentioned on the tape."

Yontz got a call on the other phone line and he told Baird what he always told reporters interested in getting the scoop.

"Call me anytime if you need more information. Call me at home, if you need to."

Later that night, Yontz glanced over at the pile of evidence strewn out on top of the table covered by the skin of Bernie the black bear. He spotted the tape he really wanted to use if Dennis Roy Yancy forced a trial on December 6. He wanted to listen to Tape Number Five one more time because it was different in one important way from all the other audiotapes. Most of David's tapes had a clever little introductory disqualification that started out with the words "This tape was designed to be used for entertainment purposes."

Not Tape Number Five.

Like all six audiotapes, this one addressed what Jim Yontz imagined was a "live" captive, fresh off the streets or the dusty back roads, paralyzed with fear and probably wondering whether she would live or die. Listening to David Ray, Yontz always took him on face value for what he and his friends said they were going to do to the victims. Yontz never allowed himself to think it was all make-believe. Tape Number Five opened with the sound of David's soft and friendly voice speaking over a background of what sounded like religious instrumental music.

> Hello, bitch.
>
> I'm sure you're wondering why you've been kidnapped and what's going to happen to you. That's why this tape has been made. It saves a lot of talking. It's brief, blunt and to the point.
>
> I'm a dungeon master for a local chapter of the Church of Satan, Lucifer, or the Devil, to you. You have been abducted so that your body can be used during rituals, and for sexual purposes for the congregation after the meetings. Our membership is pretty small, about twenty people, mixed male and female. Our meetings are pretty much what most people imagine—the way it is depicted in the movies.
>
> A hidden church, black robes, pentagrams, rituals, chanting, a lot of nakedness, animal sacrifices, chicken blood and a hell of a lot of sex afterward! The meetings get interesting and exciting,

to say the least. Trying to raise the demons is important, but it is the sex that keeps the church financially afloat. The high priest likes to keep everybody fired up on sex, and for that, we like fresh meat. Every couple of months we kidnap some good-looking little bitch to use during the rituals and to be kept available for everyone to use during the orgy.

Let me tell you what happens at the meetings. The orgy room is separate from the main church. It contains several couches, many mats on the floor and a refreshment center. In the middle of the room is a large wooden table with leather straps on it. Prior to each meeting, you'll be taken to the church in a wooden box, naked, in chains, and with your eyes taped shut—so you can't identify anybody.

Once there, you will be strapped down on top of the table. Your arms will be chained straight out to each side and leather straps will be buckled across your upper chest, your rib cage and your belly—so you can't move. Your legs will be spread extremely wide apart because some of our members have diversified interests in, ah . . . which hole they want to use. There is a U-shaped cutout at the top of the table and it allows your head to drop right down into it. Another leather strap will be put across your forehead so you can't move, allowing your mouth and throat to be available for sex.

Dental jaw blocks will be installed in your mouth so that you can't bite anybody during oral sex. When your mouth is wide open, members will just shove their dicks down your throat and hump your face until they come.

After the meeting is over in the church, everyone will move into the orgy room and take their robes off [*laughs*]. Now everybody is fucking naked! And they'll surround the table. You're definitely going to be the center of attention, especially at the first meeting when you're the new girl. Everybody is going to want to feel you up and try you out. Anyway, the high priest will move to the bottom of the table with a large wooden box that contains the dildo—what we call "the devil's dick." The tip is small, so it'll start in the vagina easy, but the thing is tapered. It widens enormously at the base to about three inches thick, and the whole thing is pretty close to twelve inches long. It's a real pussy stretcher.

Once it starts to go in, the high priest will chant:

The Devil fucks!
The Devil fucks!
The Devil fucks!

A half a dozen people will help hold your body still while the high priest forces the dick up all the way inside you. There will be a sudden blast of pain between your legs and it's not unusual at all for a girl to pass out while this is being done.

Next the high priest will rape you. After he gets through, your body will be available for everybody's use. They'll take turns using you in various ways, and during the course of the evening, most of them will come back for seconds and thirds. You'll probably be raped forty to fifty times.

The next morning, after everybody goes home, I'll take you back to the dungeon, wash the sperm out of your body and clean you up. I'll give you a bath and let you build your strength up so we can do it all over again [*laughs*]. You're gonna be used for three or four meetings. By then, a captive is pretty well worn out and everybody's tired of fucking with her.

Remember, your body is the property of the

Church of Satan. The church is going to have you one night every two weeks and I've got you the rest of the time. Now, the dungeon belongs to the church, and it's very well equipped. They spent a ton of money buying all sorts of specialized equipment, about anything I asked for. They even gave me medical supplies to patch up girls in case the high priest tears some slut's pussy with a big dildo, and that doesn't happen too often. One of my duties is to prestretch a girl's vagina so the dildo won't tear it. There have been a few occasions when we've kidnapped a bitch and had to take her to a meeting that same evening. Usually when that happens, the devil's dick tears the fuck out of her vagina. Then I have to patch her up afterward.

A few years ago, there was a certain period of time that we didn't do that. During that time there were instances where the fellows caused so much vaginal damage that the girl hemorrhaged, and sometimes didn't survive. And it caused some problems within the congregation. Nobody likes watching a girl bleed to death.

Well [*laughs*], now you know what this is all about. You're not exactly a sacrificial virgin. I don't imagine you're a virgin anyway. Virgins are pretty hard to come by. During the years that I've been dungeon master, for variety we sometimes snatch some pretty young girls . . . thirteen, fourteen years old, and even with that, we've only had two virgins.

Well, so much for that. You know how you're going to serve the church.

Now let's talk about how you're going to serve me.

It is within my power to make your stay in the dungeon reasonably easy, or a living hell. There are going to be some rules, and whether you like them or not, you will learn to obey them. You're going to find that I don't have any patience at all with pretty little girls that forget and make mistakes.

Crying is acceptable, as long as you're not too loud about it. Most of the time I expect you to keep your mouth shut. You need to tell me, however, when you have to use the rest room, because if you make a mess, whether it be a piss or a crap, you're going to be forced to lick it up.

Don't bite. There are no second chances. If you bite, I cut.

As far as kicking goes, I really don't have a set punishment for that. If you should hurt me with your feet, the punishment shall be whatever I decide. That's not fair, but that's life.

When the church is done with you, the high priest will advise me when you are to be released and I will initiate a process that will take about two days. You're going to be injected with a combination of drugs and then brainwashed until you don't remember the church, me, this place or any fucking thing about what's happened to you. After the hypnosis has taken effect, you'll be taken near some town and turned loose.

Everything will heal up in two or three weeks. It will probably take just a little longer for your vagina to shrink back to normal size, but, ah [*laughs*] . . . that too will come to pass.

Now this is the beginning of a very trying ordeal for you. This experience is going to be very traumatic. The nights when you are taken to the church are going to be the worst by far. Each time you are going to experience about ten hours of pure hell.

Satan is a harsh taskmaster. . . .

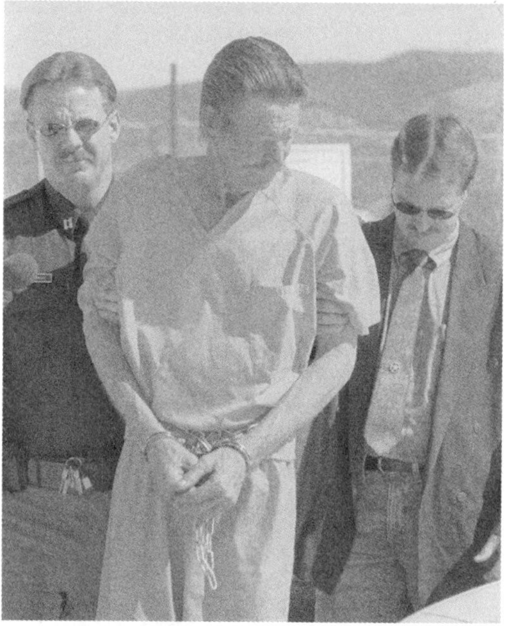

David Parker Ray on his way to be arraigned, two days after his arrest in March 1999. *(Courtesy of Frances Baird,* Sierra County Sentinel*)*

Ray, just before being found guilty in April 2001. *(Courtesy of Judd Bradley)*

Cyndi Vigil narrowly escaped death at the hands of David Parker Ray.
(Courtesy of Bertha Vigil)

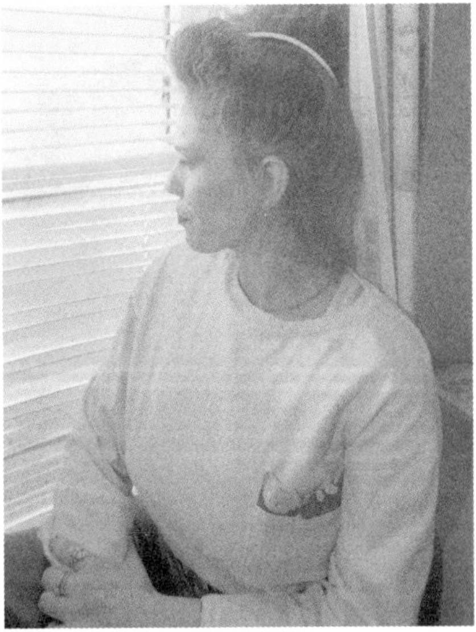

Angie Montano, another of David Parker Ray's victims in April of 1999.
(Courtesy of Thomas Herbert)

Marie Parker was killed by Roy Yancy in 1997.
(Courtesy of Thomas Herbert)

Marie Parker's children.
(Courtesy of Thomas Herbert)

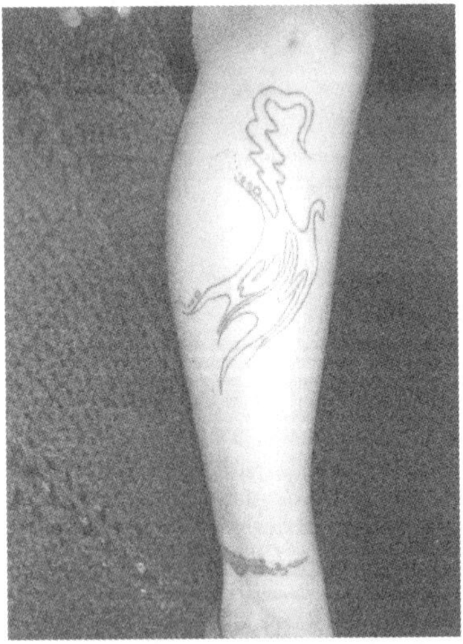

Kelli Van Cleve and Clay Hein, 1997. Kelli provided dramatic testimony about her ordeal at the hands of David Parker Ray.

Kelli's swan tattoo, visible in Ray's torture video, became an important piece of evidence.
(Courtesy of Kelli Garrett)

Kelli was able to move on in her life despite the memories of her brutal attack. *(Courtesy of Kelli Garrett)*

An aerial view of David Parker Ray's property in Elephant Butte, New Mexico. At right of center is the "toy box," his torture chamber.
(Courtesy of Thomas Herbert)

FBI crime scene investigators remove evidence from David Parker Ray's home. *(Courtesy of Thomas Herbert)*

The "toy box" being removed by FBI agents. *(Courtesy of Paul Tooley)*

Digging for bodies and other evidence. *(Courtesy of Thomas Herbert)*

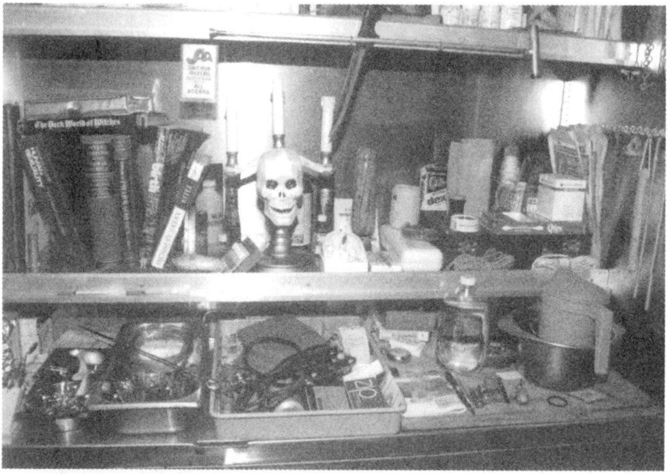

Inside the "toy box"– investigators found the devices and paraphernalia that David Parker Ray used in pursuit of his depraved desires. *(Courtesy of Sierra County District Attorney)*

Padded coffin from inside Ray's house. Victims were forced to spend painful hours within its confines.
(Courtesy of Sierra County District Attorney)

This gynecology table played a major role in Ray's videos.
(Courtesy of Sierra County District Attorney)

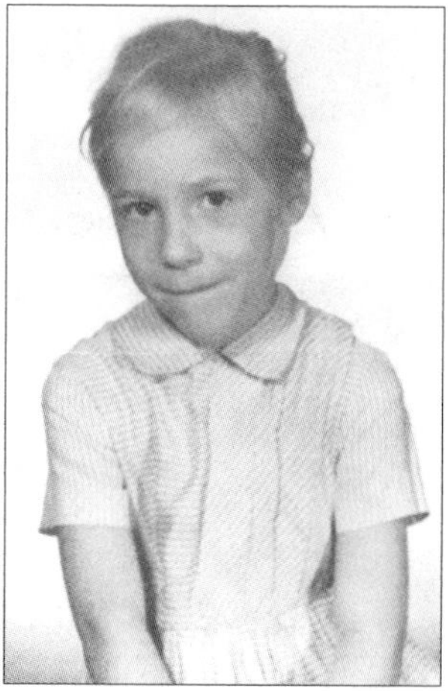

Cindy Hendy at six.
(Courtesy of Hendy family)

Hendy became David Parker Ray's accomplice in his crimes. *(Courtesy of Richard Hart)*

Hendy's arrest in March 1999.
(Courtesy of Frances Baird, Sierra County Sentinel)

Ray's daughter Jesse visiting her father.
(Courtesy of Frances Baird, Sierra County Sentinel)

Jesse after her arrest for her role in her father's crimes.
(Courtesy of Paul Tooley)

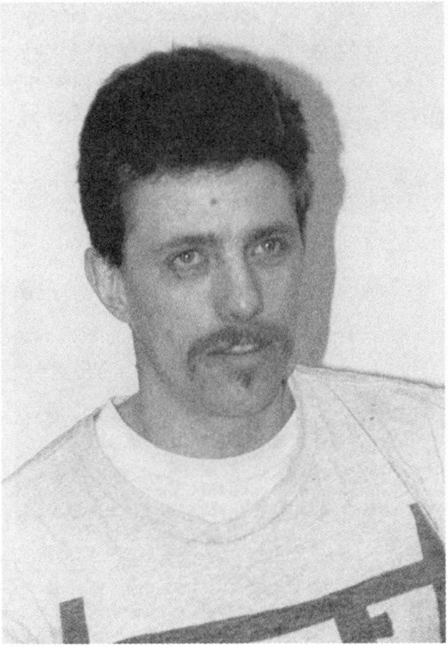

Roy Yancy, a member of Ray's circle of friends.
(Courtesy of Paul Tooley)

Cyndy Vigil in court, May 2000. Her testimony brought tears to the spectators' eyes. *(Courtesy of Paul Tooley)*

Judge Neil Mertz, May 2000, the day he sentenced Cindy Hendy to thirty-six years in prison. *(Courtesy of Paul Tooley)*

Ray and attorney Jeff Rein. *(Courtesy of Paul Tooley)*

Ray with attorney
Lee McMillian.
(Courtesy of Gerald Garner)

Prosecutor Jim Yontz of the Sierra County District Attorney's Office.
(Courtesy of Judd Bradley)

Judge Kevin Swaezea presided over David Parker Ray's murder trial after the sudden death of Judge Mertz.
(Courtesy of Judd Bradley)

Frances Baird, seventeen-year-old reporter for the Sierra County Sentinel, covered the David Parker Ray case with skills worthy of a veteran journalist.

Frances Baird married Manny Sanchez in 2001.
(Courtesy of Frances Baird)

Jim Yontz had heard enough. He turned down the volume and let the tape run down. There was no way Judge Mertz would ever allow this tape in a Yancy trial. There was also no way to know how deep Dennis Roy Yancy had sunk into the cesspool that substituted for David Ray's mind during the ten years they had known each other. The tape was made on July 6, 1993, and by that time the young man had known the old man for nearly four years—more than enough time to start a downhill slide toward becoming a violent criminal. A descent that didn't stop until Dennis Roy Yancy admitted killing Marie Parker.

Yontz remembered what Yancy had told his wife and the interrogating police officer right after he rolled over. "I feel better," he said, "getting this off my chest." Yontz thought that Yancy had shown at least a flicker of remorse. That was better than nothing, which was about all the police had been able to get from the other three suspects.

Just before Yontz got ready to call it a night, he flipped Tape Number Five over on the backside and noticed the FBI had labeled it A CHRISTIAN SERMON. He figured this was probably David Ray's idea of a joke, but he'd never listened to it, so he slipped it in the tape recorder. A soothing male voice greeted him. It was soft, but it was not the voice of David Parker Ray.

> I'm not perfect. If you find a perfect person, send 'em to me. I'd like to meet 'em. There's no one on the face of the earth that is one hundred percent perfect. The only perfect person is the man in Heaven. But each and every one of you can work harder every day at becoming perfect.
>
> I want everyone that is listening to this recording, if you're shy, if you're bashful, if someone calls you stupid or says that you won't amount to anything, if you ever feel insecure or inferior, I

want that burden to be lifted from your brain right now. I want you to feel the light coming down right now from the heavens.

Accept Jesus as your savior—ask him to save you.

Three days later, Jim Yontz got a call from Gary Mitchell saying that Dennis Roy Yancy did not want a jury trial and was ready to plea bargain. Yontz and Mitchell prepared the paperwork for Dennis to sign that would spare Yancy a life term in prison plus another 46½ years in exchange for pleading guilty to murder in the second degree. Instead of a trial on December 6, Judge Neil P. Mertz would hand down the sentence on Thursday, December 2. All Jim Yontz could hope for was a fair and reasonable sentence.

The night before the sentencing, Frances Baird called Jim Yontz at home. She wanted the update on Yancy for the following Wednesday afternoon edition of the *Sentinel*. Yontz filled her in on the details and then told her how Marie Parker's mother, Kate, had called and lobbied him not to let Yancy off the hook. She wanted Dennis prosecuted on charges of murder in the first degree. Yontz recalled his last conversation with Kate Parker, the grandmother now raising the two young daughters whom Marie left behind.

"Marie's mother called the other day," he told Baird. "She told me she wanted me to take Yancy to trial on first-degree murder because she felt like Jesus Christ would talk to the jurors." Jim Yontz paused.

"I told her Jesus doesn't want to mess with a jury in the state of New Mexico."

CHAPTER 20

"I think he had no respect for women—that's for sure."
Frank Jackson, talking about his best buddy at Hot Springs High School.
November 9, 1999.

Frank Jackson was bowling alone at the Chili Bowl Lanes in Truth or Consequences. It was the night before Dennis Roy Yancy was due to be sentenced by Judge Mertz up in Socorro. The next morning was going to be the worst morning of Yancy's life. Jackson finished his 222 game and walked up to the bartender and ordered a beer. Then he unloaded some pent-up feelings about a person he knew only too well.

"Roy Yancy was my best friend in high school," he admitted.

"We used to sneak into Raymond's Lounge and drink and listen to rock and roll. Roy liked to listen to heavy metal—he was into a heavy-metal band called King Diamond. And in this town anyone who listens to that stuff—well, they think you're into Satanism. I guess Roy diddled a little bit in devil worship, but I know it was all an act. Roy just didn't give a fuck. Anything he could do to fuck with other people's heads he'd do, because that was what people expected from him. Roy liked being the crazy man.

"He joined the navy right after high school, and when he used to come home from San Diego, he'd go out to Hot Springs High School and try to recruit kids. The teachers didn't like him because of all that shit that happened back in 1987, and they'd ask him to leave.

"He was serving on the USS *Texas,* and after a couple of years, he got in a lot of trouble with the navy. I guess he was making illegal weapons, like machetes and big ole knives, and they found all this stuff hidden under his bunk. Anyway, they asked him to leave before his time was up. I heard that the government gave him a dishonorable discharge, and after he came back from the navy, I stayed away from him for a couple of years. He was just too goddamn crazy.

"One night I was in Raymond's Lounge and a guy named Pablo Nunez was in there tryin' to cash a bad check. He was drunk and he asked me for a ride home and I was ready to give him a lift back to his place, when suddenly Roy Yancy comes up and gives Pablo a big kiss—right on the lips, for Christ's sake! It really grossed me out."

Frank Jackson was divorced now and the single life was taking a toll on him. Life had gone downhill since the glory days when he used to hang out with Dennis Yancy and Sidd Dodds and sneak into Raymond's for free beer.

"Sidd Dodds is now the town drunk. A few years ago, he got pissed off at his mother and slugged her in the face and now she won't let him sleep on her floor no more. The last time I saw him he was over at the cowboy bar, the Pine Knot, with a lesbian friend of his. A third of the people in this town are gay and most of the men go over there. I guess it's easier to pick up a cowboy than it is a rocker.

"The rest of the people here are old farts. Dating in

this town is very much a problem. I don't go out much anymore, and when I do, I just dance and come home. There aren't any more women to date—they've all been used up. After this winter I'm leavin' and never comin' back."

Frank Jackson was trying to make sense out of the fact that his old friend Roy killed Marie Parker, a woman he was once engaged to marry. He was trying to forget that one of her orphan daughters, Kathleen, was actually his child. Thinking about it too much made him really depressed.

"I never had a paternity test done—there just wasn't enough time, you know," he told the bartender. "If I'd known Roy was going to kill her mother . . .

"Heck, my wife and I used to go over and play spades with Roy and his wife. That was only two years ago and he seemed fine to me, but then . . ."

Frank put down his beer and looked out at the bowling lanes.

"Roy was a . . . really good bullshitter.

"I think it all started with his mom. When he was a little kid, she'd pick on him. Every time he tried to impress her, she'd put him down, big time. She'd call him worthless. I guess he looked too much like his real dad and she didn't like that at all. Roy told me one time his old man went to prison for murder when Roy was just a little boy.

"I think Roy had no respect for women, that's for sure."

On December 2, 1999, Judge Neil Mertz sentenced Dennis Roy Yancy, twenty-eight, to twenty years in the New Mexico State prison system, to be served at the penitentiary in Los Lunas. Yancy was convicted of second-degree murder and first-degree conspiracy to commit murder, in the murder of Marie Parker, twenty-two, during a wild drug orgy at the home of David Parker Ray. Court records said it was "on, about or between" the fifth day of July 1997 and the ninth day of July 1997.

Jim Yontz had done all the dirty work on the Yancy case, but when the newspapers and television stations showed up to get answers for the public, his boss, DA Ron Lopez, took over and passed out the official story.

"After a drug deal gone bad," Lopez told the press, "Mr. David Ray tortured Ms. Parker while Jesse Ray held a gun on Marie. When David turned to Roy Yancy and said, 'You have to get rid of her,' Yancy took that to mean he had to kill her.

"Yancy told the police he strangled Marie Parker using a rope or a cord on orders from David Parker Ray. He indicated she was killed in the trailer—what you would call the sex/torture chamber—of Mr. Ray. They placed the body in Mr. Ray's truck, wrapped the body in a blanket or some type of tarp, and took her out to some type of remote area and that's where they buried her.

"We wanted to get Mr. Yancy for first-degree murder, but without a body and without any evidence, you can't try and convict a person in the state of New Mexico.

"You can't prosecute a person on a confession alone.

"There were also mitigating circumstances, including extensive drug use by Roy Yancy and Marie Parker, and because Roy cooperated with the police and helped us tie together other loose ends in the David Ray case, we cut him a deal and recommended a lighter sentence."

After Yancy was led away in chains, Frances Baird was waiting outside the courthouse and caught up with Marie Parker's mother, Kate. She was holding hands with two little girls, four years old and five years old, and she was very bitter about Yancy slipping away on a plea bargain.

"I don't feel it's fair for Dennis Roy Yancy to serve

twenty years when both my granddaughters have been given a life sentence.

"Because of this mean young man, my grandchildren will never have their mother home to read them a book at night or go to an afternoon dance recital at school."

Jim Yontz walked back to work that morning feeling both good and bad at the same time. He knew too well that there were always secondhand victims no matter how well the American justice system worked, and he tried not to let those people rattle his emotions. But he still felt sorry for Kate Parker and the girls. He had a fourteen-year-old daughter himself from his first marriage and she was his only child, living up in Canada with her mother. Yontz only saw her in the summers. He knew how much the smile of a child can make your life come alive all over again after it seems like you're all washed up.

Even so, he felt like he'd hammered out a small victory.

When he got back to his office after lunch, there was a message from Frances Baird, so he gave her a call at the *Sentinel.* He noticed she had not been in the courtroom, but he told her he'd do his best to fill her in on the proceedings. Her first questions were about the sentencing.

"Why did Dennis plead guilty when he could have told a big pack of lies like all the rest of them?" asked a puzzled Baird.

"I think he truly felt guilty about what he did," Yontz answered calmly.

"Poor Marie, she was just four years older than me."

"She had a tough life," added Yontz. "A lot of people don't know this, but when she was a young girl, she turned her older brother in to the police on a murder charge. He's serving life in a Nevada prison right now. I don't think at the time Kate Parker could forgive her daughter for that, and that's why she kicked Marie out of the house when she was only fourteen years old. Now Kate hates herself for that, and she can't find it in her own heart to forgive herself."

"What was Roy like in court?" asked Baird.

"He wept," Yontz said.

"He got a pretty good deal, didn't he?"

"It was the best we could do, Frances," said a weary Yontz.

"But doesn't he get out in a measly ten years with good behavior?"

"Unfortunately, that's the law in New Mexico."

"Some law . . . "

"Remember, Frances, the law cuts both ways."

"What do you mean?" asked Baird.

"If we'd gone to a jury trial without a body and without any evidence at all, Mertz might have let a killer walk. I've seen that happen before."

"I guess Roy has to live with his own nightmares now," said Baird.

"Without Marie Parker's body, our hands were tied."

"Do you think you'll ever find Marie's body," asked Baird.

"No."

"Too bad."

"I don't think we'll ever find any bodies," added Yontz.

"I hope your case against David isn't crumbling," Baird said, in her own blunt way.

"David Parker Ray was a pretty smart cookie," Yontz told her. "He fooled a lot of people."

"Yeah, he sure did. Runnin' around in his little Ranger Rick outfit with that little Howdy Doody badge and all," Baird muttered.

Yontz smiled to himself as he listened to her comments.

"Jeez, one woman in town kept saying she talked to him every day, and as far as she was concerned, he was just 'normal, normal, normal,' " Baird added sarcastically.

"Nobody knows what a real killer looks like," Yontz noted.

"Well, I know one thing," Baird said with authority.

"What's that?" asked an amused Jim Yontz.

"He sure wasn't the Mr. Goody Two-Shoes people seemed to think he was."

Yontz shook his head and laughed a big hearty laugh. His first real laugh in quite some time.

"No, he wasn't, that's for darn sure."

He and Frances Baird finished talking and she thanked him for the time. He was cordial, as always.

"No problem. Call anytime you need to know something."

He said good-bye, hung up and leaned back in his chair, letting out a deep breath. A minute later, he got up and grabbed his briefcase and headed for the door and the drive home. He figured he owed it to himself to take the afternoon off. On his way out of his office, he stopped and gave Bernie a pat on top of the head.

"Well, big fella, one bad guy down—three to go."

CHAPTER 21

"In jail, David Parker Ray would read paperback books about serial killers, write his name on 'em and send 'em down to the girls in their jail cells."

Gail Astbury, T or C jail inmate.
April and May, 2000.

Just before Christmas Day, 1999, Jim Yontz took an evening off and drove up to Santa Fe, where he'd been a prosecutor from 1991 to 1997. He wanted to enjoy the Christmas lights and forget his messy office in Socorro littered with boxes of dirty deeds by David Parker Ray and his friends. He once thought Santa Fe was the most civilized town in America, and even though cop killers had changed his attitude, he still liked to go back and look at the streets and rooftops lined with *farolitos* during the holidays. The "little lanterns" made by weighing down a small brown paper bag with sand and placing a glowing candle inside were popular with the tourists and for just one night Jim Yontz wanted to pretend he did not have to live and work in New Mexico. Driving through the candlelit streets sure beat listening to any more of Ray's audiotapes.

For one night he put the mastermind Ray and his obedient daughter on the legal back burner and strolled the adobe-lined streets of a town over 400 years old. At least Santa Fe reflected the kind of old-fashioned Christianity that Yontz used to be able to count on to lift up his sagging spirits.

He bought his wife a pair of rawhide cowboy boots at Lucchese's Western Store, and on the drive home down I-25, he tried to shift gears and focus back on the case that one local Associated Press reporter was now calling nothing more than "a shadow of a murder." A year from now, Yontz hoped to have Daddy and "Daddy's Little Helper" in prison where they belonged and everyone else off his back so he could return to prosecuting a few stray rustlers down in Socorro.

Right now, though, he needed to get back to work and round up Cynthia Lea Hendy and put her away. She was a flake and using her to testify against David Ray was now out of the question. Yontz just hoped that Mertz would rule against Hendy and Carmen Garza, Cindy's new public defender.

On January 26, 2000, Yontz got his wish.

Judge Mertz sided with him and ordered that Hendy couldn't change her guilty plea. Yontz made plans to schedule a sentencing hearing for Hendy sometime before the spring thaws.

All around Sierra County, the local ranchers were worried about wolves, and momentarily they set aside their concerns about the Ray case. Thirty years ago, the Mexican Gray Wolf had been exterminated after being shot, trapped and poisoned for decades and now the federal government had a pack of Mexican Gray Wolves they'd tried to reintroduce into eastern Arizona, with no luck. The animals had killed off a few local livestock, so the plan was to move them across the border and into the Gila Wilderness in the Black Range Mountains of New Mexico, just west of Truth or Consequences.

Yontz picked up *The Sentinel* on February 9, 2000,

and grinned as he read the bold headline: **NO TO WOLVES!!!**

The panic-driven piece of reporting stated that parents in Glenwood, New Mexico, wouldn't let their children go outside and play because on January 13, the wolves had killed a 1,500-pound Black Angus bull and people were up in arms. One local cop summed up the neighborhood point of view.

"These wolves have no fear of humans," he said.

Over a thousand people were planning a local rally to protest against the wolves. Yontz always wondered how people got so excited over losing a few dumb cows and yet could care less if David Ray and his human wolf pack killed a few hookers—poor souls from rotten homes who ended up wasting their young lives walking Highway 66 selling their bodies for drug money.

Yontz was enough of an outdoorsman to know that wolves had never killed a human being in the United States and he figured people just needed a bogeyman to fight off. He smiled as he read about local citizens getting up in arms over a little pack of eight scrawny wolves trying to do what comes naturally. At the rally two days later, a Forest Service naturalist from Silver City tried to tell the locals not to be afraid—he even pointed out that New Mexico had lots of herds of elk, the preferred dinner for wild wolves. The advice fell on deaf ears.

Yontz had some advice for the wolves, the same advice he always gave his friends. Never go in the woods in New Mexico without a loaded handgun—there are a lot of dangerous people out there. Yontz always carried a Smith & Wesson .357 and he occasionally loaned it out to timid writers covering the Ray case.

By February 15, 2000, Jeff Rein, David's public defender, was filing motions to have the one large trial including all three victims—Cyndy Vigil, Angie Montano and Kelli Van Cleave—split up, so he and David Ray would have a fighting chance to beat them off, one at a time. David was facing thirty-seven felony counts and Rein told Mertz at one hearing that "it would create incredible prejudice, with the accumulation of evidence in one single trial." Yontz countered, telling Mertz that the "state of New Mexico trial rules allow similar offenses to be lumped together in one case." Yontz knew Mertz did not like the newspaper and television reporters who had covered the story in the spring of 1999 and he told the judge there might be a couple more real good reasons not to split the trial in the spring of 2000.

"There will be a media feeding frenzy," he warned Mertz. "Plus, three trials will greatly increase the costs to the state."

A stern Neil Mertz told the lawyers he would hold a hearing, consider the matter and rule shortly.

On February 21, Jim Yontz and Ron Lopez left for a five-day trip to Washington, D.C., to study the habits of sadistic killers at the FBI Crime Laboratory in Quantico, Virginia. Yontz noticed Lopez getting more interested in the case and he welcomed the help. Mary Ellen O'Toole, the specialist on sadism, took them through the ropes at the same facility where Thomas Harris studied before he made up his famous intellectual killer, Hannibal Lecter, hero of his three books on fictional sadism. David Ray, of course, was the real thing. Both prosecutors were impressed by the profile the FBI had done on Ray. He was the genuine article, moving over the years from torturing willing partners to torturing and killing unwilling partners. The FBI told Yontz and Lopez they felt David Parker Ray was one of only five "true" sadistic serial killers ever studied by the ninety-two-year-old agency.

Mary Ellen O'Toole had been on the scene in Elephant Butte right after David was arrested and Yontz planned to use her profiling skills and call her as a key witness in the big supertrial scheduled for March 28 in Tierra Amarilla, the tiny village up in the mountains of northern New Mexico.

What Jim Yontz did not count on was the decision Mertz handed down while he was gone. On Saturday night, February 26, Jim got a call from his office secretary in Socorro with the news.

"Mertz ruled today that you have to try David three separate times," she said. "One trial for each girl."

"Shit" was the first word out of Yontz's mouth.

Yontz and Lopez flew home two days later and made quick plans to try the three cases, starting from their strongest victim witness down to their weakest victim witness, beginning with Cyndy Vigil on March 28, and then going to trial with Kelli Van Cleave in the summer and, finally, with Angie Montano in the fall. Yontz was hoping David would "plea out" after they beat him in the Vigil trial, thereby eliminating the need for a Van Cleave trial or a Montano trial.

As soon as Jeff Rein found out their plans to start with Cyndy Vigil, he started filing motion after motion to have evidence thrown out. Rein knew Vigil had not been in the torture chamber and he also knew most of Yontz's strongest documentation was gathered from inside the toy box.

One day Yontz was pecking away in frustration on his computer when Frances Baird called for an update. He told her he couldn't talk for more than a minute, he was "too damn busy."

"I'm busting my butt trying to stop Jeff Rein from having Mertz throw out all my best evidence," he told her.

"Are you going to appeal Mertz's ruling on three trials?" she asked him.

"I doubt it—it wouldn't do any good."

* * *

Ten days before the first trial in Tierra Amarilla, David Parker Ray came down with a serious case of heart problems. The jail doctor in T or C sent him to the Sierra Vista County Hospital four different times in four days. It was the same facility that had treated a naked and bruised Cyndy Vigil in March 1999 and some of the nurses who bandaged up Vigil had a hard time behaving in a professional manner when they saw David Ray being wheeled through the front door. It was March 17, exactly a year to the week from the time they'd taken care of the terrified young woman with the dog collar around her neck.

The local doctors checked Ray's irregular heartbeat and high blood pressure, along with tests showing a weakened heart muscle. They were convinced his problems were serious enough that they decided to send him to a cardiologist at the Memorial Hospital in Las Cruces, seventy-five miles south of T or C. Ray spent two days in intensive care in Las Cruces before returning to his jail cell back in Truth or Consequences on March 24.

The next day, on March 25, Mertz held a hearing on media access to the process for picking the first David Ray jury. The judge's decision was to ban the media from the jury-selection process. It would just be himself, Yontz and Rein in the court chambers interviewing potential jurors—no reporters. The New Mexico Press Association and the Foundation for Open Government were both furious. Frances Baird, most of all, was livid. When she heard from Yontz what was going on, she got on the horn and called the *Sentinel* offices. She told her mom how she felt about a man who had once been a father figure to her.

"Mertz has banned the media from going to jury selection!"

"What!" gasped her mother.

Three days later, on March 28, Mertz issued a ruling that prevented Yontz from using any FBI interview material from their 1986 investigation into Jesse's allegation that David was smuggling girls into Mexico as part of a prostitution and slavery ring. He excluded volumes of toy box evidence, including pornographic drawings David Ray had made of his brutal electronic breast-stretching machine. He refused to let Yontz show jurors any of the "how-to" torture drawings posted on the walls of the torture chamber. He pretty much limited Yontz to using evidence collected from the house trailer itself—the spot where Vigil was tortured. Yontz felt the toy box showed David Ray's true intent to commit serious crimes in other parts of his torture compound, but Mertz simply did not agree. Yontz felt Mertz was making it almost impossible to get a conviction in the Vigil case.

Yontz usually tried hard not to drag his family into his work, but that night around the kitchen table, he had to tell his wife about some of his frustrations.

"If the victim couldn't describe it or remember it, Mertz tossed it."

But the most infuriating loss, Yontz told his wife, was to lose the testimony of Max Hauck, the FBI agent who specialized in hair analysis. Mertz would not allow him to testify because Yontz had failed to send Jeff Rein what Yontz called a few "nitpicky" documents. The police had found tons of evidence in Ray's big red recreational vehicle he'd used to kidnap Vigil. They found chains and a chain-tightener, a metal I bolt, a handsaw in a brown sheath, pieces of rope, a jar of Vaseline, a twelve-inch hunting knife, stainless-steel tape, six condoms—but the most important piece of evidence they found was a piece of crumpled-up duct tape with a smudge of lipstick and one human hair sticking to it. The police gave it to the FBI for DNA testing and Yontz wanted Agent Hauck to nail David to the wall in court.

"What were the results?" asked his wife.

"It was Vigil's hair," he told her.

Yontz and Lopez put their heads together and decided to appeal Mertz's decision to the seventh district court of appeals in Santa Fe. They knew it was risky business because they might not hear back from the higher court for six to nine months, thereby poisoning their strongest case against David Ray. Yontz felt they had to do it or run the risk of letting David Ray and Jeff Rein win the first head-to-head battle—a loss that could be deadly to the other two cases.

As soon as Mertz learned of their appeal, he plugged the Kelli Van Cleave case into a new date, May 23, 2000. He also set jury selection for an available courthouse in Espanola, seventy-five miles south of Tierra Amarilla.

Back in Truth or Consequences, it was April Fools' Day and Gail Astbury was celebrating the fiftieth anniversary of the town's name change. She was hanging out at Andy's Bar, a tavern she called "the Old Farts' Bar," drinking Old Milwaukee and puffing on cheap cigarettes nonstop.

The national media had completely lost interest in the David Ray case. In fact, one *Globe* editor, Craig Lewis, was facing bribery and extortion charges in Colorado, which meant he might be spending nine years in prison himself. As a result, Gail didn't have too many tabloid reporters to talk to. But she had a lot of opinions, as usual. She had plenty of good friends who hung out down on Austin Street in the steam baths and sweatshops, and she'd spent many lazy afternoons talking to people whom *Vanity Fair* magazine liked to call "the underclass" about the fate of the criminal her friends liked to call "Mr. Ray" or "Big Dave."

Gail polished off her can of cheap beer and, in a voice loud enough to be heard from T or C to Albuquerque, let all the weathered, old cowboys playing pool know what she thought of Ray's chances.

"I believe he's going to walk," she told the bartender. "And so does everybody else in town."

CHAPTER 22

"She said she'd like to take the breath out of one."
John Branaugh, discussing his old friend Hendy
November 9th, 1999

May in New Mexico is the time when the winds are still blowing, but the sun warms up the Sandia Mountains next to Albuquerque and everybody seems to be smiling a lot more. One night after dinner, Jim Yontz took his horse for a ride just so he could trot up to the foothills and watch a blazing purple-and-orange sunset reflecting off the watermelon-shaped ridge north of the city. He was mildly satisfied that the sluggish legal system was beginning to deal with the nagging and troublesome case of David and Jesse and give them what the law required—swift justice.

David's trial was scheduled for May 23 in Northern New Mexico and Jesse's trial was set for July 10 out on Old Highway 66 in Gallup, seventy-five miles west of Albuquerque. Yontz knew all about the old warning to beware of all the best-laid plans, but he couldn't have ever predicted what would happen in the first two weeks of May 2000.

Not in his wildest dreams.

On May 4, the federal government attempted a "controlled burn" to get rid of underbrush and small trees threatening to make for a bad fire season west of Los Alamos. In the process they started the biggest and most destructive fire in New Mexico history. Before it was all over, 450 people watched their homes burn to the ground and 11,000 more had to be evacuated out of their homes to escape the raging inferno.

The nuclear laboratory at Los Alamos, home to more Ph.D. scientists per capita than any town in America, had to be evacuated and parts of the town were covered with six inches of black soot. Small private planes flying into the small airport on the mesa had to turn around and go home. Many carried scientists from around the world. Old, dilapidated buildings, where parts of the original atomic bomb were assembled for the Manhattan Project during World War II, were burned to the ground.

Yontz and Rein both called Mertz, who was following the nightly television coverage. The David Ray jury selection was scheduled to begin on May 23 in Espanola, right in the path of the rampaging fire. Both lawyers recommended that the judge call the Rio Arriba Courthouse and have the local judge clear his court calendar so they could begin the jury-selection process by May 23 in Tierra Amarilla. Mertz agreed and the 125 juror candidates were notified to be in Tierra Amarilla by the end of the month. Many of them lived in Espanola, so Mertz had his office staff tell them to carpool.

Frances Baird didn't shed any tears over the jury selection being moved out of Espanola. She'd read in the *New York Times* that Espanola had the highest rate of heroin overdose deaths in the United States—higher than New York, Miami and Los Angeles. And the *Times* didn't even know that Espanola was where ten people got murdered in one month back in the spring of 1995. Nor did they know that a twenty-nine-year-old woman working as a substitute teacher in an Espanola junior high school had been arrested last year for getting stoned on black-tar heroin in the school parking lot. When Baird heard they were not going to select jurors there, she called Yontz to tell him the wildfire probably helped his case.

"Espanola is a rat hole," she announced.

"I remember the first case I prosecuted there a few years back," replied Yontz. "They had three homicides in one weekend."

"The place is populated by a mean and violent class of people," added Baird.

"Are you sure you're not talking about some of the people who live in Truth or Consequences?" he kidded her.

"I'm beginning to wonder," she said.

"It doesn't make any difference where we ask questions," Yontz explained. "We always send out a questionnaire and more than half the people we plan to interview are going to be people living in and around Espanola."

"Bummer," said Baird.

"Are you coming up to cover the Kelli Van Cleave trial?" he asked.

After an uncharacteristically long pause, Baird said: "No, I don't think so."

"Why not?" asked Yontz.

"Ron Lopez said it would be good if I wasn't there. He said some of the evidence was going to be really graphic. He thought it would upset me and thought it might be better if I didn't show up."

"Well, we'll miss you, Frances—you're a heck of a reporter."

"Yeah, I know," she replied with a giggle.

* * *

Three days after the wildfires started, another bombshell landed in the laps of the prosecutors in the David Parker Ray case. On Sunday night, May 7, Jim Yontz was sitting in his living room watching the ten o'clock evening news when the anchor caught him completely off guard with a breaking news flash.

"The case against alleged rapist David Parker Ray just suffered a severe blow tonight when Angie Montano, one of the three living witnesses prepared to testify against Ray, was rushed to an Albuquerque hospital with pneumonia and died an hour later of heart failure. Angie Montano was twenty-eight years old. She left her home in Truth or Consequences right after David Ray was arrested, and for the last year she's apparently been working as a prostitute on Central Avenue. She leaves behind a six-year-old boy living with friends in Truth or Consequences.

"Ms. Montano claimed Ray kidnapped her on February seventeenth. . . ."

Yontz clicked off the television and went to bed. He knew the morning was going to be hell. He always felt a little tongue-tied when he faced the press. He got up the next morning feeling clear-headed and didn't miss a beat when they asked about the crumbling Ray case. In a cool and confident voice, he explained how the prosecutor's office would deal with the setback.

"We will try David for kidnapping and torturing Angelique Montano by using videotapes made of her testimony at a preliminary hearing held on April fifteenth and sixteenth of 1999."

Later that morning, he talked to Angie's grandmother by phone. She told Yontz the supermarket tabloid the *Globe* never did deliver on their promise to pay for Angie's eye operation so the poor kid could have two brown eyes instead of one brown and one blue. Angie's granny also felt like the stress of being tortured by Ray, and then knowing that nobody would believe her, eventually led to her granddaughter's abuse of drugs, and her death. Yontz told her how sorry he was, but he didn't tell her that he felt Angie made some very bad choices in her short, unhappy life. He figured the grandma already had suffered a broken heart and that was more than enough pain for one day.

Yontz locked himself into his office for the rest of the day and got ready for what he figured was going to be a tough week. In three days he was going to try to get a long jail term for Cindy Hendy, and with the Ray case bouncing all over the place, he didn't want to answer any more of those hypothetical questions popular with the press.

Yontz wasn't the only one feeling heat from the press.

On Tuesday, May 9, Judge Mertz tried to face down a challenge by the New Mexico Foundation for an Open Government over his previous decision to ban reporters from the Ray jury selection. After a brief tussle, the judge backed down rather than give the reporters what he figured they really wanted—a fight over freedom of speech. He admitted that he had misread New Mexico law. Then he ruled that the media would, in fact, be allowed to send representatives to the jury selection due to begin in less than three weeks. He used a previously untapped pocket of charm to try and smooth it over with the press, joking with one Associated Press reporter that he was "only kidding" back in March when he first kicked them out.

Before he buried David Ray in Tierra Amarilla, Jim Yontz still had to take care of some unfinished business in Socorro.

* * *

On Thursday, May 11, Mertz called a hearing to sentence Cindy Hendy for her part in the kidnapping and torture of Cyndy Vigil and Angie Montano. It was the first time Cyndy Vigil and Cindy Hendy had been face-to-face since the afternoon of March 22, 1999, when Vigil stabbed Hendy in the neck with an ice pick and bolted down the hall and out into the sun, running for her life. Hendy sat in the courtroom with her straight brown hair falling down the side of her pasty white face, split ends showing everywhere. She showed no emotion during the proceedings. Vigil sat next to her grandmother Rosa with her hair tied back in a ponytail, six months pregnant with her first child and fresh out of drug treatment in California. Her urine had been "clean" for over nine months and since January she'd been holding down her first real job as a cashier at a local Pic-N-Save grocery store on Highway 66 in Albuquerque.

Cindy Hendy wanted to make one more pitch to the judge and the prosecutors to let her change her plea from guilty to innocent and Mertz agreed to listen. Hendy let her public defender, Carmen Garza, do all the talking. Garza made mention that during one period when Hendy was applying for welfare benefits in Washington State, a 1996 report by the Social Security Administration cited the fact that Cindy Hendy was "below normal intelligence." Garza also told the judge that Hendy had suffered through an awful childhood and she'd been in a number of abusive relationships with men. Garza said that helped explain how she got in a fight with her former lawyer, Acosta.

"Cindy was intimidated and frightened by her lawyer Xavier Acosta, and she didn't understand what the guilty plea would mean," Garza told the judge.

Jim Yontz scoffed at the results of the tests by sociologists and psychologists up in Washington. He looked Mertz right in the eyes and bluntly stated his case for immediate sentencing.

"Why are we looking at a 1996 report when the crimes took place in 1999?" he said. "A psychiatric report ordered months ago here in New Mexico found no evidence of mental disorders. They said Hendy only had mood disorders. Nowhere in that New Mexico evaluation does it state that Cindy Hendy did not know the difference between right and wrong."

Mertz studied the documents and came down on the side of Yontz, ruling against Garza and her attempts to save Hendy from doing hard time. Before he handed out the sentence, Mertz listened one more time to Yontz and Garza debate the role that Hendy played in the two kidnappings. Yontz was unbending in his attempts to hold Hendy responsible for her actions. Discussing the kidnapping and torture of Cyndy Vigil in March 1999, he pounded home his point.

"The court needs to know that Hendy was not simply along for the ride. . . ."

Switching to the kidnapping and torture of Angie Montano in February 1999, he made even more pointed remarks.

"The victim was held, tortured, placed inside the white cargo trailer, strapped into a chair and had a variety of terrible things done to her person. I don't know if the Marquis de Sade would have had better tools for torture than the devices found within that cargo trailer."

Mertz listened to Garza try to explain how "Cindy Hendy is a victim of her past" and then he let the victim, Cyndy Vigil, speak to the court.

Fighting back a wave of tears, Vigil urged Mertz to give Hendy the maximum sentence. Then she turned one last time to the woman who laughed at her while she was being tortured. Cyndy Vigil looked deep into the face and eyes of Cindy Hendy, while the woman who helped David place dildos inside of Vigil's body simply sat motionless and looked at the floor.

"There is not enough time that you could serve in prison," said Vigil. "There is no excuse for what you and David did."

Then with tears streaming down her cheeks, she leveled the ultimate criticism at her sadistic captor.

"I was molested as a child," she said, "and I don't go around kidnapping and torturing people."

After the victim finished speaking, Judge Neil Mertz sentenced Hendy, the forty-year-old mother of three (and grandmother to a one-year-old grandson) to serve thirty-six years in the New Mexico State prison system, at the women's penitentiary in Grants. Hendy had pleaded guilty to five counts of kidnapping, criminal sexual penetration and conspiracy in April 1999. After handing down the thirty-six years, Mertz did admit that Cindy Hendy grew up in a set of "wretched circumstances" that would challenge almost anyone to walk a straight-and-narrow line. But he added that she "made choices to be part of a shocking set of circumstances that go far beyond what is found in most sexual-assault cases."

He also told her she could get out of prison in only eighteen years if she behaved herself.

Outside the courthouse Frances Baird caught up with Cyndy Vigil and her grandmother Rosa. She didn't know it until later, but at exactly that same time of day, Angelique Montano was being lowered into the ground inside a pine casket at a small cemetery in Albuquerque. Cyndy Vigil had never talked to the press and Frances Baird wanted to know if she had anything more to say about Hendy getting thirty-six years. She did, and so did her grandmother.

Rosa spoke first, telling Baird what she said to Hendy as the convicted felon was leaving the courtroom in handcuffs.

"I told her, 'I hope Satan has a place for you in Hell and you burn forever.' "

Vigil then told Baird how she felt about the other victim Montano, and the very real possibility that Hendy might only have to serve half her time in jail.

"I'm happy that because of the judge's ruling, Hendy won't be able to do this to anyone else," she told Baird. "I'm also happy I got away.

"I'm also very sad that no one seemed to believe Angelique's story. She was a real good person and didn't deserve to go through this, either. I'm going to say a prayer for her tonight and I sure hope she is smiling down from Heaven right now.

"I feel Cindy Hendy didn't get a heavy enough sentence. If it were up to me, she would have to serve the rest of her life in prison. Not twenty or thirty years, but the rest of her natural life.

"Justice was only half served today. It will only be totally served when David Ray gets locked up.

"My only hope is that he, too, rots in Hell."

CHAPTER 23

"I think David Ray loved his dogs."

Frances Baird, November 6, 2000

Rio Arriba County is the largest county in northern New Mexico and is graced by the magnificent Brazos Cliffs, 2,000 feet of sandstone rising above the pine-scented forests surrounding two small towns, Chama and Tierra Amarilla. Jim Yontz was fond of saying, "When God goes on vacation, He goes to Chama." He liked to tell a story about a local judge who got frustrated with a slow-moving murder trial and told the jury one day, "Hurry up! I've got a date with a big brown trout on the Rio Brazos this afternoon."

Entering Rio Arriba County from the east, a visitor has one last chance to fill up his gasoline tank at the Mustang Station in Tres Padres. The big woman behind the cash register has a less-than-scenic attitude about living in the poorest county in the state. The mean income: $11,000 per household. She isn't too thrilled about living in the whole state of New Mexico, in fact, where people suffer from the lowest per-capita income of any state in the United States, even lower than Mississippi. It breeds violence. The woman goes on to tell a stranger a story about a local guy who will stand trial in front of a local jury later this summer.

"He pushed two tourists off the Rio Grande Gorge Bridge four years ago," she says. "They fell five hundred feet into the river canyon below and splattered all over the rocks. Nobody knows why he did it. I can't say for sure, but I think that guy is gonna walk.

"You get more years for killing an elk up here than you do for killing a human being."

Driving west into Rio Arriba County, a traveler's eye is drawn to the entrance to a small cattle ranch a few miles out of Tres Padres. There is a ponderosa pine gate with a black-and-white sign overhead that says DAD'S DREAM RANCH. The tall pine post on the left has a small black sign with white letters that says KEEP OUT! Hanging from a metal rod sticking out from the pine post is a life-size dummy dressed in cowboy boots, jeans, blue T-shirt and sunglasses. He is suspended by a hangman's rope around his neck, his head tilted to the side and his feet dangling eight feet above the ground. Right behind the dummy is another black-and-white sign telling first-time travelers how this rancher feels about private property rights. The sign is a monument to vigilante justice and tells everyone how people up in Rio Arriba County support the age-old New Mexico reputation as "the last lynching state": WE DO IT THE "OLD WAY."

Winding out of the breathtaking mountains covered in alpine fir and spruce down into the tiny village of Tierra Amarilla (the yellow earth, in Spanish), drivers are greeted by a large wooden sign with paint chipping off on all sides. It's a holdover from the revolutionary year 1967 and simply says LAND, OR DEATH. The reference is to Reies Lopez Tijerina, a forty-one-year-old local Evangelical minister who led a violent raid on the courthouse to arrest the local district attorney. The date was June 5, 1967. He thought the DA should have enforced an 1848 agreement between Mexico and the United States agreeing to give heirs of Mexicans living in Rio Arriba County after the Mexican-American War the lands they rightfully owned. Tijerina and his gang bombed and shot up the courthouse, leading to the biggest manhunt in New Mexico history.

A jailer and a state policeman were wounded, but nobody was killed, and Reies Tijerina was eventually tracked down and arrested by federal troops swarming all over northern New Mexico. Tijerina spent years in prison and was last seen living in the village of Coyote, New Mexico, before moving to Mexico in the early 1990s. He told his followers he had given up on Tierra Amarilla justice.

Walking the dusty road leading from the highway to the newly remodeled Rio Arriba Courthouse is depressing. Dilapidated wooden and plaster buildings from the glory days are fenced in by tumbleweeds. Windows have been broken out of nearly every building by children throwing stones. Dirt covers everything that was once alive. It looks like a scene out of a village in Mexico, where hope is gone and despair reigns.

One local artist who makes and sells Navajo drums to rich tourists in Santa Fe and Taos shakes his head when the subject of Tierra Amarilla and his violent neighbors comes up.

"This is not America," he says in a whisper.

"There are a lot of people living up here who will kill you at the drop of a hat. When you walk down the streets, be careful not to make eye contact. If they get mad and decide they don't like you, they will shoot you or burn your house down. A man stole a dog last month and his house is now a pile of ashes."

Rising up in the middle of this misery is the Rio Arriba Courthouse, which literally mean's "up the creek" in Spanish. Outside, tattered flags of the United States and the state of New Mexico hang on a pole above the paint-chipped building. Inside, it's a gilded and golden mansion of a building, originally constructed as an ornate salute to frontier justice back in 1917. When the local authorities heard there was going to be a big, well-publicized trial sometime in the year 2000, they got right to work and remade the Rio Arriba Courthouse to look exactly like it did in 1917. At least on the inside. It had been completely redecorated in the original Art Deco decor, gold trim and all. They tried to cover all the bullet holes from 1967, but a visitor with a keen eye can still find traces of Reies Lopez Tijerina.

Some of the locals are not impressed at all by the new construction project, preferring to remember their local hero from the courthouse raid over thirty years ago. Just a few blocks down the street from the courthouse is a shabby white plaster building covered in red graffiti from the late 1960s. Splashed in big red letters across the front of the building is a testament to the spirit of rebellion still hiding in the dusty doorways of bars and cafés in town. It reads: THE DYNAMITE KIDD!

Jim Yontz rode into town on May 23 hoping for fast action putting David Parker Ray behind bars. Neil Mertz had moved the trial up here in order to find a jury that wasn't too media savvy and didn't have too many set-in-stone opinions about the case. Jeff Rein just wanted to get away from all the people in Truth or Consequences who already thought Ray was guilty. All three men expected the jury selection to go smoothly. Little did Yontz, Mertz and Rein realize it would take nearly five weeks to corral 125 juror candidates and narrow the group down to a mere eighteen men and women needed for the jury pool.

The first week started with Mertz interviewing jurors

individually, instead of in groups—slowing everything down to a crawl. Yontz saw what was coming and complained to Chris Roberts of the Associated Press, the lone reporter sitting in the courtroom watching the proceedings.

"This idea of interviewing three or four candidates a day and then leaving early really sucks," he told the reporter. "Mertz can't even say hello in less than ten minutes."

As far as Chris Roberts was concerned, every day in court was just as boring as the day before. As far as he could see, all three men stuck to their scripts. Yontz wanted to know if they had any negative feelings toward the police. He also wanted to know if they understood what "reasonable doubt" meant. It was important to him that the jurors understood that they didn't actually have to nail it down completely. Rein wanted to know if they realized some people enjoy sadomasochistic sex and that almost all of David Ray's "weird toys" were not illegal.

Mertz always wanted to know the same two things: What did they know about the case and where did they hear it? He heard people say flat out, "I don't read the newspapers and I don't listen to the radio or watch televison and I'm damn proud of it." He didn't worry about those people. Other people would tell him that they read the papers and watched television and "thought" they knew what was going on. Mertz would take those opportunities to nail the real people he thought were the culprits in distorting the facts of the case—the media itself. He knew Chris Roberts was the only media representative covering the jury selection and, in his dry sense of humor, he would try to prick the memories of potential jurors with two of his favorite questions.

"Do you think maybe the media screwed up?" he would say, turning to Roberts and grinning.

"Do you think maybe the media got it wrong?"

* * *

On Friday, June 2, Jeff Rein informed Mertz that his stepson had tried to kill himself by firing a loaded handgun into his open mouth. Rein had to join the rest of his family at the hospital in Albuquerque. Mertz called off jury selection for two days and then a week later, on June 10, Rein's son died. Mertz decided to call off selection for the entire week following the death so Rein could make the funeral arrangements.

Later that night, Kathy McClean, the court clerk, was driving with Mertz down Interstate 84 and back to their homes in southern New Mexico. She lived in T or C and Mertz lived in Socorro and it took them six hours one way to make the tedious trip. The all-night road construction on I-84 made the drive painfully slow. Halfway home, a thin slice of a summer moon rose up over the sandstone cliffs that were once the home to the landscape painter Georgia O'Keeffe. McClean looked over at the unusually quiet Mertz and waited for him to speak. He didn't, so she vented some of their mutual frustration with the case that just seemed to be dragging on forever.

"Boy, this sure has been a case from Hell," she said.

A weary Mertz responded, "You can say that again. Even David Ray looks tired."

"I see a look of pleasure in his eyes," offered McClean.

Mertz kept quiet, his eyes glued to the road.

After everyone returned on Monday, June 19, Yontz, Mertz and Rein tried to kick it into gear and finish up selecting jurors. Three days later, Mertz had it narrowed down to seventeen jurors and was ready to seat the eighteenth and final juror when Chris Roberts asked to have a private word with the judge. Roberts had discovered a man he called "the Christian juror" had been going over to the jailhouse across the street from the courthouse and trying to preach "the word of God" to David Parker Ray through the bars in the window of Ray's cell.

Mertz tossed the man off the jury pool and replaced him with a twenty-one-year-old female alternate juror—Cheri Archuletta from Espanola.

Chris Roberts filed weekly stories on jury selection and toward the end of the five weeks he was feeling exhausted. He'd filed over fifty AP stories during the previous fifteen months and still couldn't predict if Jim Yontz had a jury that would find David Ray guilty. A lot of the potential jurors were dropping out. Public interest in the so-called serial killer was at an all-time low. After all, when the case first hit the airwaves, the *New York Times* was carrying it on page A18 and now Roberts was lucky if he got his stuff to run in the *Albuquerque Journal.* Even the *Journal* had refused to run one story because they considered the subject matter too lurid and seedy.

One afternoon near the end of interviewing people, an Indian from the nearby Jicarillo Reservation seemed to sum up how an awful lot of jurors felt. In a quiet voice he told Mertz he could not serve on a jury hearing evidence and then make a judgment about a man like David Parker Ray.

"As an Apache," he said, "I cannot sit on a jury like this one. It goes against my sacred laws."

Roberts tried to interview jurors as they left the courthouse to find out how they felt about the details of the case. His own frustration at being "stuck" up in Tierra Amarilla for nearly five weeks spilled over in some of the headlines he wrote introducing his stories. One stuck out like a sore thumb: RAY CALLED SCUM OF THE EARTH!

Chris Roberts did not want to spend another three

weeks inside of David's head and he finally applied for a new AP position in El Paso, Texas. What he really wanted to do was buy a new Harley-Davidson and ride it all over the wasteland of West Texas. Get lost for a few weeks.

One day before the Ray trial was set to begin, on June 27, 2000, the Associated Press finally decided to hire Roberts to be its correspondent in El Paso, covering crime on the Texas-Mexico border. Two hundred women had been murdered in Ciudad, Mexico, during the previous three years, so he had plenty to write about south of the border. The day after he landed his new job, he went out and bought a brand-new black Harley-Davidson Road King and headed down the always dangerous I-25 for the Texas border. He pulled off in Truth or Consequences and rode down to Andy's Bar, where he bought an expensive bottle of Herradura Silver Tequila. Then he got back on his chopper and motored out of town and merged with the freeway traffic heading south.

CHAPTER 24

"One book that gave me alot of new ideas was Perfect Victim *by Christine McGuire."*

David Ray, talking to FBI Agent John Schum (March, 1999)

On May 25, 2000, Frances Baird, along with her twenty classmates, graduated from Geronimo Trails High School in T or C. A month later, she was at work at the *Sentinel* when her new boyfriend, an NMSP trooper who had worked on the Ray case in the summer of 1999, brought in a copy of a glossy men's magazine called *Maxim.* He wanted her to see the big article written about the Ray case, an article that focused on the dark side of life in and around the dual towns of Elephant Butte and Truth or Consequences. The title said it all: THE EVIL IN ELEPHANT BUTTE.

After Baird read what certain local citizens had to say about her beloved hometown, it made her sick. The national article referred to T or C as "Shithole U.S.A." The author went on to say that "jobs are scarce and mobile homes are the rule." Then the writer made the point that Truth or Consequences used to be a "town of retirees," but "it is now famous for sexual sadism." One longtime resident of T or C said the town was "real white trash" and described the after-hours drug scene down on Austin Street, not far from Geronimo Hot Springs, as totally grim. "It's a world of alcoholic speed freaks," the source said. After she was through reading, Baird told the new cop in her life that *Maxim* made everyone in town sound like a "bum." Her boyfriend lived and worked in Las Cruces and saw T or C through a different set of eyes. After looking at a mock-up photograph of the toy box and a fake X ray of what the authors thought the inside of the toy box looked like, he just shook his head and told Baird about his first impression a year earlier when he was investigating the case.

"The first time I drove into T or C, I would have never guessed all the things that were going on in such an out-of-the-way little town."

Up in Tierra Amarilla, things were about to get even uglier for Jim Yontz and his high hopes of squeezing David down to size in another out-of-the-way small town. One day before Yontz was planning to present his case, Mertz refused to tell him what evidence would be thrown out in the Kelli Garrett case (Van Cleave had married twice since spending three days with David in 1996), so Yontz filed an appeal with the New Mexico State Supreme Court. Over the weekend of June 24 and 25, the state supreme court ruled that Mertz had to make up his mind on suppressing evidence before the trial could begin and the lawyers gave their opening statements. When Mertz saw the paperwork in court on Tuesday morning, he was very humble in front of the jury.

"Needless to say, orders of the New Mexico Supreme Court are to be obeyed. I don't want to turn around and get caught staring down the barrel of a contempt citation by the supreme court."

He dismissed the jurors until Thursday morning.

On the morning and the afternoon of June 27, 2000, Yontz and Rein fought tooth and nail over dozens of pieces of evidence, even witnesses, and when it was all over Yontz had blood on his face and Rein came away clean as a whistle. Mertz's decisions cut Yontz's case in half, leaving Jim Yontz and Ron Lopez wondering if they had even a snowball's chance in Hell of winning.

First to go was a photograph of the gynecological table discovered in the toy box in 1999. Mertz said there was no proof it was there in 1996, the year of the crime. Next to go was a picture of the giant veined dildo attached to a portable generator. Yontz called it a "dildo affix" and Mertz said it could be easily moved, making it difficult to prove it was there in 1996. Mertz then tossed a photograph of a gun found in the 1999 search. He said there was no evidence of anyone using a gun in 1996. The ankle-and-knee spreader that the cops found in David Ray's middle bedroom in 1999 was also eliminated because Mertz said that there was no proof it was there when the crime was committed in 1996.

By this time Yontz was sitting quietly at the prosecutor's table and nobody in the courtroom trying to watch his face could tell his gut was churning. Ron Lopez sat next to him, saying nothing. Yontz knew he had to prove that Kelli was drugged because her memory was poor, at best. He tried to introduce a bottle of Hot Damn! Schnapps that the cops found in a toolbox along with a fake badge and a big hunting knife. Yontz told Mertz that the alcohol in the bottle had been laced with a powerful "date-rape" drug. Mertz refused to let the bottle in as evidence because he said it was discovered in 1999 and "everyone knows that around your own house, consumable items are typically used for immediate consumption."

Next Yontz tried to introduce the ugly audiotape he had played at the preliminary hearing for Vigil. He said the tape showed that David had "evil intent," and without blinking, Mertz threw it out, saying that "there is no evidence the defendant played this tape for Kelli Van Cleave in 1996—and I notice the tape also has a description of bestiality, not charged here or elsewhere."

Yontz wanted Cynthia Vigil to testify because she had not been drugged as badly as Kelli and her memory was much better. Mertz got a pained expression on his face when he recalled the young woman who had cracked up under pressure and broke down screaming and crying in his courtroom when she faced David Ray in April 1999 and Cindy Hendy in May 2000. He dismissed her as a potential witness.

"This court has twice seen the witness and both times remarks by the witness were vitriolic and hysterical. The state's confidence to confine this witness to authenticated testimony has not been demonstrated."

Yontz prided himself in knowing how "not" to lose and he kept his voice matter-of-fact as he plodded forward trying to introduce evidence and witnesses.

He hoped his next witness would surely be a slam dunk. He brought up FBI profiler Mary Ellen O'Toole and Mertz listened as Yontz rattled off her qualifications to prove David Ray was a sadist. Yontz pinpointed a capsule summary of the behavior of a criminal sexual sadist: chronic, learned, acting out on fantasies—first with inanimate objects like dolls and then with nonconsenting teenage and adult females. Mertz waited until Yontz was done and then threw out O'Toole as an expert witness because she had the wrong kind of college degree to be an expert.

"A doctoral degree in public administration is not a good enough background. The jury will not be told David Ray was a sexual sadist. They can look at all the evidence and then, if they want to, come to the same conclusions as Mary Ellen O'Toole and the FBI.

"They can find this information on their own," he told Yontz.

Jim Yontz had one more piece of evidence he wanted to introduce, but by this time he had little hope that Mertz would allow him to use it. David Ray gave the FBI statements way back in 1986 when his daughter, Jesse, accused him of kidnapping and selling slaves in Mexico. In the interview David voluntarily told the FBI that he was suffering from some wicked fantasies and he thought he needed to get psychiatric help. "The defendant could be dangerous because of the fantasies he indulged," Yontz told Mertz. He claimed the statements again showed David Ray's criminal intent and went on to say that the statements were "an admission of future dangerousness." And one more time Mertz told Yontz and his evidence to "get lost."

"These statements are unfairly prejudicial to the defendant and will lead to confusion by the jury," he ruled, tossing the 1986 interview.

The last item on Yontz's wish list was the toy box itself, sitting in a parking lot in Albuquerque. He wanted to bring it up to Tierra Amarilla and have the jurors walk through to get a good feeling of what kind of terror the girls felt. When the subject of a private viewing came up, Mertz got testy, noting that he himself had not seen the inside of the box. "The court is without capacity to store large, bulky exhibits," he huffed. Then he showed a genuine interest for the welfare of his jury.

"I have concern for the safety of the jurors, noting that there are probably large step-ups and step-downs that might be productive of slips and falls."

Before Yontz was willing to give up, he challenged Mertz one more time on several of the decisions to eliminate evidence and witnesses. Mertz dismissed him with a wave of the hand, refusing to hear any more challenges to his authority.

"I don't see where we need to go back and replow that ground," he said, just before adjourning for the day.

The day had started out very hot. In fact, June 27, 1994, is on record as the hottest day in New Mexico history—122 degrees Fahrenheit. During all the legal wrangling on June 27, 2000, the weather had changed from hot to a cool breeze and, finally, windy, ending with a series of rolling thunderstorms marching from one side of the courthouse to the other. It was not unlike the experience Yontz felt he had just gone through. As he was walking out the front door and into the dusty streets, Lopez asked him what he thought. The two prosecutors had twenty-four hours to make up their minds if they wanted to go to trial. Yontz had already made up his mind.

"When Thursday morning rolls around, I'm going to tell Mertz, 'You gave David everything he wanted in pretrial; now give us what we want and sentence him to everything he deserves.' "

On the opening day of trial, June 29, Jim Yontz walked in wearing a big animal-print tie sporting a big white polar bear. He knew what everyone else didn't—polar bears eat baby seals for dinner on the ice flows of Manitoba, up in Canada. He was going to do the same to David Ray's defense. Jeff Rein wore a small diamond earring in the lobe of his left ear and had his full head of silver hair blow-dried back in a sexy wave just like a male model right out of *Gentleman's Quarterly* magazine. Both lawyers (and their partners) stood as the jury was marched in. Mertz seated the eighteen jurors, commenting on the architectural splendor of the "new" Rio Arriba Courthouse.

"Perhaps this is one of the more elegant courtrooms I've ever been in," he said. "And it's elegant because of its simplicity."

Mertz then went on to lecture the jury on how to make a fair decision.

"You will be permitted to take notes. They can be of considerable assistance to you. You will not be permitted to take the notes with you. At the end of the day, court staff will take the notes and give them back to you the next day. The notes will be destroyed after the trial is over.

"You should rely on your memory and not your neighbor's note taking."

Yontz and Rein both gave their opening statements, and after it was over, it was clear to Jim Yontz that Jeff Rein had decided not to use the "S-M between consenting adults" defense for David. Rein immediately pointed out that in the six minutes of video the prosecutors were going to show the jury, "You don't see any sexual penetration, any dildos, any sexual toys, any hitting, any pinching—in other words, nothing illegal." Rein went on to pound home the fact that "Kelli did not tell anyone about these claims for three years—she didn't tell the police; she didn't even tell her own family." In his closing comments Jeff Rein turned to the jury and paraphrased Walter Scott: "You will see what a tangled web we weave when we try to deceive. . . ."

Yontz spotted Jeff Rein's standard public-defender strategy. Try the victim—not the criminal. Yontz had been prosecuting criminals for years and he'd seen it again and again. In other words, the defense attorney was going to attack the credibility of Kelli Garrett—trick the jury into paying attention to the victim with a bad memory rather than focusing on the overwhelming amount of the state's evidence showing that the defendant committed the crimes.

Yontz was only able to introduce two witnesses (a state cop and an FBI agent) before David Parker Ray himself decided to become an active player in the trial. By noon on the first day, Ray was complaining to his lawyers of "chest pains," and after a brief recess, Mertz sent the jury home for the afternoon, telling them:

"Some time ago the defendant was diagnosed as having a heart condition. It was treated at that time in Las Cruces. As we recessed for ten minutes, the defendent complained of chest pains. The EMT was called, and based on their observation, he was taken to a local clinic here in Tierra Amarilla.

"He has been released, and we will recess for today and convene tomorrow, Friday, June thirtieth, but not before one P.M."

The next day, Yontz showed up wearing another big tie with a huge brown grizzly bear standing upright in the woods. Jeff Rein was sporting a gold earring in the lobe of his right ear. David Parker Ray, looking tired, sat slumped in his chair, wearing his standard outfit of black square-toed cowboy boots, brown jeans, a gray-silver-and-white striped cowboy shirt and a pair of square silver-rimmed eyeglasses that could have passed for a mirror duplicate of the pair Mertz was wearing.

Another FBI agent, Tony Maxwell, testified about the short videotape that had been found in the white cargo trailer. He carefully traced the movement of the tape through normal channels of evidence gathering. Maxwell had been sent to T or C to round up all the vital evidence in the case and keep it in safekeeping. "For custody of the property," he explained, "the New Mexico State Mounted Police guarded the property." He was also in charge of three 8-man teams he called the "men in white," also known as the Evidence Response Team. He explained they were a group of twenty-four FBI agents, each with different tasks.

"I was overall team leader," he pointed out. "I set up the command post."

After Yontz briefly questioned Agent Maxwell, Mertz called a recess. Yontz and Lopez had both practiced in Mertz's courtroom before and knew this was just a smoke screen so Mertz could go out in the courtyard and take a smoke break himself. He was a chain-smoker. David Ray immediately leaned over and started flirting with Cathy Love, a buxom blond public defender helping Rein with the case. All of a sudden, David Ray stood up, wobbly, and turned to Love, telling her he didn't feel so good.

"I don't think I can make it," he said.

When the jurors came back twenty minutes later, David Ray was sitting in his chair, straddling a narrow three-foot-tall green oxygen canister hooked to two sets of plastic tubes winding around the back of his head, over his ears and up into each nostril. He fumbled with the valve, controlling how much oxygen he needed as Yontz introduced the next piece of evidence, a picture of the inside of the toy box when the police first found the videotape. Maxwell identified the photograph, and after the agent stepped down, Mertz had had enough for the day. In his typically polite and jury-friendly, charming manner, he smiled at the jurors and sent them home for the weekend.

"Ladies and gentlemen, it's a little after four-fifteen. I'm going to recess for the day. This will happen from time to time. I have to talk to the attorneys. When you drive home, take your time, be careful, buckle up. . . .

"And remember, when you get home—do not discuss this case with anyone."

It was a very long five-day Independence Day weekend, so Mertz told the jurors to report back for a 1:00 P.M. convening of court on the following Wednesday, July 5.

Sometime over the weekend of July 1 and 2, a wild black bear broke into the Rio Arriba Courthouse and left a mess, with footprints all over the new floors and paw prints all over the new gold doorknobs. Not to mention scratch marks on the walls and the Coke machine. When the jurors came back for jury duty, there was a boarded-up broken window next to the door where they entered the courthouse.

Yontz, unfazed, passed it off to Lopez as no big deal.

"It was probably a little cub being chased by some dogs and it was just looking for something to eat," he told the DA.

"He won't be back anytime soon."

CHAPTER 25

"David told me he was in some kind of satanic group and that they had been watching me for a long time and they wanted me for a sex toy."

Kelli Garrett testifying to Jim Yontz
July 6th, 2000

In New Mexico you can wear your gun in your holster and your holster on your hip and walk down any street in any town. You can walk into a bar, but you just can't walk into a grocery store "packing," as they say. Jim Yontz, never trusting too many people, kept a .357 Magnum in the trunk of his car, along with all the boxes of notes he needed to use in the prosecution of David Ray. In the courtroom itself, his only weapon was his tie.

On Wednesday afternoon, July 5, he was wearing a navy blue suit, dark blue shirt and a light blue tie sporting three mean-looking maroon grizzly bears. Rein showed up a "sharp-dressed man" wearing a charcoal gray suit, minus earrings. David Parker Ray enjoyed another day in "civvies," a benefit enjoyed by many felons who, according to Yontz, "get a kick" out of going to court because they get to wear street clothes again. "Felons don't make deals before a trial," he tells people, "To them, it's like going on vacation." Ray was still looking pale and attached to the green oxygen canister, and the jurors seemed to be looking over to see if he was going to keel over and kick the bucket right there on the spot.

Yontz kicked off the afternoon by calling two more state cops to lay the foundation for the first public viewing of the six-minute videotape—the one David Ray had forgotten to erase from the longer tape found in the toy box. Soft-spoken John Briscoe testified: "I was the first person to go inside the white cargo trailer just before the videotape was discovered." He went on to say, "Agent John Schum of the FBI seized all the videotapes for the laboratory in Quantico."

The straitlaced state trooper K. C. Rogers told the jury how he set up a command post in Elephant Butte to help coordinate the NMSP part of the investigation. He testified that he had seen the videotape "forty or fifty times" and "it was fairly apparent that Kelli was not a willing participant." He also explained how the police identified Kelli from the videotape.

"At the time we thought the tattoo on her right ankle at first looked like a peacock, but later we determined it was a swan. The ID was very difficult. Her legs were spread wide apart and only a fraction of the tattoo could be seen on her ankle."

Rogers then went on to explain how the police used the FBI Rapid Start System (computerized information about potential crime victims) and came up with the first name Kelli. Rogers did a cross-reference of "Kelli and white female" and came up with the tip phoned in by Kelli's mother-in-law, Janet Murphy. Murphy had told the FBI that the woman then known as Kelli Van Cleave had several tattoos, including a swan on her ankle. Rogers tracked Kelli down in Craig, Colorado.

"I contacted Kelli via telephone. You have to be careful when you're contacting a victim. You don't want them to 'build on' the information you give them and give it back to you. I asked her if she'd lived in Truth or Consequences in 1996. I asked her if she knew David Ray. I asked her how she was dressed back on July 25, 1996. I asked her if she had a swan tattoo on her right ankle. As soon as I was sure she was the woman in the video and the woman described by the mother-in-law, I told her we had pictures of her and that it might bother her to look at those pictures. I asked her if she'd be willing to talk to two investigators and then I called NMSP agent Carrie Parbs and the FBI and told them to go to Colorado and talk to her. I didn't know the FBI had already talked to her two weeks before I did."

With preliminary background information out of the way, Yontz stood up, ready to show the brief videotape. As he held the tape in his left hand, he watched the jurors carefully, somehow managing to look each one right in the eye. Ron Lopez positioned the rolling cart carrying the VCR and small twenty-one-inch television screen ten feet in front of the jury. Mertz moved and sat in the witness chair so he could get a better look, and the only person in the hushed chamber who was not in a position to look at the videotape was David himself.

All eighteen jurors leaned forward in their seats, many of them with pencils in hand, ready to take notes for the first time in the trial. Jurors ranged in age from twenty-one to sixty-one and there were ten men and eight women. Sixty percent of the residents of New Mexico are Hispanic and the jury reflected the geography of the state as well as Rio Arriba County. The fate of David Ray was in the hands of the following eighteen people:

Cheri Archuletta	Simon Martinez	Donald Archuletta
Phyllis Ortiz	Raymond Lujan	Carla Leivas
Amanda Garcia	Frank Sandoval	David Maestas
Annie Vasquez	Reynaldo Chavez	Stella Randall

Cynthia Gallegos	Enriques Sanchez	Jonathan Kingson
Deborah Cordova	Robert Lucero	Mark LeDoux

Jim Yontz strolled over and put the videotape in the VCR and pushed PLAY. At first the jurors could only see and hear David Ray doing sound checks. His voice was not timid at all, but assertive and knowledgeable about electronics. He was trying to get his camera positioned just right so the angle for future viewing would be satisfying for him when he later decided to look at his work.

Everyone watched, waiting for the action. The scene spliced to a monotonous shot of the soundproof ceiling inside the toy box. Yontz made no attempt to speed up the viewing. Mertz asked Yontz how many minutes the jury would have to spend staring at the ceiling of the white cargo trailer.

"About thirty minutes," Yontz answered calmly.

Mertz ordered him to fast-forward the tape, and a few awkward minutes later, at 3:21 P.M., Yontz told everyone the long-awaited segment was ready for everyone to see.

The camera-eye view of Kelli Garrett was no less than a "crotch shot," filmed from a camera mounted up near the ceiling. The jury saw twenty-two-year-old Kelli, naked, strapped "spread eagle" to a black leather weight bench and tied down with red plastic straps. Her legs were positioned wide apart, knees up in the air, her ankles in stirrups. Her arms were tied down behind and above her head. There was a two-inch-wide piece of gray duct tape over her mouth and another two-inch-wide piece of tape over her eyes.

She appeared to be dazed and confused, moving her head slowly from side to side.

David Ray was dressed in blue jeans, black cowboy boots and a blue-and-white vertical-striped cowboy shirt—not tucked into his pants but hanging outside. He was talking to Kelli, but the videotape had no sound and nobody could read his lips. He walked over to her from the left side and put his middle finger of his right hand up inside her vagina, acting like he was a doctor examining her. Then he used both hands to rub her breasts. Following that, he knelt on the floor and fondled her belly with both hands, and this time he leaned over her and slid the first two fingers of his right hand in and out of her vagina. Then he stood up, walked around to her other side and checked the duct tape on her face. The tape over her eyes and mouth had come loose and he fastened it down. He stood up and pawed her breasts again. She moved her head from side to side, as if to say no.

He walked around to between her legs and stroked the inside of her uplifted legs, checking the tie-downs on her ankles and the red straps over her upper legs. He fastened the strap on her right leg and then fastened the strap on her left leg. He then took off the square-rimmed glasses and laid them down on a nearby table.

Now he walked back up to her head and got behind her so he could unfasten her hands. First the right wrist, then the left. She moved her arms slowly and then rubbed her sore wrists. The tape ended with her crossing her arms over her breasts and then putting both hands over her face, as if to "hide."

David was standing and talking down to her, but the jury still couldn't read his lips.

Yontz turned off the television set at 3:27 P.M. and many jurors had their heads down, taking notes. One juror, Phyllis Ortiz, was not taking notes at all. All the women on the jury were wearing black. Mertz could tell everyone was emotionally drained, so he called off court in the middle of the afternoon and excused the jury, once more reminding them not to talk to anyone about the case. He reminded them that court would resume hearing witnesses at 8:30 A.M., Thursday, July 6.

* * *

Patrick Murphy was the first witness the following day. He was married to Kelli for thirteen days back in 1996. Yontz and Rein videotaped their deposition with him in Mertz's courtroom in Socorro back on April 13 and the jury saw that testimony. Patrick was wearing his white navy uniform and was Hollywood handsome at twenty-four years old. He showed no nervousness about having to answer questions about his love life as a young man back in the summer of 1996—when he was only twenty years old.

I'm stationed now on the USS *Santini,* an attack cruiser, in San Diego, California.

I met Kelli late in the spring of 1996. I was having a beer with my friend Jay at a place called Raymond's bar in T or C. I took one look at her and I said, "Hi, how're ya doin'?" We just hit it off—right away. She told me she had these tattoos and she showed me her tattoos and I showed her mine.

[*Patrick smiled, remembering the Mickey Mouse tattoo on her left breast.*]

She'd say, "I've got a mouse—would you like to see it?"

We spent the next couple of weeks together. It was kind of an understanding that we were a "thing." She liked to ride in my Jeep. She was out of work and living outside of town with some friends in a trailer. As far as the trailer was concerned, it was in bad shape. She had some money in the bank, but I told her that sooner or later the money was gonna run out.

"You gotta think of the future," I said.

I was staying with my parents at the time, and so I'd bring her over and we'd hang out. My mom thought she was a nice person but hung out with the wrong group of people. Kelli was hanging out with bums—a lot of burned-out druggies, friends of Jesse Ray. She and my mom, well, they had a strange relationship. Kinda like a mother and a daughter. It was weird.

I liked Kelli. I never did see her drunk, and she didn't use drugs. I liked that. Her nickname was "Sassy"—she's just one of those women who doesn't mind being sassy with you. At the time I drank a lot of alcohol and one day I made it real clear how I felt. I said, "Alcohol's all right, but this drug stuff is illegal." I couldn't afford to mess up my career in the navy. I was real stern when I told her, "I don't do those things," and I told her we would be all over as a couple if she did drugs. She understood.

One afternoon, in July, we were just drivin' down the road and I looked over and asked her if she wanted to get married. She looked at me and said, "You're jokin', aren't you?" I told her I didn't want to know anything about her childhood and I didn't want her to know anything about mine.

"This is ground zero," I said.

We got married the next day. My mom was "floored" that I was gettin' married. Me and Kelli moved into my parents' house and it was a few days after we got married that all the trouble started. We had a big argument over sex. It hurt her to have intercourse. The night before she vanished, I "laid into her" about it. She didn't want to have intercourse. Something in her made it painful. That night she just watched television all night and fell asleep on the living-room couch.

The next morning she left around nine or ten. I got real pissed-off about the situation—started ranting and raving—and then I drank a lot. The whole rest of that day, I drank a lot more. I went to the VFW Hall and I drank a lot. I went to Raymond's bar and they told me she was at the bowling alley. I was underage and one other time I'd been kicked out, so I went out to Hot Springs Cove and looked for her there. I drank some more alcohol and fell asleep on the beach.

I woke up in the middle of the night thinking about her.

That morning when she left, she had shorts on, shoes, a wedding ring, a bracelet and her hair was all fixed up—my little sister, Kimberley, had braided it that morning. Her hair was all over her head, like a little poodle.

The next morning, I got up and vomited, and went home. I tried calling missing persons. I filed a missing-persons report with the local police department. Then I went out and drank a lot more beer.

Later that day, Cassandra Witt called me up with information about where Kelli was (getting stoned with her friends) and I went over to see Cassy. She told me Kelli was over at the bowling alley and some guy in a red truck was trying to "hit on her." Some guy named Todd. I took Cassy over to talk to my parents. Looking back on it, I think she was trying to form a wedge between me and Kelli. I left when Cassy was talking to my family. She was just sittin' around telling my mom some nonsense about me and Kelli.

Cassy was always telling me my marriage was too much like a fantasy—you know—the prince takes Kelli from this godforsaken town and finally gets her out of the slum of Truth or Consequences and off to California.

By the end of the day on Saturday, I thought Kelli had left me for good. I made plans to dissolve the marriage per the "How to Get a Divorce" guide. Cassy actually was the one who showed me where to get all the paperwork to file for a divorce. Most of the rest of the day, I just went out target-shooting with me and my rifle.

After that, I just went back to drinking a lot of beer.

About nine or ten o'clock Sunday morning, Kelli shows up with Jesse Ray's dad, David Ray. He's driving a company truck and wearin' his forest ranger outfit—beige-style shirt, long brown pants and boots. Cassy was in the house and I wanted her to confront Kelli. When she saw Kelli and David, she freaked out. She got scared—I thought she was gonna piss her pants. She went into the back room and hid, and the last thing I heard her say was, "Oh, shit, Kelli's here!"

Kelli got out of the truck and went over and sat on our porch. She was "out of it." She wasn't of a sound mind, that's for sure. She wasn't wearing shoes or her wedding ring or her bracelet. Her hair looked real messed up. She had body odor and the whole thing wasn't like her at all.

At home she "lived" in the shower—took two or three showers a day.

I was instantly infuriated. Pissed. Enraged with the whole situation. It looked like she was under the influence of a narcotic or something. She was dazed, tired, mopey—out of it. Mr. Ray said he'd found her on the beach and took her out for a sugared-up cup of coffee before bringing her home. I believed him because his daughter was Kelli's good friend and he had just brought back my soon-to-be ex-wife. He told me he found her layin' in the sand at a Hot Springs beach. The whole thing struck me as odd. This would have never been possible with the person I thought I knew.

If someone is layin' there in the sand, you're gonna have sand on your body.

She didn't.

All this time she sounded very sad. She kept putting her hands on her head. She had bumps on her head and at one point she started crying—she was almost in a state of what I would call "pure crying." All she could remember was going off with Jesse and then coming back to our place—three days later. There was nothing in between. When my mom asked her where she'd been she kept saying the same thing over and over.

"I don't know."

"I don't know."

"I can't remember."

The next day she came back with one of her friends to get her toothbrush and stuff. Most of our conversation was real heated. It was mostly me being a smart ass. I had to get out of there. I was gettin' hotheaded. I was beyond reasoning.

A few days later I got together with Cassy Witt and we got married—I think it was July 31, right before I had to go back to San Diego. The marriage only lasted six months. On October 11 I left for the Persian Gulf and when I came back six months later I was in financial ruin.

She wrote several thousand dollars in bad checks.

She wrecked my Jeep.

She ruined my credit card.

Once I got rid of Cassy, I realized I'd made a great mistake when I dumped Kelli. I went back to T or C in April of 1997, and Kelli and I tried to get back together again. She moved into our house for a while. A week later, my mother told me Kelli was still hanging out with Jesse Ray, so I broke it off. After that spring, I . . . I just tried to forget about Kelli. I knew we were all washed up.

I just returned to California and went on with my life.

CHAPTER 26

I grew up with my mother telling me, 'There is no bogeyman, there is no bogeyman,' and one day I discovered that the bogeyman does *exist.*

—"Unidentified" woman overheard talking to another woman in Judge Mertz's courtroom, 7/06/2000

On Thursday, July 6, it was hotter than Hell. Judge Mertz ordered the bailiff to find additional air-conditioning to help out where the graceful, slow-moving 1917 ceiling fans left off. It was all business that morning with Yontz and Rein, and observers could see their faces glisten in the dry desert heat as the testimony of Kelli Garrett drew closer and closer. David Ray sat in his chair with a blank look on his weathered face. Just before the morning session started, Jeff Rein turned to Cathy Love and said he thought David Ray looked a "little pooped."

The morning proceedings started out with a bang as the obviously stressed-out Neil Mertz zeroed in on the media for a stern warning. Photographers had been moving benches so they could set up their tripods and cameras in preparation for Garrett's testimony. Mertz looked at the Associated Press cameraman and reporter and shouted all the way to the back of the courtroom:

"Turn that camera off! Put the furniture back! I'm not gonna have today what I had yesterday. Once these proceedings start, nobody is gonna leave except during a recess. If these rules are not satisfactory, then you can leave now. This public event is being staged for the jury—not the newspapers or the television stations. As best I can manage it, there are not going to be any distractions."

Janet Murphy testified first and the guilt written across her face was obvious to everyone in the courtroom.

Next was Todd Thompson, "the guy in the red truck" whom Patrick Murphy had talked about the day before. He told Yontz what life was like for the young and the restless in T or C back in 1996.

"There was nothing to do—unless you go bowling or go out to the lake.

"I'd known Kelli for a while and on July twenty-fifth she stopped by my work with Dave Connolly. She said she was having troubles with her new husband, Patrick. I was with a group of people that hung out with her later the same night—the night she disappeared. It was me, Cassy, Dave, Clay, Sonja, Steve, Tres, Kelli and Jesse Ray. We shot pool, danced and had a few beers before me and Cassy Witt went home early, about midnight. I kept running with the same group of friends over the weekend, and when we didn't see Kelli for the next two days, I got concerned. Finally, on Sunday afternoon, July twenty-eighth, I saw Kelli with her friend Dave Connolly. She didn't look like the same girl at all.

"She looked scared, messy—her clothes were wrinkled, the braids in her hair were dirty. I was surprised. She usually took pride in how she looked. She seemed upset, shaky and very nervous."

When Jeff Rein got his hands on Thompson, he tried to make quick work of him. He got Todd to admit he and Cassandra Witt had been dating during the first three weeks of July 1996 and then Rein asked Todd who he was dating by the last week of July.

"I was going out with Kelli—it only lasted about seven weeks and then she broke up with me by the end of September '96."

"Thank you, Mr. Thompson, I don't have any more questions," said Rein.

Out in the corridor, a small (five feet one inch), slender woman with long, straight blond hair falling over her shoulders clutched her stomach and talked to her older sister as she got ready to enter the Rio Arriba Courthouse and face down the man she claimed had imprisoned her for three days back when she was twenty-two years old. Kelli Garrett, now twenty-six, was taking deep breaths and crying softly just before the bailiff came out to get her and lead her into what she later told friends was "another torture chamber," Mertz's courtroom.

As she walked in, the female jurors, all dressed in black, watched her every move. By the time she was sworn in, she had regained her composure and was ready to tell Jim Yontz how the whole story had unfolded. She had practiced telling the story in front of Yontz many times before, so she was pretty much ready for him to take her through it step by step.

"My friends and I would all go to the bars and play pool and dance," she began.

"Right after I met Patrick, we decided to get married. It started out as a joke. We went down and bought these two fake rings. Little silver bands. We had this mutual friend Cassandra Witt and we decided to play a trick on her. We decided to tell her we were going to get married. She'd been telling everyone she was going to take Patrick away from me, so we bought this cheap cake and these cheap wedding rings. We knew Cassy was going to come by—she always did. I knew Cassy wanted Patrick for herself, but I knew he didn't want her. Patrick's parents were even in on the joke. . . . Except, in the end, we really got married.

"Cassy even stood up for us!

"A few days later, we started fighting. We fought quite a bit. It was over sex. I have 'female problems' and sex hurts. He got real mad at me because I wouldn't 'give him any.'

"We were staying at his parents' house and one night I got mad at him and went out and slept on the couch. The night before, he'd told me he was tired of not getting enough sex. He said when I did give it to him, I cried too much. So the next morning I decided to go for a walk. It was about ten o'clock and I didn't have a driver's license or a car, so I knew I couldn't go far. I was wearing my wedding ring, a watch, a necklace and earrings. I had my hair in little bitty braids all over my head.

"I walked over to this girl Becky's house and we walked over to Cassy's place. She had a pickup truck and we drove over and got Dave and we went to Rocky's bar in downtown T or C. Jesse Ray showed up and we spent a few hours there. I didn't drink because I was the designated driver.

"Around four o'clock we drove over to Raymond's bar and met up with Todd Thompson. Everyone drank, except me. I was still the designated driver.

"Around nine o'clock we went over to the Blue Waters Saloon in Elephant Butte and met up with everyone else. I had one beer. People started to go home just before midnight. I drove Dave Connolly home in his car and Todd left Cassy and Jesse alone in the bar and came and got me and brought me back to the Blue Waters. He was driving his red truck. Right away him and Cassy got in a fight, so they just up and left. I didn't have a ride home, so Jesse said she'd take me home on her motorcycle.

"I think she took me to her dad's house."

Jim Yontz stopped Kelli and asked her if Jesse's dad was in the courtroom today. Cool as a cucumber, she looked David Parker Ray right in the eye and pointed him out, then she went on with her story.

"We were sitting on the living-room couch, and suddenly David and Jesse went into the back room for about ten minutes. When they came out, one of them put a knife to my throat. I can't remember which one. They took me outside to another trailer.

"I remember being tied to a bench. It was like a weight bench—I had my arms up over my head. I had my legs spread apart. Every time I moved, I thought I was gonna fall off of it.

"Right away he started using the dildos on me. He tried to force them inside me and they wouldn't go—they'd go partways inside me, that's all. The dildos felt like they were the size of a can of Copenhagen snuff. I had duct tape over my eyes and mouth, but I knew it was David. I could hear him talking and one time the duct tape came off my cheek and I leaned back and I saw David. Before he could adjust it, I looked up at the walls and ceiling for a minute. He had all kinds of 'things' on top of a medicine cabinet and more 'things' hanging on the walls.

"He was puting his fingers in me, trying to find out why the dildos didn't work.

"It was like he was trying to play doctor.

"He came back to the toy box six different times. He tried to force the dildos inside of me at least thirty different times. He would leave me tied to the table, and then when he came back, he would start all over again. I kept telling him I didn't want him to do it. I kept saying, 'No! No!' and I kept telling him I didn't want to be there, I just wanted to go home. I was trying to tell him to quit. I was crying.

"When he let me go, he drove me over to Earl's Diamond Gas station for a cup of coffee, and on the way there, he told me why I had been taken and why I was going to be released. He told me he was in some kind of satanic group and they'd been watching me for a long time and they wanted me for a sex toy. He said when the dildos wouldn't go in, I'd be no use to them—so he decided to let me go.

"He took me to Janet Murphy's to release me and he told the two of them he found me on the beach. I was confused. Patrick and his mother wouldn't let me in the house, not even to get my toothbrush. They wanted to know where I'd been and at the time I couldn't remember anything. They made me go away with David and he drove me down to the Dam Site Tavern and my friend Dave Connolly took care of me for the next two days.

"Ray hurt me so bad, I bled for three or four days afterward."

Yontz stopped Kelli Garrett again and showed her a picture of the swan tattoo the police used to help identify her. He asked her if she could identify the person in the picture. She looked at the photograph of her leg and ankle, and what she called her "tribal swan" tattoo, and pointed to it.

"That's my leg!" she said. "I've had memories off and on over the last four years. I didn't know if it was true. I thought it was a nightmare and most of the time I didn't want to believe it.

"Then Carrie Parbs came up from the New Mexcio State Police and showed me pictures taken from the videotape. After she showed me the photographs, I realized it wasn't a dream anymore. It was reality, and at first I couldn't deal with it. . . ."

Yontz interrupted her one more time and handed her two more pictures, each showing her naked and tied down "spread-eagle" on the weight bench. The first picture showed only her, blindfolded, and the second showed her and David Ray in the same frame. Yontz asked her if she could identify the woman in the photographs. She clutched her stomach and a sick look crossed her face. Her pale cheeks were suddenly red and flushed. She held her head in her hands and small tears began to trickle down her cheeks.

She reached for a Kleenex.

"Yes, that's me," she said in a faint whisper.

"Did you ever see the video?" asked Yontz.

"Nope," she said, sounding more confident.

"Who is the other person in this picture?" asked Yontz. Kelli Garrett's lips narrowed down to a thin white line as she struggled to hold back her rage. She pointed to the defendant sitting by himself, legs straddling his green oxygen canister.

"David," she said as David Parker Ray looked away.

"I got divorced the day after I came back from the trailer. I used to be called 'Sassy' and now I don't like to be around other people. I used to be outgoing and I'm not anymore. I don't go anywhere. I don't sleep with my husband, Mike, anymore—and we fight about sex. If I'm alone in the house, I always have a pistol sitting right beside me. If I look out the window and see a car or a truck with a New Mexico license plate, I freak out."

When it was time for cross-examination by the defense attorney, Garrett tightened up.

Jeff Rein was soft-spoken and used a very gentle style to question Kelli Garrett. He relied on his yellow legal pads to make sure he didn't forget anything and he always treated the witness with respect, attempting to disarm her. He approached Garrett with kid gloves, but it was clear from the start he was going to attack her memory, thereby making it the prosecution of Kelli Garrett rather than the defense of David Parker Ray.

"Where did you buy the wedding cake?" he asked right off the bat.

"I can't remember—I think it was Bullocks Grocery store."

"You thought Patrick was twenty-four years old, right?"

"Right," she says.

"But he was only twenty years old, wasn't he?"

"Yes, that's true."

"Can you describe the wedding rings?"

"Just a couple of silver bands."

"When you left the Blue Waters Saloon, do you remember going?"

"No, I don't remember leaving the bar."

"You said he used thirty dildos—do you remember any single one of those situations?"

"No, I do not."

"If you can't recall one individual incident, how can you remember six sessions?"

"He just came and went, came and went. . . . I could hear his keys jingling every time he unlocked the door of the toy box."

"You said when he brought you back to Janet Murphy's house, you were missing your watch and your wedding ring—what do you remember about them?"

"My watch was gold and my wedding ring was silver."

For nearly an hour, it went back and forth between the public defender and the young woman. Jim Yontz had been building his case on the assumption that the trauma from Kelli Garrett's experience with David Ray had thrown a monkey wrench into her emotional life; Rein wanted to prove her trauma might have been caused by other factors. He waited until he thought he'd worn Garrett down to hit her with his best shot. He pointed out that she got married to a man named Clay in September 1997 and then went through a messy divorce a year later. Then he reminded her that she fell for another man named Jim Hibbard in 1998 and in October of that year, tragedy struck her life one more time.

"You said after David kidnapped you, nothing else could have caused your fear of being alone," Rein began. "But isn't it true that your fiancé Jim drowned right in front of you six months before David Ray was arrested?"

"Yes."

"Jim had just proposed to you on the day he died, right?"

"Yes."

"The boat swamped and Jim didn't make it to shore, right?"

"Yes."

"Has that been traumatic?"

"Yes."

"You told your friends what happened, right?"

"Yes."

"Then why did you wait for over three years to tell anybody about David Parker Ray kidnapping and torturing you?"

Kelli Garrett paused a long time before answering the question. She was looking down at her trembling hands, and finally she raised her eyes and looked at Jeff Rein.

"I thought if I didn't tell anybody about the nightmares, they would go away," she said.

Rein sat down and Jim Yontz got a chance to ask one more question on redirect. He walked over next to the jury box and turned to Kelli Garrett and in a calm voice asked her about the nightmares going away.

"Is that why you are here today, Kelli, because they didn't go away?"

"Yes."

Kelli Garrett stepped down and slowly walked out of the courtroom. Every female juror seemed to be fixated on Garrett as they watched her shaking all over, clutching her stomach and looking down at the floor.

Mertz called it a day at 4:14 P.M. on Thursday, July 6.

CHAPTER 27

"Old David would never hurt a fly."
Co-worker John Martinez, August 10th, 1999.

Mertz's mechanical air-conditioning generators were put into the open windows on Friday morning, July 7, and it wasn't long before a cool-but-noisy breeze was blowing through the courtroom. In the meantime, things really started to heat up with the lawyers. Yontz, stripped of much of his best evidence by Mertz, still had plenty of ammunition and he got ready to toss everything in the direction of the jury before they had a chance to go out for lunch and digest his evidence. Anticipating the morning onslaught, David Ray came across as a well-dressed man. He wore black cowboy boots, dark brown jeans, a beige shirt and a very classy black cowboy sports coat with little leather arrows on the pockets.

Yontz called State Trooper John Briscoe to the stand right away. He'd been the first man on the scene inside the toy box and he'd taken a number of the initial photographs of some of the most graphic evidence. Briscoe looked at a series of photographs, identifying bloody dildos hanging from the ceiling, an aluminum drawer with a "cot" inside, stainless-steel medicine cabinet and lots of padlocks, chains and straps. The last photograph showed aging pictures of several women in bondage and right next to the naked ladies, there were two lists, one handwritten and the other typed. Yontz remembered his own gut reaction the first time he saw the handwritten list and he asked Briscoe, a short man with a hefty build and a loud voice, to read the first document to the jury. Briscoe stood up and read the handwritten list first. For lack of a formal title, Briscoe called it the "Remember" list:

R–E–M–E–M–B–E–R
A WOMAN WILL DO OR SAY ANYTHING TO GET LOOSE!

THEY WILL:
KICK SCRATCH BITE

Yontz sat back in his chair and watched the jurors as Briscoe rattled off the list in a bold voice. Most of the jurors were getting tired and Yontz noticed a couple of men had sort of a bored look covering their faces. Briscoe had a tone of outrage in his voice and Yontz figured the jurors might have the same feeling he had listening to David Ray rattle off his "standard excuses for sob stories." After all, men in captivity might try to use some of the same tricks to escape—I'm sick; I have to work; I have a sick kid; I have a sick parent; my doctor told me I have a bad heart; I'm missed by a friend; my boss tells me I can't miss work. . . .

Briscoe completed the "reminders" by emphasizing David Ray's most telling advice for his followers:

– – – – DON'T LET HER GET TO YOU – – – –
IF SHE IS WORTH TAKING – – – SHE IS WORTH KEEPING
AND
SHE MUST BE SUBJECTED TO HYPNOSIS BEFORE THIS WOMAN CAN BE SAFELY RELEASED.

< NEVER TRUST A CHAINED CAPTIVE >

Briscoe finished and sat down. He went on to identify several pictures he'd taken of several miscellaneous items, like wrist clamps, gloves, more big and small dildos. Right after Yontz held up the last photograph for the jury to see, he walked back to the prosecutor's table and pulled a huge wooden item out of a plastic bag and asked Briscoe to identify it. It looked like a rolling pin used by a pastry chef to make pies. It was about ten inches long and it tapered from $1\frac{3}{8}$ of an inch at the narrow end to $2\frac{5}{8}$ inches at the wide end. The whole tool was mounted on a T-shaped metal handle. Briscoe got a little embarrassed and stumbled over his words identifying the object.

"It's a vag-vaginal stretcher," he said.

Yontz put the rolling pin back in the bag and handed Briscoe another list to read. It was a one-page neatly typed list of eighteen instructions, presumably guidelines for the other members of Ray's satanic cult. Unlike the first list, which was scrawled in felt tip pen, this one looked like just another corporate document. Briscoe turned to the jury and read it with the same boom in his voice as before—except this time he read it even louder.

PSYCHOLOGICAL AND PHYSICAL PROCEDURES
INITIAL HANDLING OF A CAPTIVE
PERSONAL FETISH

1. The new female captive should be gagged and blindfolded with wrists and ankles chained.
2. Move her into the Recreation Room. Place her body under the suspension chains.
3. Stand her up under the chains and lock her wrists well above her head.
4. Place the neck chain around her neck and lock it in place. IT IS PERMANENT.
5. Clip her leg irons to the floor chains.
6. Use scissors to slowly remove her dress, blouse or sweater. Cut and remove the bra. ??
7. Fondle and abuse her breasts, nipples, and upper part of her body.
8. Keep her blindfolded to increase disorientation. Use verbal abuse. (Dumb Bitch, Slut, etc.)
9. Slowly unzip, open, and remove the lower clothing. Cut or rip the panties off.
10. Fondle and abuse her sex organs. Continue the verbal abuse.
11. Attach the over head suspension straps to her body. Ankles, waist, hips, and upper chest.
12. Remove the leg irons and tighten the ankle straps, pulling her legs upward, until the middle part of her body is horizontal. (THE ANKLE STRAPS WILL FORCE HER LEGS WIDE APART).
13. Tighten and adjust the waist, hip, and chest straps until the middle of her body is straight. Clip the short floor chain to the bottom ring on the waist belt, so she cannot jerk or lift her body upward.

14. At this point, the captive is suspended at a convenient height, immobilized, and fully exposed. She is very uncomfortable, disoriented, and probably terrified. Don't cut her any slack. Continue a lot of verbal and physical abuse . . . Keep her mentally off balance.
15. Play with her sex organs. (Vagina or anus). Force large dildos deep into both holes. Use clamps, needles, or other devices on her tits and sex organs. (Clit and cunt lips). Whip her and use Electro-shock.
16. Don't give her time to collect her thoughts. Use her body agressively, during the first hour or two. She will sweat, struggle a lot, and exhaust herself. Particularly if the Electroshock machine is used extensively.
17. Intensify her fear. Tell her how she is going to be kept as a Sex Slave. Describe, in detail, how she will be continuously raped and tortured. Work on her mind, as well as her body.
18. Keep her body suspended two or three hours, then roll the Gynocology Bench directly beneath her. Lower her body down on the bench. Release one arm or leg at a time, and secure it to the bench, until she is strapped down. Buckle all the straps on her body, until she is totally immobilized, feet in the stirrups, and knees forced wide apart.

NOTE: THE SHOCK VALUE OF DISORIENTATION, PLUS CONTINUOUS VERBAL AND PHYSICAL ABUSE, DURING THE FIRST FEW HOURS OF CONFINEMENT, WILL HAVE A GREAT INFLUENCE ON HOW DOSCILE AND SUBDUED THE CAPTIVE WILL BE DURING THE REMAINING PERIOD OF CAPTIVITY. IF IT IS DONE PROPERLY SHE WILL BE INTIMIDATED AND MUCH EASIER TO HANDLE.

John Briscoe finished up and when Jeff Rein stood up and got ready to ask the one question that the public defender figured would spell doom for the other side, Briscoe's face seemed to knot up.

"Do you know if any of these items were there in 1996?"

"I don't know," said Briscoe, and the tone of his voice seemed to say it didn't make a damn bit of difference.

Just before the jury came back from lunch, Yontz and Rein approached the bench with a request that upset Mertz so much the judge's face turned purple. Yontz wanted to use Kelli Garrett's therapist, David Spencer, as a last-minute witness and Rein knew all about it ahead of time. Mertz chewed out both attorneys for not telling him Garrett's psychotherapist was a potential witness.

"I am absolutely livid!" he scolded them. "Apparently, this is the kind of trial you want. . . ."

When the jury returned to the courtroom, the judge smiled as he told the jury there was a "development" that made it difficult to continue for the day, while at the same time he frowned at both lawyers. As soon as the jurors had departed, Mertz told Yontz and Rein exactly how he felt about spending the rest of the afternoon fighting over one witness.

"Well, come on, let's get on with it."

Mertz listened to David Spencer, a therapist from Craig, Colorado, give his opinion of Kelli Garrett in order that Mertz might decide if Spencer was qualified to provide expert testimony on the mental state of the victim after the alleged crime. Both lawyers spent the afternoon grilling Spencer and this is what he told Mertz about the mental condition of Kelli Garrett after he started "seeing her" in September 1999.

"She came to see me because she was suffering from anxiety and depression. She was having trouble sleeping. She was losing weight. She couldn't work. During our first session together, she told me she was 'in a fog' over what David had done to her. I tried to make her feel safe and protected. She had isolated herself from the whole world.

"She felt people from Truth or Consequences could harm her—a person she had known for years [Jesse] helped another person abduct her. Kelli was so scared she kept a gun next to her and had a couple of large dogs.

"I came to believe she has post-traumatic stress disorder.

"People with PTSD become hypersensitive. Occasionally paranoid. These people have trouble sleeping soundly, or not at all. Kelli told me once that she often gets only one hour of sleep a night.

"When she was a child, she was Daddy's girl. By the time she was seventeen, she was no longer Daddy's girl. She left high school before graduation and moved in with Greg, a boyfriend who was extraordinarily abusive to her—he locked her in the house, threw the phone at her and hit her over the top of the head. She still has a terrible scar on her forehead where he hit her with the phone.

"Years later, after she got divorced from Patrick and Clay, she was engaged to a man named Jim who drowned in a boating accident on the Colorado River in 1998. After the boat sank, other people on the river didn't do anything to help save him. Kelli dove underwater three times herself trying to save him and at that point a friend grabbed her and kept her from drowning. Right before she came to the surface, she saw Jim go under . . . for the last time."

When Rein questioned Spencer, he reminded the psychotherapist that it was imperative to prove that Kelli Garrett had undergone "great mental anguish" in order to show that she was a victim of David Parker

Ray's—and not her past bad luck. Yontz took the next opportunity to point out to Mertz that this was an unfair criteria to use against Kelli Garrett. Sarcasm wasn't his suit, but he pointed out to the judge that Rein's standard couldn't be met.

"The only people who haven't suffered anguish are newborn infants, who haven't had any life experiences at all."

At this point, Mertz injected a question for the witness. He wanted to know if there could be "multiple causes" of PTSD. Spencer said yes and went on to explain that in some cases there is an "immediate onset" condition and in other cases patients suffer a "delayed onset." The judge was satisfied that David Spencer knew what he was talking about and gave the "green light" for the therapist to testify as soon as court resumed on Tuesday, July 11.

"The court finds that by education and training and experience, the witness, David Spencer, is suited to render expert opinion on this, case."

Over the weekend of July 8 and 9, there was an attempted jailbreak across the street from the Rio Arriba Courthouse. It was the same facility that housed David Ray.

On Saturday night, July 8, a riot broke out about eight o'clock, after guards tried to break up a fight between two inmates. Inmates from all three "pods" rampaged through the detention areas, destroying plumbing and shower fixtures, beds and mattresses, television sets, video cameras and the Rio Arriba jail electronic monitoring devices. They also ripped up welded steel tables from the lunchroom and used rebar from concrete pilings to smash all the security glass within reach.

Shortly after midnight on July 8, the fifty-nine inmates were surrounded outside the jail by over a hundred NMSP officers who had circled the facility. Just before 2:00 A.M. on July 9, the riot was brought to an orderly conclusion. The only reason the inmates couldn't break out and terrorize the community was because the last of the three sets of steel doors was under the control of a command-center computer they couldn't get their hands on.

Cost of damages from the six-hour uprising was estimated to be over a quarter of a million dollars and the next day County Commissioner Hector Morales suggested that in the future violent prisoners such as murderers should be kept in another facility.

"We should not have these tough guys here—they don't care about anything anymore," he told the local paper, the *Rio Grande Sun*. "They've given up on life."

One inmate who had not given up on life was David Ray. Many in the community thought Ray was behind the jailbreak, but jail boss Valdez tried to reassure the neighborhood by stating that "Ray was being held in isolation inside the jail and this didn't affect him at all." In fact, David Ray was the first inmate to be sent away—driven to Santa Fe in the middle of the night. He returned after things had calmed down and was back in his cell by Tuesday morning, July 11.

Both Yontz and Rein knew there was going to be a battle brewing in the minds of the jurors over Kelli Garrett's "state of mind," and on Tuesday morning, at 9:01, Yontz put David Spencer on the witness stand. Spencer elaborated on the mental health of the victim.

"She moved up to the Vermillion Cliffs in Colorado to get away from people she once thought were her 'friends' in T or C. She is still suffering from her contact with Jesse and David. She will sometimes fly off the handle and sometimes she takes out her anger on her pets. She is hypersensitive. If she sees a program on television about sexual abuse, she has to turn off her television set.

"She has a great fear she could be kidnapped again. She can't take a shower unless her husband is home. At one time in her life, she regarded herself as being 'street-smart.' After all that has happened to her, she doesn't feel like she can go out on the street and be safe.

"She fights going to sleep in order to prevent the nightmares. Victims quite often do that. If you are in a deep sleep, you might not be able to protect yourself. That's the way she thinks."

Jeff Rein calmly tried to focus Spencer on the fact that Kelli Garrett seemed to have what Rein called a "fuzzy memory." He got Spencer to admit that "you don't question whether what she tells you is true or false, do you?" He also confronted Spencer with his own take on the counseling sessions, concluding, "It is fair to say you don't know much about Kelli's life before Patrick, do you?" And just before Rein finished with David Spencer, he made the pointed comment that Spencer "didn't know much about Kelli's life right after Patrick, either.

"Would it surprise you to know that within a few days after her divorce Kelli started dating a guy named Todd Thompson?"

"No, I didn't know that," admitted Spencer.

Jim Yontz decided to haul in one more piece of evidence before wrapping up his case against Ray. In the spring of 1999, police investigators had found a rusty weight-lifter's bench press leaning up against a shed out behind David Ray's place. It was rigged with D rings and lots of red elastic straps and it looked like the same piece of equipment seen in the six minutes of video that Yontz had shown the jury. The bench press was unfolded and placed on the floor so the jurors could see the similarities. Jeff Rein asked Trent Peterson, the state cop who found the evidence, if there was any proof that the press was on David Ray's property back in July 1996.

"No," the officer admitted.

At 1:36 in the afternoon, Judge Neil Mertz turned the proceedings over to Jeff Rein and the defense team for David Ray. Without calling a single witness, Rein stood up and addressed the judge.

"Your Honor, the defense rests. . . ."

The next morning, July 12, Mertz gave a stern warning to everyone in the courtroom before allowing Yontz and Rein to take one hour each to give closing arguments.

"There are to be no visible reactions to remarks made during closing arguments—no grimacing, no grinning, no shrugs, whatever—if you are unable to do this, leave my courtroom right now."

Yontz started out strong and was prepared to finish the second half of the summary and give his closing when DA Ron Lopez leaned over and told him he wanted to do the final closing, Yontz figured it was because Lopez was running for reelection in November. Plus, he knew Lopez's father had called the night before and told his son he was coming up for the last day of the trial, and Yontz figured Lopez wanted to show off a little. Lopez stood up and delivered a hard-driving and emotional attack on David Ray, quite often turning and pointing his finger only inches away from the defendant, who looked tired as he sat slumped in his chair. Lopez saved his best lines for last and hammered home the entire prosecution case near the end of his oration.

"The facts show David's guilty. He knows he's guilty. We know he's guilty. And the worst thing of all is he knows we know he's guilty!"

Jeff Rein used his entire hour to attack Kelli Garrett one more time, and he tried to sum up the defense case by a couple of well-chosen comments about the woman with loose morals and a notoriously poor memory.

"Let's take a look at the laundry list of her boyfriends, husbands and lovers—let's see, there was Lamont, Patrick, Todd, Patrick again, Clay, Jim and now her third husband, Mike. Her track record with men wasn't very good. And we've seen where her memory isn't very good, either.

"If you're tellin' the truth, you don't have to remember anything," he said. "Your story makes sense. Kelli Garrett's story does not make sense."

Judge Mertz then read off the secret list of the final twelve jurors and excused the six alternates, thanking them for their time. He then outlined the twelve felony charges against Ray, explaining in detail kidnapping, sexual penetration and conspiracy. After he was done, he reminded the jury about the conditions they needed to consider in order to convict David Ray on any or all of the counts.

"You must be convinced that Kelli Garrett suffered great mental anguish, marked by an extreme change in her behavior," he told them. "Any criminal activity by David Ray must have been an attempt to intrude on the bodily integrity of Kelli Garrett. You are the judges of the facts—your sole job is to get to the truth of the case. Each crime should be considered separately. Your verdict should not be based on conjecture. To convict, you must be satisfied beyond a reasonable doubt, but not beyond all possible doubt."

For the next thirty-six hours, over a period of two days, the jury voted on each of the felony counts. David Ray's fate was solely in their hands. They had to decide if Ray was going to spend another sixty years in prison for the sixty hours he spent with Kelli Garrett back in the summer of 1996.

Out in the dusty streets of Tierra Amarilla, people

waited. Just after noon on the second day, June 13, 2000, Amanda Garcia, an alternate, was talking to a group of court spectators. She had carpooled from Espanola with two other female jurors chosen to be on the jury and she seemed to let the cat out of the bag when she was overheard telling an unidentified woman how she and her two friends felt about the testimony of Kelli Garrett.

"That little blond bitch was lying. . . ," she told the shocked woman.

CHAPTER 28

"Never put young women on a jury in a rape case—they never believe other young women."

Karen Yontz, March 10th, 2001

Jim Yontz once got a murder conviction in less than seventeen minutes, so he knew the longer the jury was "out," the worse it looked for the prosecution. The David Parker Ray jury had already been out for over twenty-four hours, and when the jury finally returned to Mertz's courtroom late Thursday afternoon, July 13, Yontz could tell by the long, drawn look on the foreman's face that they were not a happy group. As soon as Mertz started questioning Frank Sandoval, jury foreman, Jim Yontz knew the battle was lost.

"As to all of the charges, the jury has been unable to agree?" asked the distressed judge.

"Yes, sir," said Sandoval.

"If deliberations were to continue tomorrow," asked Mertz, "would the jury be able to reach a unanimous decision?"

"No, sir, I'm afraid not."

Mertz went on to ask each individual juror how they

voted on each of the twelve individual felony counts against David Ray, and when it was all over but the shouting, the Rio Arriba County jury had voted 11–1 in favor of conviction on kidnapping and 10–2 in favor of conviction on criminal sexual penetration and conspiracy. It was a lost case, so Neil Mertz brought it to a quick and bitter end.

'"The court now makes the finding . . . that this trial is declared a mistrial. Mr. Ray is remanded to the Rio Arriba County Detention Center."

Kelli Garrett, her long blond hair tied back in a ponytail, stood with her sister Becky, NMSP officer Carrie Parbs and FBI agent Larry Houpt, the bodyguard who had been watching over her throughout the two-week trial. Slowly the blood left Kelli Garrett's face and she began to cry. As she watched the jurors leave the courtroom, she had a look of disbelief on her face. Soon her whole body was rocked by uncontrollable sobbing.

A moment later, Jeff Rein and Cathy Love were out in the hallway talking to the dissenters: the two youngest women on the jury, twenty-one-year-old Cheri Archuletta from Espanola and twenty-three-year-old Phyllis Ortiz from Chimayo. Both young women were giggling as they talked to Rein and Love. The two public defenders smiled and laughed as they talked to them.

After the lawyers left the building, the two young women stood and talked to a reporter from Reuters. Neither juror beat around the bush when talking about why they refused to find David Ray guilty. Cheri Archuletta, tall and attractive, did most of the talking. Phyllis Ortiz, short and heavyset, stood in the background, just nodding. Ortiz was the only juror who refused to jot down any notes during the trial, and after the verdict was in, Sandoval said she "didn't say much during deliberation—she didn't even give her reasons for her vote—she just went along with Cheri Archuletta." And out in the hall, her tall friend in the bright yellow sweater had a lot to say about the hung jury.

"I know a lot of people who like rough sex," Archuletta told the stunned reporter.

"I know people who enjoy whips and chains and being tied down. When I was watching the videotape, I had a hard time because I couldn't see Kelli's face. When she was tied to the table, I couldn't tell if she was laughing or crying. There wasn't any evidence it wasn't consensual. Anyway, I think she was on drugs.

"What Kelli said on the stand didn't make sense. She doesn't seem to remember a lot of details. She couldn't remember anything—so I would have to say she was lying. During jury deliberation, they all tried to change our minds. They even raised their voices. It was terrible in there, but I knew we were right.

"I have no doubt Kelli was lying—not one bit."

When Archuletta was pressed if she thought David took advantage of Kelli Garrett, the youngest juror stood her ground, stating that in her mind the prosecution did not present enough evidence to convict him. Just before she and her friend Ortiz walked away, Cheri Archuletta turned around and made a shocking admission about her attitude toward the crimes of David Parker Ray.

"Yes, I think he did kidnap other women and I think he did torture other women," she said. "But not Kelli Garrett.

"And I just don't think he ever really killed anybody."

Outside the courthouse, dusty winds blew between the small groups of idle curiosity seekers. Nobody interviewed Jim Yontz, but Ron Lopez told the small gathering of television and newspaper reporters that this was not the end of the *State of New Mexico* v. *David Parker Ray*. He told the media that David would be retried by November.

* * *

Later that night, Jim Yontz drove home to Albuquerque, resigned to do it all over again in six months. He'd seen juries do unpredictable things before and after all these years in the business of crime fighting, nothing really surprised him. He and Ron Lopez drove south on Interstate 84 and out of Rio Arriba County for the last time. It was quiet in the car. Just before midnight Jim was driving through Espanola when he saw two men stagger out of the Saints and Sinners Liquor Store. He chuckled out loud and Lopez looked over at the black-and-white shadows crossing Yontz's face.

"Next time we'll get him," said Lopez.

"What do you mean 'we'?"

"For Christ's sake, Jim, don't bail out on me now."

"Don't worry," said Yontz. "I finish what I start. Anyway, this thing looks like a career job for us."

Ron Lopez shook his head as they left Espanola. "Did you see those drawings David was making in jail while he waited for the jury to come back with a verdict?" he asked. "They were black-and-white pencil drawings of giant lizards torturing women."

Yontz looked out the window as they headed down I-84 toward the lights of Albuquerque. They were passing a long stretch of junk cars parked next to the freeway. Rusty and dead as a doornail. He chuckled and told his boss, DA Lopez, what he thought of good old David.

"The best thing I can say about David is . . . he's biodegradable."

On Friday night, July 14, a large gathering of public defenders attended their annual summer meeting in Albuquerque. Lawyers who defend the bad guys are wildly unpopular in New Mexico, a state with a high crime rate. These low-paid defenders of the people from the wrong side of the tracks know they have to stick together and compliment themselves whenever possible. They realize the public has no interest in giving them a pat on the back for keeping criminals out of jail. On this particular night they had a good reason to celebrate. Jeff Rein had just won a highly publicized victory for David Parker Ray in Tierra Amarilla, and when Rein walked into the ballroom, they did what came naturally.

They put down their drinks and gave him a long standing ovation.

Jeff Rein smiled, looking uncomfortable in the spotlight.

CHAPTER 29

After me and Kelli got divorced, one night I got shit-faced drunk and went out and rolled my truck seven times.

—Clay Hein, former husband of Kelli Van Cleave's, 8/08/99

Clay Hein was slouched over a tall, cold bottle of Budweiser up at the bar at the Chili Bowl Lanes. It was the first Saturday night in August 2000, and it was midnight and the air temperature outside was still over a hundred degrees. He and Frank Jackson had bowled together after work and Frank had gone home early, so Clay pushed back his cowboy hat and watched the eleven o'clock television news with the bartender. Clay sipped on his Bud Light bowling pin–shaped bottle of beer and settled back in his chair to watch the tube.

The big issue that summer was the endangered silver minnow, a small fish going extinct along the Rio Grande, all 160 miles upriver from the headwaters of Elephant Butte Lake. The river was so heavily used by farmers and ranchers in the summer that it usually went dry by the first of August. This summer the federal government was ordering the state of New Mexico to keep the water flowing so the fish could survive.

Nobody at the bowling alley cared much about the little fish, and Clay and the 'tender waited for the next story. When the Albuquerque news anchor started talking about how the former Mrs. Clay Hein was going to have to testify against David Ray all over again during the November 27 retrial, the bartender turned off the TV. Everybody in town knew Clay and Kelli got married at a cowboy ceremony at Chili Bowl Lanes in the fall of 1997 and a few of his friends knew Hein still carried a picture of Kelli around in his wallet. Clay Hein was a hardworking and honest man of very few words. It was common knowledge that he did not like to discuss Kelli and the thirteen months he spent married to her between 1997 and 1998.

Six tall, ice-cold bowling-pin beers later, he was ready to talk about her.

"She was a nice, sweet person," he told the bartender.

"When she first came to town, she was quiet. I guess she had an ex-boyfriend who beat her up real bad for nearly three years. She was kind of afraid of men, but I liked her. She wasn't into drugs. She wasn't into all that kinky sex people around here like to mess with. I used to drink like hell before I met her. After we started goin' out, that kinda changed. I didn't drink as much when I was with her—not as much as I do now.

"She kinda kept me in line.

"For the first two months I was married to her, it worked out pretty good," he told the old guy pouring the drinks.

"Then I found out she was seein' someone else.

"One week she was with me, and the next week she was off with someone else. Screwing around. It was usually like that. It's kind of like an everyday deal with her. When we were married, I worked up at the volcanic-ash gravel pits at Saint Cloud Mining. I made seven dollars an hour. We were always out of money, and one night I came home real tired and pissed and I told her, 'Hey, I bag kitty litter eight hours a night and I don't make enough to have a wife runnin' all over town spending all my money.'

"She can't ever stay with anybody for very long.

"You never know about the people in this town—one minute you think they're the greatest person in the world and the next minute you don't even want to talk to them.

"I never been to Craig, Colorado, but after she moved there, she called me one night. She never told me about bein' with David before we got married in 1997. So she tries to tell me. She told me she don't remember nothin' for three days. And now she's afraid of Jesse. She told me she was worried Jesse's friends were going to come up and kill her.

"I told her to go out and get herself a gun."

Not everybody in town believed in toting a gun. Some people believed in fighting back with words.

After the media zeroed in on T or C one more time in the summer of 2000, the respectable citizens were fed up with the blemish David Ray and his friends had left on their small town. Frances Baird was tired of her town taking a beating. By the end of August, people were still talking about the "wonderful" editorial Frances Baird wrote after *Maxim* magazine trashed the town. Copies of her spirited defense of the common folk of Truth or Consequences got passed from hand to hand wherever the decent local citizens hung out—the Roadrunner Antique Car Club, the Tumbleweeds Ladies Golf Club, the Cowbelles (the local chapter of the wives and daughters of New Mexico ranchers) and the New Mexico Old-Time Fiddlers Association. Most people knew crime was simply the result of bad individual choices and they didn't like the fact that law-abiding community members were getting smeared with David Ray's dirt. As the summer of 2000 wore on, Frances Baird was the talk of the town. She had been able to put in words what many of them had been feeling but were unable to express for almost eighteen months.

The editorial was written one week before she turned nineteen years old, and it was written from the heart. The title was: I'M STILL PROUD.

> I am extremely upset about what was printed about Sierra County with the assistance of some "locals." I am referring to an article entitled *The Evil in Elephant Butte* published in the June edition of *MAXIM* magazine.
>
> I have lived in Sierra County all my life. Having been raised here I am very proud of the community and the people who live in it. I am not always proud of the actions of some residents but I realize they are responsible for their own mistakes. The judicial system will punish them accordingly.
>
> I have no problem with an article being written about David Ray and the crimes he is accused of committing, but if someone is going to write a story about him and his family and friends, don't take down the community in which the rest of us live.
>
> The story was written by Gil Reavill and it notes that "Jobs are scarce." Well, if Mr. Reavill had done his homework he would know that Sierra County has more jobs than people to fill them. By taking a quick look at the Help Wanted section in one of the three local newspapers he would have found that statement to be false.
>
> It was also mentioned in the article "that mobile homes are the rule, not the exception." I and the majority of the Sierra County residents don't see any problem with calling a mobile home

"home." Many of the mobile homes built today are much nicer than site-built homes and have the same luxuries at half the price.

To be "thrifty" is no crime.

He said "the depressed economy is boosted only slightly by the drug corridor running from Juarez, Mexico." The largest percentage of the drugs taken on the Interstate never make it to T-or-C, but have a final destination of Albuquerque. To say that the economy is somehow boosted by those taking drugs through Sierra County is like saying T-or-C needs a snowplow.

Reavill states that "Ralph Edwards probably never ventured onto Austin Street at night, when trade prospers in the sole locally produced product, methamphetamines." He makes it sound as though EVERYONE in Sierra County goes to Austin Street after dark and buys meth and gets high.

He obviously has forgotten that one bad apple doesn't necessarily spoil the whole barrel.

Sierra County's number one industry is recreation. But Mr. Reavill slammed that, too, in his article—reporting that "locals worry that the fish of Elephant Butte Lake are feeding on something other than each other. Some have sworn off eating fish from the lake altogether." Granted, this statement may be true, but only a fool would think that the only bodies in the lake were put there by David Ray.

Numerous people have drowned over the years (1916–2000) in Elephant Butte Lake and never been found.

It will never be announced to the readers that T-or-C and Elephant Butte, New Mexico, has more than 355 days of sunshine a year. That it usually snows once a year and the snow is melted before noon the following day. Readers of *MAXIM* magazine will never get a chance to know that we have the prettiest sunsets God ever made.

But as far as *MAXIM* magazine is concerned we are all probably a bunch of devil worshippers.

I just hope the readers of *MAXIM* magazine realize that it depends on what side of the street you walk on. What you find on your journey greatly depends on what you are looking for.

If you are looking for smut, that's all you're going to find.

A week after Frances Baird wrote her editorial, Gail Astbury got released from jail. The police had finally caught up with her, and a local judge in T or C agreed that the Florida charges were "old as dirt" and only gave her four months for her assault crimes she committed back in 1990. By the end of the summer, she was hanging out at Andy's Bar with all the old cowboys, going out of her way to shock people by telling them, "That guy who is tending bar is having sex with his own daughter right now."

When she visited with her good friend Jesse Ray in jail one afternoon, Jesse gave her a necklace with a tiny man in the moon hanging from a leather thong. Except there was a woman sitting on top of the man, straddling his penis. Gail Astbury wore it every day and always laughed her loud laugh when showing it to friends.

When the bartender at Andy's asked her one night what she thought of the hung jury up in Tierra Amarilla, she only had one thing to say: "I told you so."

Then she quickly added, "I sure hope Jess gets off."

As the summer wore on, David Ray's daughter sat in jail, rotting, according to friends. Jesse Ray's trial had been set for July 15 in Gallup, but because of David's partial victory, it looked like Jesse's day in court was going to be pushed clear up to March 2001.

And her dad wasn't doing much better.

Right after Labor Day, he got a visit from his public defender with some numbing news. Jeff Rein had mulled it over during his August vacation and decided to quit practicing law for at least a year. Rein was part of the Capital Crimes Division of the Albuquerque Public Defenders Office, and since it didn't look like David Ray would ever be charged with murder, Jeff Rein didn't see any reason to continue on the job. Originally, he told his client he was worried Ray might have to face the death penalty, and Rein was fiercely opposed to capital punishment. New Mexico had never executed a killer since 1960 and Rein wasn't about to ever let any of his clients, young or old, be the first to hang. Anyway, he had been working for David Ray for nearly eighteen months and he told Ray he was badly in need of some well-earned rest. He told Ray not to worry, there were a number of excellent private attorneys who would probably be more than happy to help him with his defense against the crusading Jim Yontz. Jeff Rein shook hands with David Ray and wished him well.

On September 15, 2000, Jeff Rein quit his job as the public defender for David Parker Ray and made plans to change careers. To many observers in and out of New Mexico, his choice of a new location and job spoke volumes about how repulsed he must have become in defending David Ray—a man who many people, rightly or wrongly, felt was a hard-core, sadistic killer.

Jeff Rein flew to Antarctica in October 2000 and almost immediately jumped into his new blue-collar job at the South Pole.

Driving a forklift.

CHAPTER 30

"For talking, I punish a girl in one of two ways. You'll be whipped or have your tits and sex organs worked over with an electric cattle prod."

David Parker Ray audiotape, July 6th, 1993

Just before he left for Antarctica, Jeff Rein called his good friend Lee McMillian and asked him to take over the David Parker Ray case. McMillian, thirty-seven, a tall, beer-bellied lawyer more comfortable in cowboy boots than Brooks Brothers suits, had a tough reputation as a very aggressive defense attorney who split his practice between Texas and New Mexico. Rein also knew that McMillian presented a real problem for the prosecution: he'd never lost a case in front of Judge Neil P. Mertz.

"I asked the public defender's office to take me off the case," Rein told McMillian. "They refused, so I just quit. I needed a break. I've been doing this for twelve years and I'm tired."

After McMillian made the lowest bid and was awarded the case, Rein made arrangements to have the entire eight boxes of background information shipped to McMillian's small one-man office in Albuquerque, sandwiched between the new Interstate 40 and the old Highway 66.

McMillian, a seasoned attorney with thirteen years' experience under his belt, jumped into the case feet-first.

"I'll tell ya one thing," he told friends. "David Ray is in no way a 'balls-out' sadist. I wouldn't want him dating my daughter, that's for sure, but when the trial gets going again on November twenty-seventh, I'm going to present a whole new defense for David. All I need to do is find a couple of women who enjoyed having rough sex with David and I know I'll have a strong case. And I'm sure some of those 'babes' really enjoyed fooling around with the old boy. You just know some of those old girls were consenting partners and not the unwilling victims Jim Yontz wants everyone to believe they were.

"It's not against the law to be interested in dominance and submission," he told Amy, his young, red-headed office secretary.

"It's called consensual sadomasochism."

McMillian's first job was to meet and have a little talk with David Ray. He drove down to the Sierra County Jail in Truth or Consequences in early October. For over five hours the thirty-seven-year-old balding attorney and the sixty-year-old mechanic with the full head of hair had a good chat. They talked about everything under the sun. When McMillian returned to Albuquerque the next day, he strolled into his office sporting a big smile, threw his arms up in the air and declared that he had really taken a liking to the old geezer. Lee leaned over and tapped his pencil on Amy's desk.

"He's the nicest client I have ever represented,"

McMillian said. Looking over the rim of his wire glasses, he quickly added: "Yeah, he's a pervert—but we're going to go to the wall for this guy."

McMillian, always one for a good story, then strolled back to his office out of the earshot of Amy and called a college friend and described his trip to southern New Mexico.

"I was down at the jail in T or C," he told his friend, "and David and I are walking along with a guard when some crazy female inmate throws her panties out the bars of her cell and says, 'Eat me, David!' We all laughed our asses off! Everybody down there really likes David."

McMillian had been practicing law in New Mexico for the past six years and he knew the emotional terrain like the back of his hand. In his opinion, there was a long-standing class war going on in the state and without a middle class there was always bound to be extreme violence. Some of his friends thought of New Mexico as the "Murder Capital of America," and if cornered, Lee McMillian was hard-pressed to disagree. He liked to hike and fish the Pecos River in northern New Mexico and he never went anywhere without his Colt .45 tucked in his briefcase. He liked to tell his friends how New Mexico was different from his old stomping grounds in Texas.

"It attracts nuts!" he used to say.

The retrial of the Kelli Garrett case had been scheduled for Estancia, a small town in cattle country, just southeast of Albuquerque. McMillian felt he knew the people who lived there inside out.

"There are no liberals down there," he used to tell other lawyers. "I'm a dyed-in-the-wool adrenaline junkie—I like to bungee jump and skydive—and I was real pleased to get this case. I know those people down in Estancia. It's a real ultraconservative community of German ranchers and I know how they think. They won't like the idea of government prosecutors looking into David's private life.

"Anyway," he concluded, "I'm the hired gun for the redneck community in New Mexico!"

For weeks McMillian pored over the volumes of notes and photographs, looking for female witnesses to help him with his S-M defense. Early in his research he found photographs of a woman named Candy Frairs, who had since nearly vanished off the face of the earth. According to friends, she was hiding up in Ruidoso—living with some Mescalero Apaches—but McMillian was unable to find her. He did, however, have the handwritten notes she'd scribbled to David on the back of two nude photographs found on the bulletin board inside the toy box.

And to the new defense attorney for David Parker Ray, they sure did not sound like the sentiments of a woman who hated or feared David. They sounded like the words of a woman who really liked rough sex. Not unlike 2 million other Americans who are attracted to the ultrakinky, but not illegal, sexual practices. Each note was printed in big black letters. One night McMillian held the pictures under the lamp on his desk and read the words out loud to himself. The first note got right to the point:

I LOVE WHAT YOU DID TO ME
YOU KNOW "THE ROPES."
SOME OF THOSE BIG THINGS HURT, BUT
I MUST HAVE CREAMED 15 TIMES.
MY BACKDOOR IS STILL SORE, BUT
IT'S READY FOR MORE.

McMillian smiled a sly smile as he contemplated the legal possibilities of reading both notes out loud in court. The second note mentioned some of the sex toys and asked David Ray to give Candy Frairs more of the same:

GREAT FOR SPANKING, HUH.
OR FOR ANYTHING ELSE
THAT YOU HAVE IN MIND.
THOSE BIG "TOYS" THAT YOU
PUT IN MY BUTT STRETCHED
IT A LOT, BUT ITS O.K. NOW,
AND READY FOR MORE ACTION!

Later that day, McMillian was leaving the office when Amy asked him if he really thought he had a chance to get David Ray off the hook a second time. McMillian shrugged his shoulders and came back with his casual "win-win" philosophy.

"If I lose, I've lost a case that was impossible to win," he explained to her. "And if I win—well then, I will have won a case that most people thought was impossible to win."

The next week, he went back to T or C looking for a live witness he could put on the stand. He had to prove that not all the ladies "ran for their lives" at the sight of David Ray. He found a thirty-nine-year-old woman named Cindy Asbell, who claimed to have lived with David and Jesse for a short time. She told McMillian that she "enjoyed" the times David Ray tied her up, whipped her and inserted a few of his large collection of dildos into the private holes in her body. McMillian was overjoyed, but when he went back a week later to tape-record an interview with Asbell, she wouldn't say a word.

McMillian came back to his office, discouraged.

"People in town threatened to beat her up—hell, even her own family threatened to disown her if she testified for David," he told Amy. "I even had death threats on my life.

"People down there are nuts," he added.

While McMillian was struggling to patch together a defense for his client, Jim Yontz had moved his base of operation to a tiny office in Estancia, feeling boxed in by Neil Mertz and Ron Lopez down in Socorro. He found out the two lawyers had worked side by side years earlier when Lopez was the DA and Mertz was his ADA; he knew the two men royally disliked each other. Yontz was trying to walk the thin line between Mertz, the legal purist, and Lopez, the fast-talking prosecutor.

That November, Lopez was running for reelection in the seventh district against a rancher named Clint Wellborn. Lopez had already served eight years as DA, and a week before the election, he placed an advertisement in the *Sentinel* that pointed out to the residents of Sierra County that he had been tough on crime. Lopez claimed his overall conviction record on murders, drug crimes, sex crimes and other felonies was 91 percent. Clint Wellborn was quoted in the *Sentinel* as saying that "ninety-six to ninety-eight percent of the crime in Sierra County is drug related," and he promised to reduce considerably the proliferation of meth labs if elected the new district attorney.

On November 7, 2000, Clint Wellborn (R) beat Ron Lopez (D) by a wide margin—2,638 votes to 1,793 votes. In an article written by Frances Baird and published in the *Sierra County Sentinel,* he promised he would take a different approach to the David Parker Ray retrial and possibly use a new strategy.

"That's news to me," Yontz told Baird off the record a few days later.

The very next day, Wellborn came up and humbly asked Jim Yontz a question that Yontz always wished people in power would ask him. Wellborn admitted that he knew very little about how to "get" David Ray, but he liked the work he had seen Yontz do so far and simply wanted to know if there was some way he could assist Yontz.

"What can I do to help you?" he asked Yontz.

"Let me call the attorney general's office in Santa Fe and ask them if they can loan out Claire Harwell. I've worked with her before and she's sharp. She and I can win this case."

"Go for it," said the new DA.

Ron Lopez was bitter about losing the election. He told Yontz that since he, Lopez, wasn't out of office until January 20, 2001, that he, not Yontz, would be selecting the jurors for the retrial in Estancia. When a Reuters reporter called Judge Mertz the next day to ask what was going on, Mertz said he would look into it. After several days of undisclosed legal wrangling behind closed doors, the situation changed.

By November 27, the first day of jury selection in the retrial of David Parker Ray, Ron Lopez was no longer part of the story.

Jim Yontz was back in the saddle again.

During the first day of questioning jurors, there was a break in proceedings so Mertz could smoke a cigarette. A few minutes later, Jim Yontz and Lee McMillian ran into each other in the men's lavatory. They had dueled in court before, but always as friends. McMillian swore to other defense lawyers that Yontz was "the most honest man I know—if he tells you something is true—it's true." McMillian was still upset about the way Yontz got treated after he had been caught with a prostitute in Albuquerque back in 1998. McMillian told friends that "Jim picked up hitchhikers all the time." McMillian always made it plain that Yontz "got screwed" back in 1998.

Yontz grinned at McMillian.

"So why did you take this case?" he asked.

"The extreme challenge—and, of course, the money."

"Why did three women who did not know each other all tell the same story about David?" asked Yontz.

McMillian slapped Yontz on the back and reminded him that defense lawyers are not easily swayed.

"Remember, my good man, human memory is plastic and cannot be trusted—don't forget that."

"If that's the case, nobody would be in jail," joked Yontz.

"You guys put too many innocent people in jail anyway," quipped McMillian.

"That might be true in some cases, but I'll tell you one thing—David Ray is not one of those—he deserves to be locked away where the sun don't shine."

The next day, November 28, Lee McMillian was starting to come down with a bad case of laryngitis and a cold, so he asked Judge Mertz if they could postpone jury selection for a day so he could get well. McMillian was speaking in a whisper. Mertz shook his head over the prospect of another delay and agreed that since McMillian could barely be heard, on Wednesday, November 29, there would be no interrogation of potential jurors for the second trial of Ray.

On the way out of the courtroom, Mertz was overheard telling his court clerk, Kathy McClean, how he felt about attempting to try David Parker Ray.

"What else can go wrong in this case?" he said, with no possible hint of what was going to happen to him in less than forty-eight hours.

CHAPTER 31

Mertz has a heavy caseload and he just wants to get the David Parker Ray case off his docket.

—Prosecutor Jim Yontz, 7/13/2000

On his day off Neil Mertz went over to the small jail in Estancia to help solve a minor problem that had been festering during the two previous days of jury selection. Mertz was a stickler for fairness and David Ray had lodged a complaint with the judge. Ray was a hero to his fellow prisoners at the Sierra County Correctional Facility down in Truth or Consequences, but he was nothing but a pervert to the redneck guards up in Torrance County. Mertz had heard that the guards were "picking on" Ray, so he showed up early on the morning of November 29 to set things straight. He told the guards to "leave David alone" and warned them that he didn't plan to come back and give the same lecture twice. The guards apologized and told him it wouldn't happen again.

The next morning at approximately 8:30, Neil P. Mertz was taking his morning shower back home in Socorro when he dropped dead of a sudden and massive heart attack.

He was up early and getting ready to resume his twenty-month ordeal of trying to run a tight ship in the notorious trials of David Ray and his cohorts. When the news spread that he simply crumpled over and died, it was a shock to everyone. It was November 30, 2000, and Ron Lopez was still the "acting" DA. That afternoon he was interviewed by a television reporter from a local Albuquerque station. As usual, Lopez was at ease with the media and what he said greatly disturbed Jim Yontz. Later that night, Yontz told his wife that Lopez made one "really stupid comment."

"He told the Channel Four News that David must have made a pact with the devil."

"Are you serious?" asked his wife.

"He just can't keep his mouth shut," answered Yontz.

Publicly Jim Yontz tried to take it all in stride. Privately he told a reporter for Reuters how he felt about moving ahead in the Ray case without Mertz.

"He always wanted to be in charge. He was used to being his prima-donna self. We had to live with him, and now, I guess you could say, we'll have to live without him. Normally, we'd have to live with all his positions in court, but not any longer."

Judge Neil P. Mertz died on a Thursday morning and the following Monday afternoon, December 4, there was a standing-room-only funeral at the ornate Garcia Opera House in Socorro. Important movers and shakers inside the New Mexico legal community were there. Yontz attended, as did Lopez. Mertz, fifty-five, was the youngest of the three sitting judges in the seventh judicial district. He left behind a wife of thirty-three years and a grown son and daughter. When asked before the funeral about his interests outside of work, his longtime court clerk and friend, Kathy McClean, said: "His hobby was work."

The eulogy was given by the Honorable Gene Franchini, judge with the New Mexico State Supreme Court, and a man who had been privately following the controversial Ray case for the last two years.

The David Parker Ray Trial was postponed until January 2001, and in the supermarkets of America, grocery shoppers were greeted by the December 5 issue of the *National Enquirer* and a full-page article titled DAD AND DAUGHTER BUSTED. The T or C sheriff, Terry Byers, told the tabloid that Ray might have killed nearly sixty people during his reign of terror along the shores of Elephant Butte, New Mexico.

Craig Lewis, the *Globe* editor who had originally said that the David Parker Ray case was the most sensational murder case in American history, had fought his own battles with the cops and prosecutors in Golden, Colorado. After the tabloid spent almost $2 million defending Lewis, the `Colorado prosecutor caved in and dropped all the bribery and extortion charges against the outspoken editor. When informed that Judge Mertz had died in New Mexico, Lewis told a Reuters reporter how he felt.

"That's good news for everybody except the dead people."

The deadline for new applicants for Mertz's job was December 18 and to fill the void, Judge Franchini appointed Judge Richard Parsons from Carrizozo to handle all of Mertz's cases. All except the high-profile Ray case. Then Franchini headed up a committee of local lawyers, judges, professors and politicians to help select a new judge to take over and possibly move the Ray case forward. Unless, of course, Judge Thomas G. Fitch or Judge Edmund H. Kase III, the two remaining judges in the seventh, decided to take on the now infamous case. Fitch and Kase also had the option to appoint a judge of their own choosing.

Just before the Christmas hoidays, the "Committee

of 13" interviewed the six applicants scrambling for Mertz's job. Ron Lopez, soon to be out of a job, was one of the six, and when Jim Yontz heard that his old buddy was trying to move up, he joked with his wife that "Ron's putting in for Mertz's spot and just to aggravate him, I told him I was going to put in for it, too."

"You better not!" warned his wife.

Right after the holidays Jim Yontz got some news that was less than humorous. The committee, evenly divided between Democrats and Republicans—with the chairman of the board, Franchini, serving as tiebreaker—had submitted the names of two Democrats to Republican governor Gary Johnson—and the name of Ron Lopez was on the shortlist. Yontz knew that Lopez would have to disqualify himself to handle the Ray case, but down the road he knew Lopez was going to create problems for him. Yontz did not want to have to deal with the possibility of a "Judge Lopez."

Just before New Year's Eve, 2001, Jim Yontz took another drive up to see the holiday lights in Santa Fe and Taos. He stopped to buy a silver bolo tie that reminded him of a Texas Ranger badge—then headed home. On his way breezing down Interstate 25, he got this sinking feeling that he was right back where he started from over a year ago, New Year's Eve, 2000. One more time it all seemed to come down to prosecuting the father and the daughter, masterminds behind the operation. Everybody else had dropped out, died or been sentenced. The list of casualties was staggering. Some nights Jim Yontz felt like he was carrying the world on his shoulders, and this was one of those nights.

When he got home later that night, his wife asked him how he was holding up under the constant pressure.

"Fine," he said, giving her a faint smile.

"I just take it a day at a time," he added. "If I think about it any other way, I'll just drive myself crazy."

Yontz was hoping that Judge Kase would appoint Judge Rebecca Sitterly to fill the Mertz job—he especially wanted to see a woman handing out a stiff sentence for David Ray. Kase wanted to save money by not appointing a judge outside the seventh, so he turned Yontz down. It was January 4, 2001.

On January 8, Kase tried to appoint Judge Fitch, and Yontz struck him. On January 10 Kase tried to appoint himself to preside over the David Parker Ray retrial, and Lee McMillian struck him. That didn't leave any further choices for the only two sitting judges in the seventh, so now it looked like the political haggling was going to drop directly into the lap of the governor, a loose cannon himself. Governor Gary Johnson was going to make the final decision and, like many people in law enforcement, Yontz didn't trust the governor.

In the fall of 1999, Governor Gary Johnson had done something no other Republican had ever done in America. He came out for legalizing the recreational use of marijuana, cocaine *and heroin*—a position so controversial that it even shocked his fellow Republicans. His chief law enforcement officer, Darren White, quit in protest a year later, in the summer of 2000. White was the official who flew to T or C in the spring of 1999 and told worried residents that "the nightmare is behind bars." By the winter of 2001, New Mexico was drowning in drug-running, drug use and drug convictions, and Johnson boldly stated that legalization was the only way to keep the jails from spilling over with nonviolent criminals.

The Democrats, as well as many Republicans, criticized him daily for his stand, and by the middle of January, Gary Johson was so uptight that one morning when he was out jogging, he fell on the ice and bruised his spine. Pressure was mounting to move ahead with the notorious Ray trials, and right after he got out of the hospital, Johnson made up his mind on how he was going to handle Mertz's replacement. He had appointed Neil Mertz to the bench back in 1993, but he was "damned if he was going to give the Democrats another judge in the seventh." On January 18, he sent the two names back to the Committee of 13 and told them to try it again.

"Here we go again," grumbled Yontz over dinner the next night.

"What a mess," replied his wife.

"He wants a Republican," he told his wife. "Someone who won't let David plea-bargain the case away."

In the meantime, there were other cases for Jim Yontz to deal with, but all the legal wrangling over the third judge in the seventh was beginning to wear on him. After Clint Wellborn officially replaced Lopez in the DA's office on January 20, Yontz felt like he was finally running the case, but he spent most of his time in a sort of no-man's-land, waiting for Governor Johnson to act.

One day he got a call from Frances Baird, who was still covering the slow-moving crime scene in T or C. He complained that the logjam over the Ray judge was cramping his style.

"It's getting rather boring in my life—because of this battle to replace Mertz, everything's on hold and I can't do anything else. I can't go out and help prosecute any other crimes. I have to farm everything out."

A week later, he got a reminder of just how much his hands were tied behind his back. Frances called him early on the morning of January 30 and told him about a spectacular murder right outside of T or C the night before. Police had found a woman's remains in the trunk of a torched car. Her body had been burned beyond recognition. Her husband had killed her, stuffed her body in the trunk and driven the 1995 Buick LeSabre out to the edge of town. Then he set the car on fire, and accidentally set himself on fire. When the police got there, the forty-four-year-old husband, Lee Uecker, made up a story about him and his wife accidentally driving off the road, but he failed to tell them she was dead, folded inside the trunk and wrapped in bailing wire. Baird told Yontz he'd beaten her with a claw hammer at home before taking her out to her car. He was in the hospital recovering from his burns and smoke inhalation. Yontz asked Baird what she knew about the case.

"She left him for another woman—and he got mad."

"I'd say so," Yontz replied, chuckling.

Baird went on to say that she was the first crime reporter on the scene.

"I asked the guy if his wife was in the car and he told me she was. I figured she'd been thrown out and I wandered around in the desert for half an hour in the pitch dark looking for her body with my crummy little Girl Scout flashlight."

"Pretty inconsiderate."

"I was so mad at him."

"I don't blame you," added Yontz.

"Why didn't he tell me she was in the trunk?"

One more time, Jim Yontz smiled when he listened to Frances Baird talk about her involvement with criminals. He wondered how such a nice girl could have such a steel-trap mind when it came to reporting on the bums of this world. And every time he started to get a little down in the mouth about David's case, it seemed like Frances Baird was there to cheer him up. He thanked her for the information and told her he'd call back as soon as he heard about whom the governor was going to appoint to replace Mertz.

Three weeks later, he had an answer for her.

* * *

On February 24 it was announced that the Committee of 13, under the leadership of Gene Franchini, had recommended a thirty-seven-year-old rancher named Kevin Sweazea to replace Mertz. The next day, the governor announced the appointment of the Republican rancher with no previous experience in presiding over a criminal trial. In fact, Sweazea instantly became the youngest judge in New Mexico history. A week later, it was announced that Sweazea would preside over the David Parker Ray retrial.

The Republican attorney had done work in settling sit-down land disputes, but his lack of criminal experience didn't seem to faze Yontz. Yontz talked to Baird right after the announcements and soft-pedaled any problems with Judge Sweazea, the new rookie judge.

"Instead of payin' somebody money for a crime," he told Baird, "somebody's goin' to prison instead."

Judge Sweazea established a new trial date of April 9 in Estancia, and Yontz and McMillian agreed to pick up the interrupted jury-selection process on April 2. Everything looked like it was going to run smoothly, so Jim Yontz, forty-nine, and his new helper, Claire Harwell, forty-two, sat down to see if they could map out a new strategy for nailing David Ray this time.

"No young female jurors," Yontz said to Harwell during their first meeting.

It was his most glaring error in the original trial in Tierra Amarilla. His wife, Karen, was a former Los Angeles cop and she had pounded home the point that in a rape trial you never pit a young female victim up against other young female jurors—the chance of one young woman not believing another was too great. Harwell more than agreed with Yontz. He hoped she could help soften the touch when dealing with selecting women on the jury—it was still painful for Yontz to admit that he'd made such a basic and foolish mistake in the first trial. There was too much at stake this time.

"And not so many grizzly-bear ties this time," added Harwell, poking fun at Yontz's favorite way of reminding the jury he was a big, hard-boiled prosecutor with a sense of humor.

"Okay," Yontz said sheepishly.

Yontz and Harwell focused their energy on a preliminary hearing in front of Judge Sweazea scheduled for March 23 in Estancia. Their primary goal was to introduce a "shorter" copy of the audiotape that David Ray played for both Vigil and Montano in 1999, but not for Kelli Van Cleave in 1996. Back in June 2000, Mertz had thrown it out and Yontz was damn sure he could win in April if the jurors could listen to David Ray describe in 1993 what Kelli Garrett remembered him doing to her in July 1996.

On Friday the twenty-third, Yontz stood in front of Sweazea and tried to stop an effort by Lee McMillian to introduce a so-called "dominatrix" on behalf of David Ray. "She wasn't there in 1996," Yontz told the judge. Next McMillian tried to introduce Cindy Asbell as a potential defense witness. "Not there in '96," Yontz again pointed out. Both times the judge agreed with Yontz. McMillian was getting frustrated and toward the end of the day he unloaded his anger on the court clerk, Kathy McClean.

"She's been running around the courthouse in T or C and telling everyone she thinks David's guilty as hell," McMillian complained.

"I've been saying that since day one," quipped Yontz.

"I can't find anyone to testify," shot back McMillian. "People in town have slammed doors in my face. Her neighbors told Cindy Asbell they'd beat her up, and her family threatened to throw her out of the house if she helped David. How the heck am I supposed to mount a defense for my client if everyone is frightened?"

Jim Yontz saw his opening and waded in with a big grin.

"Why don't you put David on the stand to testify on behalf of himself?" he told his old buddy Lee McMillian.

McMillian peered over the tops of his wire-rimmed glasses one more time and let out an exaggerated groan.

"Over my dead body, Jim."

Yontz was tempted to point out that in this case that might be the wrong thing to say out loud, but he buttoned his lip.

Judge Kevin Sweazea seemed unruffled by friendly lawyer exchanges that would have upset Judge Mertz. He told the attorneys to come back on Monday, March 26, and be prepared to debate the introduction of the audiotape. Yontz and Harwell relished the possibility. So did McMillian. He figured at the worst it would give him an opportunity to show that David Ray was a practitioner of S-M sex. Assuming, of course, that Ray's heart did not "give out" in the meantime.

That weekend Yontz and Harwell met in his cramped office in Estancia and spliced parts of the audiotape together so as to eliminate all the possible stumbling blocks that might allow McMillian to trip them up at a later date. Although Vigil claimed that Ray let a German shepherd "lick hot gravy off my naked body" in 1999, there was no evidence that David Ray had sicked a canine on Kelli Van Cleave back in 1996. Jim Yontz felt a little uncomfortable listening to David Ray in front of a civilized lady like Claire Harwell. But the two prosecutors sat down side by side and decided to eliminate the following explosive segment of the controversial tape:

> You'll be taken into the living room and put on the floor on your hands and knees, naked. Your

wrists, ankles, knees and hips will be strapped to a metal frame to hold your body in that position. The frame is designed for doggy-fucking. Your ass up in the air, sex organs exposed, your tits hanging down on each side of the metal support bar, knees spread about twelve inches, positioned similar to that of a bitch dog in heat, right in the middle of the floor, so we can sit on the couch and chairs and watch. I'm going to rub canine breeder's musk on your back, the back of your neck and on your sex organs. Now—I have three dogs, all of them males, because I don't need any fucking pups. One of them is a very large German shepherd that is always horny, and he loves it when I bring him in the house to fuck a woman. After I let him in the house, he'll sniff around you a little bit, and within a minute, he'll be mounting you. There's about a fifty-fifty chance which hole he'll get his penis into, but it doesn't seem to bother him whether it's the pussy or the asshole. His penis is pretty thin, it goes in easy, but it's about ten inches long. And when he gets completely excited, it gets a hell of a knot right in the middle of it. I've had sex slaves tell me it feels like they've got a baseball inside of them. It doesn't take long for him to come. He's going to hump you real fast for about three or four minutes. And while he's doing it, he'll wrap his front legs around your chest to hold himself in position. And in the process he'll probably scratch your tits with his claws. After he gets through, he usually turns around and tries to pull it out. The knot will usually shrink enough to come out of your pussy in about three minutes. If he's in your asshole, about five minutes.

Now, if you think all this is sick and depraved, you haven't seen anything yet. . . .

Harwell got up, turned off the tape recorder and made a face. It took about two hours for the two prosecutors to go through and reduce the tape from about forty minutes down to about twenty-five minutes. When they were done, Jim Yontz felt he finally had the ammunition in hand to bring David Ray to his knees.

On March 26, Judge Sweazea listened uncomfortably to the tape and agreed with Yontz and Harwell that it should be played in court when the trial was due to begin on April 9.

On Sunday night, April 1, Jim Yontz got a call at home from Frances Baird. It was the night before jury selection and she wanted to know the latest.

"What do you think of Judge Sweazea now?" asked Baird.

"At first I was much more concerned than I let on," answered Yontz. "The judge had never been 'practiced' in front of before and I wasn't sure if he could handle the pressure. He had tried cases, but not criminal cases. Now that I've seen him, I feel confident. At least he's not a cigarette fiend. Without taking a 'smoke break' every half an hour, the whole trial should be over in seven or eight days."

"Do you think David will plea?"

"Last year I did," said Yontz. "Not anymore."

"How come?" asked Baird.

"You have to remember that Ray is a sadist. He gets off on seeing women scared, and I think he really enjoys watching a jury trial scare the hell out of the victim."

"What about Jesse?"

"I think after we convict David that Jesse's gonna plea and get on with her life."

CHAPTER 32

They'll "get" him {David} in Estancia.
—Chief Justice Gene E. Franchini, New Mexico State Supreme Court
11/06/2000

On Sunday night, April 1, 2001, huge firestorms on the surface of the sun turned the New Mexico northern night sky a deep, crimson red. It seemed like the gods were getting ready for the second trial of David Parker Ray. Jim Yontz felt confident going into jury selection the next morning, April 2. This time there would be no mistakes.

Driving into Estancia, New Mexico, is a throwback Western experience. Cattle ranches cover the flat landscape and there is a gentle quality of life that only gets disrupted by the extreme spring windstorms. On Main Street, the Old Wind Mill Cafe serves killer coffee and has a display of 1878 barbwire—strands of split arrow, half hitch and prickly pear—that reminds visitors that out here in the wide-open spaces people mind their own business. During the week of jury selection, the locals were excited about the new Copenhagen Black snuff for sale at the Mustang Gas Station—bourbon-flavored chewing tobacco for people who probably never bothered to think of themselves as rugged individualists.

Yontz and McMillian managed to select a fifteen-member jury (only three alternates this time) in record time. It took Judge Mertz and the boys nearly five weeks in June 2000, and this time—with the help of the new judge, Kevin Sweazea—it only took five days. On the Sunday night before the trial was set to begin, Yontz took his wife out to dinner and told her he felt fairly confident he'd be able to get a conviction.

"I feel like I've got all my ducks lined up this time."

"Good."

"The jury is very much older—compared to last summer, it's like night and day. There are no kids on the jury—the youngest person on the jury is over thirty years old. There are eight men and four women. We have two younger girls, but they're both alternates and they're both married to law enforcement officers."

"Sounds solid," his wife said.

"I like our jury pool in Torrance County. I like 'em very much. It's the way it should have gone before—no hitches. Plus, this time I've got Claire—she's my ace in the hole."

Yontz and Harwell had dreamed up a new approach to presenting their case, and the next morning they called Kelli Garrett to testify first, rather than waiting until the jury got bored with all the other testimony. She was dressed in blue denim and it wasn't long before her eyes turned red. This time Claire Harwell questioned the victim and handled the twenty-seven-year-old woman with kid gloves. During the emotional testimony, Garrett told Harwell, "I was tied to the table naked. I was kind of in a position a woman is in when she has a baby—my feet were in stirrups." For the first time Kelli Garrett had agreed to identify herself from a brief clip of the videotape, and when she saw herself being pawed over by David Ray, she looked at the ceiling and started to sob. Harwell asked her if she was the woman tied down to the weight lifter's bench in the video. Kelli Garrett wiped away a steady stream of tears before she answered.

"Yes, that's me," she said.

Jim Yontz had more ammo this time and on the second day he had Claire Harwell play the full six-minutes of videotape for the jury in the morning and in the afternoon he stood up and introduced his lone silver bullet—the forty-minute audiotape that had been condensed down to twenty-five. All day the jurors watched and listened, showing very little emotion, except for one woman in the back row who covered her face and a man in the front row who seemed so shocked by the audiotape that he let his jaw hang wide open the whole time the tape was playing. His eyes never blinked as David Ray rattled off nasty comments recorded back in 1993.

"You're going to be kept in a hidden slave room. You are going to be kept like an animal. Your only value to us is that you have an attractive body."

Outside, powerful sixty-miles-per-hour winds were ripping off the roofs of houses on nearby farms and ranches. As usual, New Mexicans took the brutal daytime spring winds in stride, knowing that by nightfall the winds would die down and everything would be calm again. Same with the air temperatures—if it was 90 degrees Fahrenheit by day, they knew it would drop to 50 degrees by nightfall. Everyone involved in the trial stayed inside, except one sixty-one-year-old man who suffered through the trial just so he could step outside and puff on his friendly smokes.

During a late-morning break on Tuesday, April 10, David Ray was standing outside smoking a cigarette and he was overheard telling a guard, "Losing Mertz was a definite blow to my case."

* * *

On Wednesday, April 11, Jim Yontz spent the good part of the morning questioning a very nervous Patrick Murphy. Yontz was wearing his big maroon grizzly-bear tie and this time Murphy showed up in person, with his hair cropped short and wearing his dark blue navy uniform. He was a drill sergeant in the military now and looked every bit the part of a real tough guy—except when he sat down in the witness chair and started to talk about Kelli. Yontz talked to him man to man and Murphy admitted his uniform covered "tattoos all over my body," but there was nothing to protect him from his memory of his ex-wife. He stuttered and stammered as Yontz asked him about his brief two-week marriage to Kelli Garrett. Yontz grilled Murphy about what he did after Kelli vanished and he went out looking for her.

"I ended up passin' out at the lake," he told Yontz, "and I woke up the next morning with a killer hangover."

Yontz followed up by asking Patrick Murphy what Kelli looked like when David Ray brought her back after claiming he'd found her down at the lake on the same beach where Patrick had passed out. Murphy just shook his head.

"I came outside of the house and there she was—real weak, disoriented and babbling to herself. And she was dirty. I used to call her the 'water fairy' because she took so many showers during the day—and here she was, filthy—and it wasn't sand.

"And David—he was wearin' his park ranger uniform, but it all looked real shady to me."

Patrick Murphy was nervous under the steady stare of Jim Yontz, but he really got tongue-tied when Lee McMillian stood up and approached him for his cross-examination. McMillian wanted to bear down on the arguments Patrick and Kelli had over sex. McMillian took a folksy tone in his first question.

"Is it fair to say, that in your case, the sap was runnin'?"

"Yeah," answered Murphy.

"At twenty, you're kind of new to the game?"

"Yeah," said Murphy. "I wanted sex all the time and all she wanted to do was clock me—she'd do it real fast on the couch and then tell me, 'Get the hell off me.' "

McMillian then zeroed in on how quickly Patrick broke up with Kelli, suggesting that maybe he didn't trust her very much around other men. Murphy admitted that after listening to Kelli tell his mother how she couldn't remember what happened, he walked up to Kelli and gave her an ultimatum.

"Hey, I got your stuff; you gotta sign these divorce papers right now—we need to end this crap."

"It sounds like you didn't cut her much slack," noted McMillian, smiling.

"Yes, that's right," answered Murphy, hanging his head.

McMillian went on to ask Patrick about the shady characters that Kelli used to hang out with. Murphy, not noticing there were two men on the jury with scruffy beards and long, scraggly hair, jumped right in where McMillian wanted him to and unloaded on what he called the "riffraff" of T or C.

"I feel like if a person doesn't have enough pride—they should take care of their mustache and beard. Over at Becky Smith's place, there was a real scrubby guy outside the trailer."

McMillian challenged Patrick Murphy's memory a couple of times, and after he let Patrick go, Sweazea dismissed everybody for lunch.

An hour and a half later, Jim Yontz decided to call Patrick Murphy back to the witness chair one more time. Sensing the great burden of guilt Patrick felt for dumping Kelli, and then realizing three years later that his wife was really drugged by her friends and unable to remember much of anything, Yontz slowly led Murphy into a discussion of his ex-wife's sex habits. Patrick explained how Kelli always seemed to be in pain when they had sex, and Yontz asked Murphy if he knew she had a medical condition called a "tilted uterus" as well as a "collapsed vagina." Murphy shook his head.

"No, I didn't know," he said, "and I don't think she did, either."

Then Jim Yontz lowered the boom.

"Did Kelli *ever* ask you to take a ten-inch piece of white PVC pipe and shove it up inside her body?"

Patrick Murphy couldn't take it anymore.

"No," he said quietly. "She would never do that. . . ."

Then he broke down completely and began to cry—big tears rolling down his cheeks and onto his neatly pressed navy uniform.

Jim Yontz had made his point. He excused the upset sailor and the jurors watched Patrick Murphy walk toward the exit door, unable to hold back his sorrow any longer. The sounds of his sobbing followed him out of the courtroom.

Judge Sweazea then excused the jury for the rest of the afternoon, explaining that the prosecutors and the defense attorney had "private matters" they needed to discuss. It was 2:07 P.M. on April 11 and for the rest of the afternoon Judge Kevin Sweazea listened to an Albuquerque "dominatrix" whom the defense team was trying to bring on board one more time as an expert witness for David Ray. Sweazea had turned her away once before, but he was trying to be fair to McMillian and let the defense take another crack at it.

In the next three hours, stress began to show on the face of the young judge as he was asked to enter into a world that defense attorney Lee McMillian had once said dealt with "photos of things that most of us have never done before" and "sexual practices that none of us ever thought of before."

"All of us have taken a step into the twilight zone," said McMillian as he got ready to introduce the dominatrix.

After a short break McMillian called up the thirty-five-year-old woman and asked her to introduce herself. The attractive redhead cut right to the chase.

"My name is Michelle Marie—and, in quotes, 'Diva'—Eytcheson," she informed the judge. "I've been exploring this world for fifteen years and I've been practicing it in the public eye for the last nine years."

Hoping to nudge the judge into letting her testify that David Ray wasn't the only pervert in America, McMillian asked the "Diva" several loaded questions that he hoped would expand the judge's appreciation of sadomasochism, bondage and domination, all areas where the "Diva" considered herself an expert.

"Have you taken professional classes?" asked McMillian.

Eytcheson went on to explain that she'd taken classes in corsetry (shrinking a partner's waist to fifteen inches), body modification (pierced nipples, belly buttons and vaginal lips) and "the most popular class of all," good old-fashioned S-M 101. She explained that she had just created an Internet Web site to encourage others to enjoy the pleasures of the S-M/B-D world, but she didn't want young people peeking into her dark world. So she had a great idea—just insert a special message for people nosing around on the Internet in places where they didn't belong. The message on the screen was simple, she said: "Don't click here unless you're twenty-one or older."

"Can you explain the 'fear fantasy'?" McMillian asked.

"I like to scare them!" she blurted out. "It's fun."

Eytcheson explained that in her world there is always someone "on top" and someone "on the bottom." A dominatrix, she said, naturally likes to be on top. She struggled to find a name for the person on the bottom.

"The bottom is . . . I can't think of a better word than 'victim.' "

She went on to explain to the judge that provoking fear in the person on the bottom greatly increased her own levels of sexual arousal. Her voice trembled as she tried to capture the thrill of it all in a language "straight" people might be able to understand.

"I get a highly aroused sexual charge—sometimes it increases two hundred fold," she told the stone-faced judge.

She went on to explain that people in her circles use a "safe" word when the person on the bottom is experiencing too much pain and wants the person on the top to stop. Once the person on the bottom blurts out the secret password, the person on top eases up.

"The minute the 'safe' word is used, the fantasy stops," she added.

"What is the 'mummification' ritual?" asked McMillian.

"That's when you wrap someone from head to toe in duct tape. They need a straw to breathe with and we found out you can get them at a Home Depot store for only nineteen cents!"

McMillian felt like the "Diva" was in a groove now and he asked her if she'd listened to the 1993 audiotape. She nodded. Then McMillian asked the "Diva" how she knew the tape was a fantasy and not a threat to someone's life.

"It says right at the beginning, 'This tape is to be used for entertainment purposes.' My good friend Spencer holds seminars up in Seattle, Washington, and he always tells us, 'Always put a disclaimer in there.' "

Next McMillian asked her to hold up several magazines from local Albuquerque bookstores that specifically dealt with the kind of fetishes she assumed David

Ray was "into." She showed the judge the following glossy best-sellers: *Capture, Reluctant Captive, Pirate, Bondage, Hush!,* and *The Love Gallery.*

"All six magazines sell videos like David made—and one even sells audiotapes," she added.

There is currently no college-studies program for the kinds of things that the "Diva" knows all about, but McMillian wanted to establish her solid credibility, so he asked her about the little-known International Mister Leather and International Miss Leather contests apparently held all over the world. Proudly Eytcheson pointed out that she herself had actually participated in some of those very contests during her prime.

"I was personally Miss New Mexico Leather in 1997," she acknowledged, smiling at the judge.

Finally McMillian showed her some pictures from David Ray's toy box. She identified most of the objects, all except the large blue saw blade used to keep a girl's legs spread wide apart. Then McMillian handed her some toys. McMillian handed her the vaginal-stretcher that had been introduced at both trials and she handled it clumsily and said: "It looks like some kind of homemade penetration device."

McMillian showed her a photograph of the bench press that had been introduced as evidence. She raised her eyebrows, recalling her own days and nights enjoying a little kinky sex with good friends, and pointed out something she thought the judge probably hadn't thought of yet.

"I had dungeon games in my home two years ago and the use of a tie-down table came in handy."

McMillian saved the best for last, asking the "Diva" a question that made at least one unidentified middle-aged male spectator mumble out loud, "Ugh!"

"Can you tell the judge what 'fisting' is?" asked David Ray's attorney.

"That's when you put the fist in the anal or vaginal

canal," replied the "Diva" in kind of a soothing, matter-of-fact voice. "I actually attended a seminar on fisting in Austin, Texas, last year," she added. "It was a marvelous experience."

McMillian wasn't done.

"Is the human fist actually put in the vagina?" he asked.

"I have actually heard of ways you can enlarge the canal so the fist can be put in," Eytcheson replied.

Jim Yontz had heard enough.

For nearly an hour and a half, he had listened to this woman try to make David Parker Ray sound almost normal, and he wasn't going to have any more of it. He jumped to his feet and with an angry voice seldom used in public, he lectured Lee McMillian on defense efforts to twist the case.

"David hasn't said he's into S and M or B and D and until he does, so what?" Yontz thundered. "Nobody cares what the 'Diva' thinks! Until David stands in front of the jury to explain himself, the dominatrix cannot testify. You cannot build prejudice into the record that can be appealed later, and I think that's what's going on here."

Judge Sweazea called all the lawyers up to his bench in an effort to sort it all out. Yontz had a big white dildo with a red tip in one hand and the big brown-and-cream vaginal-stretcher in the other; during the discussion Sweazea could not make himself call the items by name, only pointing and saying "this thing" or "that thing."

"Some things are left unsaid," he pointed out to the amused lawyers.

One time Yontz went back to the prosecution table and brought another sex toy up to the bench; Sweazea swallowed hard as he pointed to the object and asked, "What's this thing?"

Yontz, mild mannered and low-key, simply said: "It's a nipple piercer, Your Honor."

During the debate at the bench, McMillian's red-headed secretary, Amy, leaned over to David Ray at the defense table and whispered a question on the minds of everyone in the courtroom.

"Do you think you could hold up in cross-examination?" she asked.

"I don't know," David whispered back.

After listening to Yontz's arguments, Judge Sweazea ruled on the dominatrix. She could testify as to the identification of items pictured from the toy box, but Sweazea warned her not to talk about her philosophy of alternative recreational sex. Essentially, the judge backed Jim Yontz.

"I'm not going to allow testimony about fetishes unless there is evidence that David was using a fetish," he ruled.

After the judge decided to call it a day at 5:01 P.M., curious onlookers were congregating in the hall outside of room 22. Lee McMillian and his secretary met next to the watercooler to discuss their defense strategy for David. Amy was blunt and told her boss, "I think we should call David to the stand." McMillian grinned, looked over his shoulder and, in a low voice, said: "Well, if we do, nobody's gonna know about it."

The next day, Thursday, April 12, the jury was back and Lee McMillian got to sink his teeth into the weakest link in the prosecution's case against Ray. After Claire Harwell finished leading David Spencer, the therapist from Craig, Colorado, through his testimony that Kelli Garrett had nightmares and bouts of sleeplessness because she was suffering from post-traumatic stress disorder, Lee McMillian rose for his cross-examination. One sentence at a time, McMillian challenged the witness by pointing out that the only thing Kelli Garrett suffered from was DSNMFD (dire southern New Mexico financial disorder). Then he tried to get Spencer to admit that other traumatic experiences (like the drowning of her boyfriend Jim Hibbard in the fall of 1998) could have played a huge role in her inability to recover. Finally he got the grandfatherly therapist to admit that Garrett might actually have shown PTSD symptoms of trauma that she never experienced.

"Isn't that the nature of human memory?" asked McMillian. "It's plastic, right?"

"I don't understand what you mean," replied Spencer.

"Isn't it possible you could have similar results regardless of whether the activities between David and Kelli were consensual or not?" McMillian shot back.

"Yes, I suppose so," answered Spencer. "If the belief was there, the symptoms could be the same."

"Thank you," replied McMillian.

Spencer turned and smiled at the jury and fired back a salvo of his own.

"To Kelli, the most traumatic part of the kidnapping was having her 'control' taken away," he said. "That terrified her."

McMillian swung around and pointed his finger at Spencer.

"But the simple truth is, Mr. Spencer, her trauma would be the same, regardless of whether anything happened to her or not. It wouldn't make any difference if she lost control or not. Isn't that right?"

"Yes," conceded Spencer. "If she believed that David had raped her, then the symptoms could be the same."

"Thank you, sir!" said McMillian.

It was getting late in the afternoon and Judge Sweazea did not want the jurors to miss enjoying their upcoming three-day Easter weekend, so he dismissed the jury and sent them home. Before they left, he reminded everyone that on Monday morning the defense would present its case.

When Monday morning, April 16, rolled around, the jury discovered that David Ray and Lee McMillian had no plans to present a defense.

"At this time, we rest, Your Honor," McMillian told Sweazea.

Closing arguments took the rest of the day. David, wearing an olive suit loaned to him by McMillian, also sported a bright yellow tie. Lee McMillian looked causal in gray slacks, blue shirt and a gray sports jacket. Jim Yontz finally decided to drop the bear ties and showed up wearing a dark brown suit and black cowboy boots. He wore a boring tie with black-and-white diagonal stripes. Compared to two years ago, his hair showed a lot more salt and a lot less pepper. Kelli Garrett came back to court wearing a light-blue dress and Claire Harwell stood out wearing a white jacket, a white skirt and white shoes. She was also sporting a big gold cross hanging down in front of her open V-necked blue sweater. Just a little reminder to all the good Catholics in New Mexico to do the right thing.

Before letting the lawyers sum up their arguments, Sweazea had to read the jurors the twelve felony charges, including criminal sexual penetration (the term for rape in New Mexico), kidnapping and criminal assault. He also had to read a very detailed description of the female genitalia, right down to the patch of pubic hair surrounding the vagina. He also had to define the vagina as "the area between the vulva and the uterus." Nervous as hell, he mispronounced "pubic" on two occasions, each time calling it "public hair."

Nobody laughed.

Claire Harwell approached the jury at 1:14 P.M., and to some observers in the courtroom, she used the power of her huge eyes along with her full-bodied voice to remind the jury that they were dealing with a very serious case against a very evil man.

"David Ray was Kelli Garrett's worst nightmare," she began.

"Rather than face the truth, for three years she preferred to think she was going crazy. David Ray doesn't look very scary today, but remember who he really is and how he made you feel when you first heard the audiotape.

"When David brought Kelli back to Patrick's mother's house on July 28, 1996, he was wearing his park ranger uniform. You know now after hearing from his boss that he didn't need to be in his uniform because he wasn't working that day, or the day before, either."

Then Harwell showed the jury a short clip from the videotape. While the jury was looking at a naked Kelli with her legs spread, Claire put an 8½-inch by 11-inch manila folder over Kelli's open vagina to try and maintain some modesty for the victim. Then, as the jurors again sat transfixed, she told them what they were seeing one more time.

"The woman in the video is sobbing. She is moving her arms slowly. If you look closely, you can see by the movement of her throat that she is gently weeping."

Harwell shut off the television and walked slowly back to the prosecution table, where she picked up a big (fourteen inches long) white dildo with a red head. She walked over next to the jurors with the dildo in one hand and a can of Copenhagen snuff in the other. She held the can up to the end of the dildo and reminded the jury what Garrett told them a week earlier.

"Kelli recalled that one dildo was the size of a Copenhagen can of chewing tobacco—look at the comparison—it couldn't get much closer."

Harwell put down the big "toy" and asked the jury to side with the prosecution.

"You can tell Kelli that her nightmare was real and it has finally come to an end."

At 2:27 P.M., Lee McMillian rose for his last chance to influence the jury. He reminded them that Jim Yontz would follow him and this was his last chance to defend David Ray. He pointed out that most of the prosecution evidence was based on photographs and "weird toys" found in 1999, three years after the crime. He held up picture after picture taken from the toy box and the trailer home and crudely threw each one on the floor, one at a time. He reminded the jury, "There is no way of knowing if this stuff was there in 1996." And then, apparently unaware that some fundamentalist Christians wear copper bracelets with the letters WWJD (What would Jesus do?) in order to prick their conscience, McMillian asked the jury to listen to Yontz and then let their memory of him prick their conscience.

"What would Lee McMillian say?" he asked.

"The prosecution has invited you to guess," he told them. "Time after time, Mr. Yontz asks you to guess. Please don't guess. The law says you're not allowed to."

Then McMillian presented what he considered to be the best evidence that Ray was innocent. He picked up the videotape, placed it in the VCR and turned on the television set. A few jurors looked surprised. He played the entire six-minute portion of the videotape for them, offering his interpretations of what they saw. He pointed to David Ray and Kelli and told the jurors that what they were seeing was just a "harmless fantasy." Soon six out of seven female jurors began chewing gum and another female juror wept. McMillian stood next to the TV and used his left index finger to emphasize the fine points of what he told the jurors was nothing more than two people doing what they both agreed to do ahead of time.

"I want you to look at the manner in which this man touches this woman," he said, using his softest voice.

"This is gentle; this is not torture. Her vulva is extended—you often see that in horses and cattle out on the ranch. Watch what happens here—is Kelli crying, or just laughing?"

When the videotape reached the part where Ray let Kelli free her arms and she folded them over her breasts, McMillian took on a compassionate tone of voice.

"Ahh . . . ," he said. "That's got to feel better."

At 3:27 P.M. McMillian sat down. Both he and David peered over their glasses riding down on the end of their noses as Jim Yontz took the floor and challenged the defense's case. Yontz played "snippets" of the grisly audiotape and asked the jurors if any of it sounded like what Kelli Garrett claimed happened to her in 1996. After playing each segment, Yontz used his most sarcastic voice to tell the jurors what was obvious to him.

"Gee, sure sounds like what we saw."

At one point in the audiotape, David Ray told his victim that her memory would be worthless once he let her go: "You're not going to be able to remember a fuckin' thing."

"Does that sound like Kelli Garrett?" Yontz asked.

Like most hard-boiled prosecutors, Jim Yontz always liked to save his best zinger for last. Just before his conclusion, he lowered his voice and stared straight into the soul of the whole jury.

"There is no more torturous thing than to be held totally nude and have another person lightly touch your sex organs," he told them.

"Take your God-given brains and common sense," he added. "Find the defendant guilty."

Judge Sweazea released the jury for deliberations at 5:01 P.M. and for the next five hours they debated the case, only taking a short dinner break to order out for pizza. The small group of court onlookers hung out in the parking lot, chatting and drinking beer. As the hours wore on, people talked less and less, wondering if Estancia was going to be a repeat of Tierra Amarilla. Finally, at 9:24 P.M., a court observer came outside with the announcement that everyone was waiting for.

"They have a verdict," she informed the friends, family and media.

People rushed back inside room 22 and quietly took their seats. The entire audience was only a mere thirteen people. At 9:26 P.M. Judge Sweazea called the proceedings to order and turned to address the jury foreman, Mr. Greg Nevelos.

"Do you have a verdict, Mr. Nevelos?" the judge asked.

"Yes, we do," replied the man who watched the video and listened to the audio with his lower jaw hanging wide open. Greg Nevelos, fifty-one, a tan and fit local high-school track coach with a blond beard and long blond wavy hair, handed the bailiff the jury checklist covering each of the twelve felony counts.

The bailiff delivered it to the judge and Sweazea spent five minutes looking over the final verdicts.

At 9:31 P.M. Judge Sweazea turned to face David Parker Ray. The tone of his voice was very grave. He looked right at David.

"As to Count Number 1 . . . Guilty in the First Degree.

"As to Count Number 2 . . . Guilty in the First Degree.

"As to Count Number 3 . . . Guilty in the First Degree.

"As to Count Number 4 . . . Guilty in the First Degree.

"As to Count Number 5 . . . Guilty in the First Degree.

"As to Count Number 6 . . . Guilty in the First Degree.

"As to Count Number 7 . . . Guilty in the First Degree.

"As to Count Number 8 . . . Guilty in the First Degree.

"As to Count Number 9 . . . Guilty in the First Degree.

"As to Count Number 10 . . . Guilty in the First Degree.

"As to Count Number 11 . . . Guilty in the First Degree.

"As to Count Number 12 . . . Guilty in the First Degree."

At 9:36 P.M. Sweazea finished speaking. Kelli Garrett broke down sobbing. Her small group of supporters gathered around her, hugging one another. David Ray's sister, Peggy, also cried, her face red and puffy, but nobody gathered around Peggy. David Ray was immediately handcuffed behind his back and led out of the courtroom. His face looked ash white, defeated.

After the judge dismissed the jury, all of Kelli Garrett's friends gave her a congratulatory hug. One tall Reuters reporter walked up late and Garrett, joyous, jumped up on top of a chair in order to give him a hug.

"You're so tall, I can't reach ya." She laughed.

"How do you feel?" he asked.

"Now I can get on with my life," she said. "Finally."

Kelli Garrett prepared a quick press release and a few minutes later the woman who served as her victim's advocate read it to the tiny media crowd.

" 'I'm glad he's been found guilty of the crimes against me. I wish I could have remembered all of this five years ago. There is still a lot I do not remember—and I'm glad for that. But what I do remember will affect me for the rest of my life. Still, I do not feel sorry for myself. I consider myself a survivor—not a victim.' "

Channel 13 TV News in Albuquerque had covered the conviction and Garrett didn't want to miss seeing the ten o'clock news, so she and her followers—two state cops, one FBI agent, two prosecutors, three onlookers and her sister, Brenda, headed down to the local watering hole, the Blue Ribbon Bar. Nobody mentioned it, but she'd been kidnapped from the Blue Waters Saloon and maybe it was fitting that she got to celebrate the trial's end in Estancia, far from the waters of Elephant Butte Lake.

Just before the gathering left the bar, a half hour later, Kelli Garrett told everyone how she felt about the possibility of David Ray spending the rest of his life in prison. She tried to sidestep her real feelings but couldn't.

"I don't want him to die," she said.

"I won't say exactly what I want. . . . Let's just say I want the guards to let him out one morning to take a shower . . .

"and then I want 'Big Bubba' to get him."

Outside, someone asked her how she felt about Jesse Ray now. Garrett didn't mention why her attitude had shifted, but she gave Jim Yontz an idea of how she saw the woman who helped kidnap her.

"I feel sorry for Jesse—I think she did it to keep her dad away from her."

While Kelli Garrett and her crowd were celebrating, David Parker Ray was seated in a back room in the Torrance County Courthouse. He was doing his first television interview in over two years. Mark Horner from Channel 4 in Albuquerque got Ray to comment on the outcome of the second Kelli Garrett trial and the possibility he might be sentenced to over 130 years in prison.

"I feel raped," he told Horner.

"If you're innocent, you're innocent. I'm an innocent man.

"My sexual fantasies are not that unusual. There are approximately two million people in the United States who have the same fantasies. Next time, I'm going to be more selective of my friends.

"When they played the audiotape, I thought it was a violation of my U.S. constitutional rights. It was a source of entertainment for me to create those tapes. I don't hate women at all. I get my sexual excitement from making women happy.

"I got pleasure out of a woman getting pleasure.

"I did what they wanted me to do."

Channel 4 also interviewed David's sister, Peggy, who stood by her brother.

"He was a loner growing up. He spent a lot of time by himself. We grew up out in Mountainair. We were way out in the country, so really, it was just the two of us—

not a lot of friends or anything. We was raised real old-fashioned, where truth is just basic—you don't even think about lying about things.

"I've known that David had fantasies and fetishes all his life, nearly. He's a kind and gentle person, though—he's always good and kind to animals. The word 'sex' is why this case got so much attention. You mix the word 'sex' with the word 'violence' and everybody's going to jump on it."

The reaction to the verdict back in Truth or Consequences was hard to measure. People had been trying to forget about David for a long time—so every time his name came up, people got edgy. They figured that once he finally got sentenced, the whole thing might just go away. Their little town had taken a real beating and everyone just wanted a little peace and quiet.

Rosemary Hoskins, owner of the Rio Grande Motel, seemed to sum up the general opinion best when she told a reporter from Reuters on Friday night, April 20, what she thought of the whole David Parker Ray case.

"It costs seventy-two dollars a day to keep the son of a bitch in jail," she snorted. "They ought to just throw him off a cliff."

CHAPTER 33

"As long as his parents are alive, he'll never confess."
Jim Yontz, March 24th, 2002

Two months later, Jim Yontz decided to give Frances Baird one last call. It had been a long and tiring two years and he suspected she didn't feel the same way about living in Truth or Consequences. In addition, he had one last tidbit of news for her. He called her at home on a Thursday night because he knew it was her "down day" after putting out the Wednesday paper each week.

"Frances, this is Jim—I wanted to let you know that Lee McMillian and I are discussing a possible plea deal for David."

"Just toss him to the general population like a piece of meat," she said.

"Don't worry," said Yontz. "He's almost sixty-two years old now. He'll never breathe free air again."

"How are you going to swing the deal?" asked Baird.

"Let Jesse go."

"Isn't she just as guilty as he is?" asked Baird.

"Yeah—but if I try Jesse, that means Kelli Garrett has to testify at a third trial. She's got a job and a new boyfriend and she seems to be getting on with her life for the first time."

"Boy, Jim, this whole thing sure has been a nightmare."

"Heck, when it all first broke, I avoided it from day one."

"I wish I'd never heard of David Parker Ray," grumbled Baird.

"I don't blame you," said Yontz. "David's been kidnapping girls ever since they put pictures of little kids on milk cartons."

"You know, I used to go walking around Truth or Consequences all the time by myself and now I don't go walking alone—not even in the daylight."

"Law and order hangs by a thin thread in T or C," Yontz added.

"So what are your plans, Jim?" asked Baird. "Going hunting?"

"No—you know, we call it hunting because we do a lot more hunting than killing. I learned a long time ago the fun ends when you pull the trigger."

"So where to?"

"I figure Lee and I oughtta be able to nail down some kind of plea agreement with old David in the next couple of weeks. If it happens, I'm going to take a vacation for the first time in two and a half years. I'm going to drive up to the cliff dwellings at Acoma with my wife and tour the town—now, there's a town that knew what to do with the bad guys."

"What do you mean?" asked Baird.

"It's the oldest inhabited town in North America—I think the Indians have been living there for over eight hundred years. The houses are perched on top of a four-hundred-foot island of rocks. When the Acoma tribe had problems with anyone acting antisocial, they would just haul the criminal over to the edge of the cliffs and toss them down on the rocks below. A couple of hundred years ago, they had problems with a Catholic priest and they threw him off the cliff, too. They don't mess around. They don't tolerate people who screw with the social order."

"Law and order," chuckled Baird. "New Mexico style."

"So what are your plans for the year?" asked Yontz.

"Well, I'm getting married in September."

"Tying the knot, huh—you going to marry a cop?" asked Yontz with a laugh.

"No way," answered Baird. "I'm going to marry Manny Sanchez—he works down at the lumber store in T or C, and we're going to have a Western wedding out at his parents' ranch on the edge of town. You're invited, too. It's September fifteenth."

"Thanks, Frances—I'll make plans to be there."

On Monday, July 1, 2001, Jim Yontz showed up in court wearing black cowboy boots, blue Levi's jeans and a white cowboy shirt with no tie. He was laughing and smiling. An hour later, he and Lee McMillian approached the bench and the two men walked David Ray through a Plea and Disposition Agreement that Ray signed in front of Judge Sweazea just before high noon. Afterward, Yontz told Sweazea that if David Ray ever got free "he'd commit another crime before he reached his front porch." Ray had pleaded guilty to the charges brought by Jim Yontz in the cases of Cynthia Vigil, Angelique Montano and Kelli Garrett. Yontz had contacted the two living victims and the mother of Angie Montano and everyone agreed to the plea deal fashioned by Yontz and McMillian.

Later that day, Yontz called down to Socorro to report the good news. The secretary on the phone informed him that just before noon they had experienced tremors and a small earthquake. Jim Yontz laughed and said: "That's Judge Mertz rolling over in his grave."

On Thursday, September 20, 2001, Judge Sweazea gave David Parker Ray the maximum sentence—224 years in prison. As part of the deal engineered by the prosecutor and the defense attorney, Sweazea gave Jesse Ray 9 years and suspended 6½—setting her free after serving 2½ years.

On Monday, October 1, Jim Yontz finally took a well-deserved vacation and got out of town. He and his wife, Karen, drove west from Albuquerque to the valley of the stone monoliths, where the Acoma Indians still lived. As they drove down into the islands of sandstone, Karen asked Jim: "Are you glad it's over?"

"I'm happy that Kelli Garrett is expecting her first child next summer."

"What about the case?"

"I'm not so sure."

"Why not?"

"The Mexicans have a saying that describes a dangerous guy like David—*Los ojos del matar.*"

"What does it mean?" asked Karen.

"It means he has the eyes of a killer," answered Yontz.

"He was a whole lot more than just a garden-variety killer," commented Karen.

"Oh, he sure was," said Yontz. "John Schum of the FBI told me they figured Ray had killed between sixty and ninety women."

"He was just plain evil."

"I used to tell my friends to try and imagine the very worst things that another human being could do to them and I told them that when it came to David—they weren't even close."

"That's all over now, Jim," his wife said, putting her arm around his shoulder.

"I know, but certain things still bug me."

"Like what?"

"We found those eight driver's licenses with pictures of girls we couldn't identify. . . ."

"You think David killed those girls?" asked Karen.

"I'm pretty sure he did—and that's the problem."

"Loose ends, huh?"

"Yeah—like no bodies."

"Maybe someday."

Jim Yontz sighed.

"I will always feel like the worst thing about the David Ray case isn't knowing what I did prove in a court of law—it's that sickening feeling of knowing what I *couldn't* prove in a court of law."

Yontz turned to his wife with a weary look on his face.

"That's what bothers me."

CHAPTER 34

The only thing that protects the rest of us from David Parker Ray is the fact that Cynthia Vigil picked up that ice pick.

—Jim Yontz, 10/15/2001

Cyndy Vigil was the last living victim to see David Parker Ray in action. Late in the afternoon on Monday, March 22, 1999, she was chained to a pole in the living room of Ray's mobile home in Elephant Butte, New Mexico. Vigil had been in captivity for two days and Ray was making plans to take her out to the toy box and finish the job he'd started in the house. Cyndy desperately wanted to escape for good and just before Ray came home from work, she made her move.

"The day I got away, David got up early and went to work and left Cindy Hendy to guard me. I was naked and tied down. He took the handcuffs and leg shackles off but left the dog collar around my neck. Before that, my hands had been tied above the bed and my feet were tied to the bottom of the bed. I couldn't even roll over without getting my feet all tangled up.

"That afternoon I was connected to a pole on the wall by just the dog collar. All I could do was sit up. The pole was standing straight up at the head of the bed. There was a small iron fence separating me from the living room. When Cindy Hendy got a phone call from David and went to the back room to talk to him, I put my body under the rail and I pulled the table toward me with my feet.

"There was this table in the living room and Cindy had left this ring of keys on top of the table. I hooked my feet between the rail of the fence and pulled the table over—you know, like you see people do in the movies. As soon as the table was close enough, I reached over the fence with my hands. The iron railing was choking my neck, but I really wanted those keys.

"It was a key chain with a bunch of keys on it. A bunch of little keys. I knew that the key to the dog collar was on the chain 'cause they always carried it with them. I seen David carrying that ring of keys around the whole time I was there. The minute I got the keys, I crawled up in a ball in the corner and started trying every key on the lock. As soon as Cindy Hendy got off the phone, she came back in the room and caught me pushing the table back with my feet. She seen the keys weren't on the table and right away she started hitting me with this big old glass lamp.

"I just crawled up in a ball and I was trying every key in the lock—even while she was hitting me. I was frightened because I knew she was carrying a gun in her back pocket. It was the same gun I saw in David's pocket all weekend. Finally the lock came loose and me and Hendy started fighting like two alley cats. She was so damn strong and she was hitting me real hard. I saw where she had dropped the phone and I ran over and tried to call nine-one-one. I hardly got a word out of my mouth when she jumped me and I dropped the phone on the bed. She was pulling my hair real hard, and all of a sudden, there was this box.

"A small box somehow got knocked over on the floor and a bunch of things fell out.

"An ice pick fell out of the box. . . .

"I picked it up and stabbed Hendy in the neck and got away."

Without the ice pick falling out of the box and onto the floor, David Parker Ray would still be out in the desert of New Mexico capturing and torturing women. Many of those women would have died alone—a cruel and horrible death.

One woman, however, would still be alive.

Special Agent Patricia E. Rust of the FBI.

EPILOGUE

"I don't give a rat's ass if they send me to prison for the rest of my life."

David Parker Ray talking to Jim Fielder
Jailhouse Interview
August 21st, 2001

DAVID PARKER RAY — During the 8/21/2001 interview in Truth or Consequences, Ray said, "Prison is like a dog pound, but at least with dogs you can kill them when they get out-of-control." Then he added, "If my heart stopped today, it wouldn't bother me at all." On May 28, 2002, Ray got his wish. He was sitting in his jail cell at the Correctional Facility in Dobbs, New Mexico, when his heart stopped and he died. He was sixty-two years old.

JIM YONTZ — On January 7, 2002, Yontz was back in Albuquerque working his new job as a Deputy DA in the Violent Crimes Unit. Work keeps him busy. "This April we had nine murders in nine days," he reported. "As far as David dying"—he shrugged—"it was untimely but not unexpected."

FRANCES BAIRD SANCHEZ — After turning down three offers to write for the Associated Press, she is still living in Truth or Consequences, New Mexico, and working as a crime reporter for the *Sierra County Sentinel.* She is married and expecting her first child (a baby girl!) on November 11, 2002. When asked how she felt after Ray died, she said, "I'd rather imagine him burning in Hell than sitting around his jail cell and watching reruns of *Lonesome Dove.*"

LEE McMILLIAN — On October 1, 2001, McMillian switched from defense to prosecutor and took over Jim Yontz's old job working as the Deputy D.A. out in Estancia, New Mexico. When asked about David, he said, "He's the meanest person I ever met—and yet he was so nice." Then McMillian added, "David created what the FBI calls THE TORTURE BOOK—only three people in the world have ever seen the hundreds of pages of text and drawings." Then McMillian shuddered. "It's too dangerous to let any other human being see—you can't read it without having nightmares."

JESSE RAY — She is a free woman, walking the streets of Albuquerque, New Mexico. "My dad was always innocent," she tells anyone who will listen.

CINDY HENDY	She is serving out her thirty-six-year sentence at the prison in Grants, New Mexico.
DENNIS ROY YANCY	He is serving out his twenty-year sentence at the prison in Los Lunas, New Mexico.
CYNDY VIGIL	She has a job working as a waitress in a roadside cafe on Highway 66 and has given birth to two healthy baby boys since escaping from The Toy Box. She lives with her boyfriend in Albuquerque, New Mexico.
KELLI GARRETT	She lives with her boyfriend in Craig, Colorado. On June 30, 2002, she gave birth to her first child, a healthy baby boy. When asked about Ray dying, she said, "My first emotion was complete shock, but it pisses me off that he died. I wanted him to live long enough to give up a few secrets—like what he did to all those other girls." Then she paused, and added, "I'm not sure how I want to feel."
TRUTH OR CONSEQUENCES, NEW MEXICO	If you have additional information about crimes committed by David Parker Ray, please call Truth or Consequences and ask for Assistant DA June Stein. Her number is 1-505-894-9033.

UPDATE 2013

CHAPTER 1

When David Parker Ray suffered a fatal heart attack in his cell at the Hobbs, New Mexico, Correctional Facility on May 28, 2002, scores of unanswered questions about his crimes were left to plague the investigators who had worked on his case.

Where were the bodies of the more than forty victims he had claimed in his journals to have kidnapped, tortured, and killed? How many of his captives might have been lucky enough to have been released alive, but with only vague, nightmarish memories of what had been done to them during their time in "the Toy Box"?

On May 2, 2003, the law enforcement community in New Mexico felt as though Ray had reached out from the grave to claim another victim—this time, one of their own. Karen Yontz, a well-respected investigator, as well as the wife of prosecutor Jim Yontz, was shot and killed following a robbery at Albuquerque's New Mexico Bank

& Trust. But Karen was not shot in the line of duty, trying to prevent the crime or apprehend the bank robber. She was killed by her fellow officers after she donned sunglasses and a baseball cap and robbed the bank at gunpoint, then fled in her service vehicle.

When officers cornered Karen in the parking lot of a restaurant, they did not realize who she was. That shocking knowledge came later—after a tense and lengthy standoff, during which Karen told them, "You're going to have to shoot me." She refused to drop her weapon, putting it to her own head several times before finally raising the gun and pointing it directly at the officers. They had no choice but to open fire, fatally shooting her at least three times.

"She absolutely knew what was going to happen," one of her acquaintances from the district attorney's office said, adding that the bank robbery could have been either for the money or perhaps Karen was "hell-bent on a destructive pattern and didn't know what to do."

At first, the officers at the scene did not recognize the woman they had shot. But when the authorities ran the license plates on Karen's car after finding a police radio inside, they were horrified to learn the vehicle was registered to the office of New Mexico's attorney general. They soon realized that the woman who had robbed the bank and then seemed intentionally to commit "suicide by cop" was Karen Yontz, a career law-enforcement officer, as well as a capable and respected investigator in the attorney general's office.

During the highly stressful time when her husband, Jim Yontz, was prosecuting David Parker Ray, Karen began going to Indian casinos in the area to play video poker as a way to relieve the escalating tension in her personal life. There had been domestic incidents and other marital problems in the past, and Karen had apparently turned to gambling as a distraction. At first, she told her friends about her visits to the casinos and spoke to them very openly about playing video poker. However, her gambling quickly began to slip out of control, and her debts started to pile up. It soon reached the point of an addiction, and Karen began to be very secretive about her gambling trips, ceasing to talk to her friends about her outings to the casinos. Acquaintances would see her there, though, and her friends knew that the gambling was becoming more and more frequent and was out of hand.

By the time of the May 2 robbery, Karen's wages were being garnished; she was being investigated for credit card fraud; she was about to be placed on administrative leave at work. According to her husband, she owed more than $100,000, and her friends believed she felt that she was at the end of the line. Jim Yontz told the press that his wife had so much pride, the situation "just ate her up."

One of Karen's coworkers told the press that Karen was in a lot of pain, "and this was the only way she knew to end everything."

A coworker said that Karen was the person who had taught her how to investigate child abuse cases, and said she was always there to answer complex legal questions.

"She loved law enforcement," the friend said. "She was a very bright person, and that's why this is all so shocking to us."

Sadly, Karen's eighteen-year-old stepdaughter said that she only wished she had known how desperate Karen had become. She remembered a caring woman whom she loved and missed, who had tucked her in at night, and who would have done anything to help her.

Would Karen Yontz have become addicted to gambling if not for the tremendous pressure that David Parker Ray's trial put on her family life? The law enforcement community believed it was a major factor, and it looked to many of Karen Yontz's friends and family members as though Ray had claimed yet another victim, even after his death.

CHAPTER 2

Author Jim Fielder's interest in the David Parker Ray case never lessened following the publication of *Slow Death,* and he kept very close track of any developments that came to light following Ray's death. He made several trips to New Mexico, in 2008 and 2009, to narrate three hour-long documentaries about Ray and his crimes. Two of those episodes were aired on the Investigation Discovery (ID) channel. One of them, entitled "Escaped," was seen by Michael Colburn, an independent filmmaker from Texas.

Afterward, his interest piqued by Ray's story and Jim Fielder's narration of the program, Colburn bought a copy of *Slow Death.* After reading the book, he began piecing together the idea of a movie. This would evolve into *The Toy Box.*

Colburn's plans began to solidify, and his film began to take shape. With a crew that involved more than eighty people, filming of *The Toy Box* began. Initially it took place in Huntsville, Texas, and then in six other small-town locations around the state.

Several of the actors pulled double duty: Jennifer Peebles, who played "Jesse," was also an adaptation writer, and Shannon Lark, who had the role of "Carrie," became a contributing producer. In the lead roles were Jeremy James Douglas Norton as "David Parker Ray" and Scott Guthrie as "Dennis Roy Yancy."

When publicizing his film, Colburn told interviewers that he had been intrigued by the prospect of someone being so cold, detached, and callous as David Parker Ray. Ray had kidnapped and tortured so many women—over such a long time—and had gotten away with it for so many years, before he was finally brought down due to the escape of his last victim.

According to those who saw some of the online trailers and clips from *The Toy Box,* Colburn's movie seemed to be quite good, but there were numerous production delays along the way. The film was scheduled at one time for an October 31, 2011, release, but at last report it was listed as being in postproduction. The release date had been pushed back to August 1, 2013. The scores of devotees who followed the case, with as much interest as Colburn, were anxiously awaiting a chance to see the film. They hoped that it would be released with no other delays.

CHAPTER 3

One of David Parker Ray's accomplices, Dennis Roy Yancy, the only person to admit to any actual murders in the case, was paroled on March 17, 2010. Despite his parole, Yancy couldn't leave the prison where he was being held. According to the prison officials, that was because the locations Yancy had chosen as the places he wanted to live and spend his two years on parole were not approved by the state.

Yancy, who had been sentenced to twenty years in prison after entering a guilty plea to the strangling death of twenty-two-year-old Marie Parker, had served eleven years of his sentence and had received good time, despite having three major misconduct reports while incarcerated.

Sandy Dietz, the chair of the Adult Parole Board, told the press that Yancy had "no place to go."

Yancy started collecting good time in March 2010; unless he found a suitable, state-approved place to live, he would have to remain in jail until March 2011. If he found a place to live that met with the parole board's approval, and was released prior to that time, he would be on probation until 2015.

CHAPTER 4

One of the missing persons believed to have been a victim of Ray's Toy Box was a twenty-three-year-old woman named Jill Troia, who was last seen while in the company of Glenda Jean "Jesse" Ray on the night of October 1, 1995. The two women had been drinking together at an Albuquerque bar and restaurant, the Frontier, one of Jesse Ray's regular hangouts. They had been dating and, according to witnesses, were having an argument that night. Jesse told the police that the last time she saw her girlfriend, Jill had been on the phone with a roommate. Jesse claimed that she left Jill and walked out of the restaurant. Jesse told police that her father, David Parker Ray, came to the Frontier and picked her up outside, but the authorities have always suspected that Jesse and her father actually kidnapped Jill and took her with them that night.

In his journals, Ray boasted about torturing and killing an "Oriental woman," and Jill Troia, who was adopted, was of Korean descent. She was a perfect fit for the description that Ray gave of his Asian victim, and the authorities felt there was a high likelihood that Jill was indeed the woman whom Ray had written about in his journals.

In October 2011, dozens of law enforcement officers

from several local, state, and federal agencies flocked to the Elephant Butte Lake area after receiving a very specific, highly credible tip about the location of some human remains that might prove to be those of Jill Troia. Quite a few searches had been conducted in that area over the years; there had been continuing suspicion that Ray could have killed several victims and hidden their bodies in the lake, or in the marshy ravines of McRae Canyon, a drained canyon adjoining Elephant Butte Lake. Six years of continuous drought conditions had left the lake very low, and many areas that had been underwater for years were now exposed. It was an ideal time to scour the edges of the lake and the adjoining canyons for new evidence.

After receiving the confidential information regarding Jill Troia's disappearance, the searchers who combed the area, once again, found nothing on the first day of their search other than a pair of glasses. They said, however, that they had no intention of giving up the search. The glasses were taken into evidence, and global positioning system (GPS) coordinates for some of the areas slated for future searches were marked and recorded.

Jill Troia's mother told reporters she hoped that the renewed search for her daughter would result in the closure her family desperately hoped for.

"We're pleased that Jill's investigation is getting reenergized, and we're just praying that we get some answers to what happened to Jill," Ann Troia said.

Personnel from the FBI's Evidence Response Team (ERT), the New Mexico State Police, and officials from the Albuquerque police told the press that although nothing substantial had turned up on the first day of the search, their efforts would continue. There was much area to cover, they said, and they were confident in the tip's accuracy.

FBI spokesman Frank Fisher told the press that their

team included some of the most experienced searchers in the country, and they all felt that the information they had received was very credible.

"We wouldn't have been out here if we didn't have a good idea of where we were supposed to look," Fisher said, adding that they felt certain that the search was being conducted in the correct area.

"We don't know who it is, we just know that there's something there," another agent said, speaking anonymously.

The unidentified agent went on to say that finding evidence after such a long time might not be likely.

"There'll probably be very little left," he said. "It's like finding a needle in a haystack."

CHAPTER 5

After watching television coverage in 2001 about the renewed search for bodies of David Parker Ray's victims, a man unexpectedly came forward with what could prove to be some very solid information on Ray's method of hiding his victims.

The man, who asked not to be identified in the media, told the authorities that he had delivered load after load of concrete to David Parker Ray over a six-year period. The concrete was ordered by Ray and had been delivered to Elephant Butte Lake State Park, where Ray worked. The man said that he had taken the loads of concrete to an area above the park, where concrete and cement-block walls surrounded an empty lot. Ray would use the concrete to fill up large truck tires, the man said. These tires were definitely large enough to have held a body, he reported.

Ray never allowed the man to get out of the cement truck or let him see inside the tires, the man told law enforcement. No one else was ever present when the concrete was delivered, he said. When this tipster asked Ray what the tires were going to be used for after they were filled with the cement, Ray told him they were going to be used at the park to anchor down the marina.

FBI agent Frank Fisher said the agency was very interested in the man's tip, saying that something was definitely suspicious because Ray did not let the man get out of his truck and walk around or look around the area. Fisher said Ray was believed to have used several different methods to dispose of bodies; encasing bodies in concrete at the bottom of the lake was a definite possibility of being one of those methods.

"Even in his own writings, he would suggest ways to dispose of bodies," Fisher said, adding that Ray had mentioned putting bodies in areas where roads were scheduled to be paved.

The man who came forward with the information about the cement-filled tires had moved away from the area before Ray's arrest in 1999. He said that he was unaware that the authorities believed that the lake could have served as a dumping ground for the bodies of Ray's victims.

"It hit me like a ton of bricks," he said, when he saw the news reports of the renewed searches for remains. "Bodies could be in that concrete."

CHAPTER 6

Another person who came forward after learning of the renewed search for evidence in the Elephant Butte Lake area was a dentist from El Paso, Texas, a visitor to the state park, who had made a discovery around a month before the searches began in 2011. While exploring in the park, he found a group of bones near the shore on the east side of the lake. The man "didn't think much of it," the FBI said, but after watching the news reports on the renewed search for Jill Troia, the dentist knew his discovery might be very important. He contacted the park rangers and gave them a group of what proved to be human leg bones, which he had found at the lake, including a foot-long section of a femur.

On receiving the bones, around fifteen agents and police officers went back to the lake to search the area where the dentist told them he had found them. They had been lying on a ledge of a rocky new shoreline, near a section of the lake that had been underwater until the past year, when the lake's level had dropped almost thirty-five feet over a several-year period due to drought conditions. There were no other bones found at the site, but a choke-chain collar was found nearby. The officers initially believed it might have been a dog's collar instead of one of the chain collars Ray typically had used to restrain his victims. They said that a dead dog had been found in the area, but other sources said the dog's body was found over two hundred feet from the spot where the chain was lying. This distance kept some of the searchers from completely discounting the idea that the collar might have been connected to one of Ray's victims.

The remains of a blue T-shirt were also found near

the spot where the bones were located. It was not known if the T-shirt was connected in any way to the bones, which were to be examined at the medical investigator's office or at the FBI Laboratory, DNA Analysis Unit, in Virginia. After so many years of exposure to the elements, the bones might have been difficult to identify conclusively. They were described by one of the officers who had seen them at the scene as being "extremely weathered."

CHAPTER 7

Around the same time the searches of the Elephant Butte Lake area were taking place, in the hope of generating even more new leads and information, the FBI released a large group of photos of hundreds of items that were collected from Ray's home and the Toy Box during the investigation of his crimes. Many of the items, the FBI believed, may have belonged to Ray's victims and could have been kept by him as "souvenirs" of his activities. The Bureau hoped some of the items might possibly be recognized by family and friends of missing persons Ray could have murdered, or even have belonged to some of his victims who had been given amnesia-inducing drugs and then released alive.

In 2011 thirty-four pages of photos of the items were posted on the FBI's website, on their Facebook page, and on the agency's Twitter account. Because of Ray's own admission in his journals that he had abducted people from states other than New Mexico, it was hoped that posting the photos on social media would draw attention and bring in more information about missing persons who might have come into contact with Ray at some time.

"The FBI, along with its law enforcement partners in New Mexico, is aggressively pursuing several leads in the search for the remains of any possible victims of David Parker Ray," Agent Frank Fisher told the media, and also posted his appeal on the agency's website and Facebook and Twitter pages. "We are asking family and friends of missing people to look over these photographs and contact us if they recognize any of these items."

It turned out to be an excellent idea to use social media to distribute information about the search for Ray's victims by posting the photos on the Internet.

"We're getting numerous tips and they're coming in steadily," Fisher said after the photos were released and began to be viewed by the public, "and our investigators are quite busy with them right now."

The hundreds of items shown in excellent detail on the postings ran the gamut from the very cheapest pieces of broken costume jewelry to custom-made, one-of-a-kind pieces, which were obviously very expensive. Being unique, these items should be very easily identifiable. The FBI remained hopeful that their venture into social media would pay off and someone would recognize items that had belonged to a missing friend or loved one. Rings, bracelets, pendants, key chains, rosaries, belts, and various other items of clothing, jewelry, and accessories have remained on the sites for viewing. To date, these images have had thousands of "hits" and "likes."

CHAPTER 8

In addition to distributing missing persons posters featuring Jill Troia, another poster with the photo of a possible victim of David Parker Ray was distributed by the FBI in their campaign to generate tips and information. The photo of a dark-haired, dark-eyed, smiling young woman had been found on a fake ID card in Ray's possession and was widely distributed to agencies nationwide. It was feared that she had come into contact with Ray at some point, and she might have subsequently gone missing.

Shortly after the photo was distributed, a Texas woman came forward and identified herself to the authorities as the person in the photo. She had lost her identification years previously, she said, and didn't remember where or when the ID had been lost. She had not been a victim of David Parker Ray's, she said. How Ray had gotten hold of the woman's photo ID was not known, but officials were quite relieved to learn that the woman was alive and well.

CHAPTER 9

When the search for victims of David Parker Ray resumed, another person contacted the authorities with a very interesting lead. A former lieutenant in the Grants, New Mexico Police Department said that he had provided information years prior to the renewed search, and his info had been ignored by the authorities.

Steve Bell said that he had met with Ray's girlfriend, Cindy Hendy, and her friend Pam Gomez, at the Grants Women's Prison on a couple of occasions between 2002 and 2006. Bell had an office in the prison at that time, and he told the press that Gomez said to him once, during an interview, that three of Ray's victims' bodies had been dumped near the dam at Caballo Lake. She even drew him a map leading to a place called "the Pit," where she told him that the bodies had been left.

Bell said that she told him, "They can drag that lake till the cows come home. They ain't going to find nothing."

Bell said he was also told that at one time, Jesse Ray had photos of the Pit in which heads, legs, and other body parts were visible in the water. Bell said that he believed that Gomez was telling him the truth, and he contacted the New Mexico State Police and the Sierra County district attorney, but his information hadn't been taken very seriously. The authorities told Bell that they had gotten so many false tips, especially those based on information that had supposedly come from Cindy Hendy, that they weren't interested. They were tired of going on wild-goose chases, they said, and didn't pursue the things Bell had told them.

Bell said that he felt vindicated when the renewed search for Ray's victims began in 2011 and the FBI, state police, and Albuquerque police all became very interested in his information. Bell told the media that he did not resent the fact that his first tip was ignored. He said he only hoped that it would now be able to help the case in some way. He said he didn't want to be thought of as an "old-timer" giving advice and telling people how to do their jobs, but he believed that there was something in the information he had received that was well worth investigating.

"If this was my case," he said, "I'd sure be digging into it."

CHAPTER 10

In an effort to generate more information on potential victims who might have escaped alive from the Toy Box, Cynthia Vigil Jaramillo spoke to reporters in the Albuquerque FBI headquarters in mid-November 2011, a month after the renewed search for leads on David Parker Ray's possible victims began. Cynthia was the last victim to be held in Ray's Toy Box, and her escape from his home had resulted in his arrest.

Cynthia told the media that conversations between Ray and Cindy Hendy that she had overheard during her time as Ray's prisoner had made her believe there were other surviving victims out there who might not have clear memories of what had happened to them due to the amnesia-inducing drugs Ray sometimes forced on his captives.

Ray told her on one occasion, she said, that Cindy Hendy "would kill me like the others had been if he got off on me"; and she said that he told her that someone named Daisy was okay, so she would be, too.

Cynthia, who is still living in Albuquerque, is the devoted mother of three young sons and has built a good life for herself—despite the horrific things she endured at the hands of David Parker Ray. She said that she hoped that by coming forward and sharing her story once again, some of the other victims who survived Ray's Toy Box might begin to be able to remember what had happened to them and also come forward.

"Please, you guys," she said, "this man was a very sick man, and these families need the closure."

CHAPTER 11

In an effort to bring closure to a family that might have a daughter who had gone missing years earlier, the FBI reached out worldwide for help in identifying one of David Parker Ray's possible victims. In February 2012, FBI press releases in the United States and Australia, as well as in Canada, France, and England, asked for the public's help in locating a man the authorities only knew as "Mark."

A letter written by an Australian man named Mark to a young woman, Connie, and her friend Candy, had been recovered among David Parker Ray's belongings, but there were no last names used in the letter and there was no remaining envelope with the address of the person to whom the letter had been sent.

Ray wrote in one of his journals about a girl he had abducted whose name, he said, was Connie. He described her as Caucasian, about five feet tall, with long blond hair and a birthmark on her chest. She was believed to have been born around 1977, and Ray claimed she had been abducted by him in December 1995. It is not known whether or not she was from New Mexico.

The letter from Mark was dated June 19, 1990, bore a return address from Old South Head Road, Bellevue Hill, New South Wales, Australia, and begins: *Greetings from Sydney, Australia.* The letter offered the following clues to Mark's identity:

1. He lived in London for about twelve months in 1988.
2. He lived in Canada for around eighteen months in 1989.
3. He worked in Sydney in 1990 in a hospital for

people with developmental disabilities, and for the AIDS Council of New South Wales.

4. He spent the Queen's Birthday holiday in Melbourne, in 1990.
5. He was studying for exams in social policy in June 1990.
6. He jogged with the gay Frontrunners around June 1990.
7. He lived in Paris, France, for about six months.

According to the letter, Mark had met the two girls at an unspecified beach somewhere in the United States in February 1990. He said that he had promised the girls at that time that he would write soon and send some photos. He had misplaced their address, he said, or would have written much sooner than the following June. At one time, the letter evidently had contained some photos, for he wrote: *I am the one in the red and black swimming trunks.* He said he had been very sunburned at the time the photo was taken.

Agent Frank Fisher, of the Albuquerque FBI, contacted the Australian Federal Police with all the details of the letter. They launched a search for Mark, hoping he could offer some further information on Connie's identity. When they were unable to locate Mark, the search went public, in the media, with appeals made to Australian citizens asking for their help in finding Mark.

"We're hoping Mark can tell us more about Connie," Fisher said on Australian television. "Her last name, for beginners. Also her friends, her family, where she hung out."

Fisher said that it was a long shot that Mark would be able to provide useful information if he should happen to be located, but the agent said that the authorities in both the United States and Australia were determined to do everything possible to identify Ray's victims.

"We continue to hear from the relatives and loved ones of possible victims of David Parker Ray," Fisher said, "and we think we owe it to them to exhaust every possible long shot and turn over every rock that we can, to try to bring closure to this case."

Fisher said that the FBI wanted to find out what happened to Connie, and said that the "big, overriding concern in the David Parker Ray case for us has been the fate of the victims. Some may have survived. Some we fear may not have survived. We want to bring closure to their families."

Fisher had earlier told the media that the FBI and the other agencies involved in the search for victims of Ray were hoping that previously unknown victims who survived Ray's torture might come forward and provide more information. Cases of missing women from the time period were being reinvestigated to see if they might be connected. Also, a new DNA missing persons database could prove to be very valuable and would help identify any remains that might be discovered.

CHAPTER 12

Thanks to David Parker Ray's deal with prosecutors to get his daughter a reduced sentence, Jesse Ray spent two and a half years in prison and then walked out on a year's supervised probation. Eventually she ended up in a small town in Kentucky, where her mother and Jesse's daughter were living. Jesse moved in with them; and in early 2009, the townspeople began to discover her background. Many of them became wary of having her in their midst. A message board for the town on the Internet carried post after post of people alternately deriding and defending Jesse; some praised her well-respected mother and showed sympathy for her teenage daughter. The arguments raged on for almost a whole year. The cyber feuding included scores of rumors about the family and the David Parker Ray case, plus an incredible amount of small-town speculation—in many cases, downright malicious gossip.

One of the first to respond to the posts telling of Jesse's presence in the town said that she was indeed there, living quietly and minding her own business. The writer claimed to have read two of the books on the Ray case: **It sure did not sound like Jesse was innocent.**

The writer said that according to the books, Jesse was supposed to have picked someone up on her motorcycle and taken the woman to her father. The Internet pundit said that if Jesse had been involved with Ray's activities, why was she not on some watch list to warn people?

I believe people can change to an extent, however crap like this is an illness and I don't think you get over it, the commenter wrote.

Another person posted that medical experts do not believe that sociopaths could ever be cured: **They are generally resistant to therapy.**

Someone else remarked that when they first discovered Jesse was in and around the area, their first thought was that she had come to the wrong place: **I would think that a ridge full of lead- and torch-packing rednecks would be the last place that she would set up camp, wouldn't you think? Clearly she has no idea of her surroundings!**

The writer said their father had been regularly attending a hymn meeting held at a local store, and one night **[Jesse] just hossed [*sic*] right in and plopped down and started picking the guitar.**

A couple of nights later, the writer said, the people

who had been at the singing were very surprised and shocked when they found out who Jesse was.

Another observer said that he had heard that Jesse was actually pretty good on the guitar when she played at the store that night.

By all accounts, Jesse's mother was liked by everyone who knew her, and she was loved by the patients she tended at the local nursing home.

One person said that Jesse's mother was one of the sweetest people around, with always a kind word to say. The writer said that perhaps Jesse had helped to bring some of Ray's victims to him, but maybe she did not realize the complete extent of his activities.

The defender went on to say that people could change, and maybe Jesse's move back to the town with her mother was such an endeavor: **[A] way of getting her second chance, having a chance to change her ways and do better in life. At least, I hope so anyways.**

CHAPTER 13

There were scores of opinions, both pro and con, on the subject of Jesse Ray and her presence in the town. One writer left an extremely long and detailed post that offered much information on this individual's view of the town, its people, and the family that, according to this writer, was being attacked unfairly on the message board.

The observer pointed out how the folks that "you villains are attacking" had a wonderful history and were probably related to the majority of the townspeople. When Jesse's mother first moved back to the town, the writer said, she brought some admirable nursing skills and love, which the town needed:

She's made our older loved ones that had to be in the nursing home during the last days, less hurtful and very full, including my grandfather before he passed on.

Many of the patients in the nursing home wouldn't let anyone else care for them, the writer said; and when the David Parker Ray case made the news many years earlier, some of the townspeople were aware of what was going on and, without her knowing it, rallied around Jesse's mother to support her.

She had remarried in 1978, and she'd had no dealings with that man in the news since. For you people to be dragging her name into this forum shows your own nature, which isn't very pretty, the poster challenged.

Jesse's champion claimed to have met her a few times and talked to her, saying she was a bit standoffish: **[But] considering things, I understand why.**

Jesse's mother had told friends that the only reason Jesse was even around her father was because she was having some major medical problems and stayed in Truth or Consequences, New Mexico, for a couple of years because of that:

But when that man was arrested, his daughter was living in Galveston, Texas, and went back up only to take care of his financial affairs because no one else wanted to get dragged into it.

The writer recounted what was believed of Jesse's work in conservation efforts and helping homeless youth and adults. The empathetic supporter mentioned an editorial Jesse had once written concerning an injured animal and her efforts to save it: **That doesn't mean she's an angel, but it gives thought for the nature of the person who wrote it.**

The writer said that actions spoke louder than words, and Jesse's actions didn't tell them they should be afraid of her: **[It] tells me there is something there that I'd like to understand and perhaps adopt as my own.**

If Jesse stood by her father out of love and obligation, as a child to a parent, despite the accusations against him—**her fortitude must be tremendous.**

The advocate closed the post by saying to the others on the board: **Unfortunately your petty viciousness can't be brought before a jury but, God forbid, this forum is open to the world and hopefully other people will be as smart as I and steer clear of your town.**

CHAPTER 14

After months of rumors and arguments on the town message board, Jesse Ray evidently grew tired of the situation and went on the board herself in December 2009. She left a long post that stated her position on many of the issues that had been brought up by the townspeople concerning Jesse and her family: **Do you really believe everything you read? I was drawn into my father's case because I couldn't keep my nose out of the investigation.**

Jesse claimed she was warned three times to steer clear, and when she tried to "decipher fact from fiction," she was drawn in for discredit. She said that if the others on the message board who liked to spread so many tales would access all the available information on the Internet, they would have discovered that her probation was supposed to be one year, supervised.

But I was allowed to work in international waters at my own discretion. Now do you really think if they thought I was truly guilty of anything of that nature that

my "conditions of probation" would state that? she wrote.

Jesse added that regardless of her father being the person that he was, she had wanted to believe something else and "had to see it through." She wrote she spent two and a half years in jail: **[That's] a long time to wait on a matter of principle.**

Jesse continued to say that she tried to live her life well and to help whomever she could. She had always been the person she was now, and yet: **Most of you folks, without knowing a damn thing, choose to try and influence my existence in my home. You need to wash your own laundry first.**

CHAPTER 15

Sadly, the message board battles eventually drew in Jesse's daughter. She apparently felt compelled to defend her mother. She left a long post in explanation of many of the things that had been written about her family:

I am the 17-year-old daughter of Jean (Jesse) Ray, she wrote. She said she could not believe that so many people would post, acting as if they knew everything about the case—when, in actuality, they only knew about "20 percent" of the facts.

For one thing, are you actually stupid enough to believe everything you read? she wrote. **Yes, many of the things they said about my grandfather was true, but not all.** Everyone knew, she said, that the media thrived on shock and sensationalism.

My grandfather was sick, but I hope with all my heart that before he died he became a Christian, she opined.

Jesse's daughter wrote that her mother had reported David Parker Ray for the first time back in the 1980s, and the information on that could be easily found on the Internet. She maintained that **[my mother had] nothing to do with those women. My Lord, she will chase a spider around the house with a jar rather than kill it.**

Jesse went to church with her, she said, and was a Christian. She said her mother's name got slurred because she got involved in the investigation: **[She] was trying to help her father whom she loved.**

I hope next time before you screw around with a family's life you have your facts straight.

One incident that had generated many wild rumors and much speculation on the message board was addressed by both Jesse and her daughter in their posts. It involved an accident that happened at their home after Jesse had been draining antifreeze out of a vehicle. She stored the antifreeze in an empty soda bottle to keep dogs from licking it off the ground.

Jesse's ninety-year-old grandmother found it, thought it was soda because of the color, and put it in the refrigerator. Later, the grandmother inadvertently drank some of it and had to be rushed to the hospital by Jesse for emergency treatment.

My grandmother has had a rough time getting over that one, Jesse posted.

CHAPTER 16

During the resumed investigation that brought renewed attention to the victims of David Parker Ray, the press was once again shown into the Toy Box, which now sits outside FBI headquarters in Albuquerque. In the twelve years that have passed since it was first discovered, David Parker Ray's $100,000 nightmare playhouse has been stripped of every piece of horrific equipment and shred of evidence. Enough of its original furnishings remain, however, to give chills to the many seasoned reporters who toured it.

FBI forensic team member Lisa Baughman's first assignment was processing the Toy Box, and her team took out and bagged all the contents of the trailer.

Baughman told the media that it was hard to look at all the instruments that were there and know they were used for torture.

"You could only imagine what some were used for and the pain it must have inflicted on people," she said. "Some of the devices had sharp objects on them—electric shocking devices—and the size of some of the objects was just horrendous."

Forensic expert Norm Cedillo was also part of the original team and was present when David Parker Ray was arrested and the Toy Box was first discovered. He and the team sorted through all Ray's homemade torture devices. Cedillo showed the reporters the wooden box lined with carpet, where Ray locked up his victims between torture sessions. He showed them the gynecological exam chair, which still remained inside the trailer. Wires, which Ray used to give his victims electrical shocks, were still attached to the chair.

Cedillo said he wondered about the women who

hadn't been found, "or that we know are out there somewhere."

Baughman told the press, "I guess that's the main thing in my head," saying she really wanted "to work hard to find them."

EPILOGUE

All of the agencies involved in the continuing search for victims of David Parker Ray are anxious to hear from anyone who might have even the smallest shred of information that could help them in the case.

The readers of this book are urged to go to the FBI website or Facebook page and look closely at all the items that are shown there. Some of those items are so unique and individual that there must surely be someone who will recognize them as having belonged to someone they knew, perhaps someone who has been missing for many years (http://www.fbi.gov/news/news_blog/fbi-releases-images-in-david-parker-ray-case).

Contact numbers for some of the agencies are listed on those sites, and those and other contacts are listed below:

- Detective Richard Lewis, Albuquerque Police Department, rlewis@cabq.gov, (505) 924-6095
- FBI Albuquerque, (505) 889-1300
- Australian Crimestoppers, 1800 333 000

AFTERWORD

When I was asked to update the late Jim Fielder's book *Slow Death,* I felt very honored. Mr. Fielder's excellent work on the David Parker Ray case had continued even after Ray's death in prison, and Fielder had narrated several videos and taken part in many television documentaries about Ray and his crimes.

There was another reason I was particularly pleased to write this update. *Slow Death* was the first Pinnacle True Crime book I had ever read, even before beginning work on my own first book, *Blood Highway.*

When I began to look into all the many developments in the case since *Slow Death* was first released, I was amazed. It was almost as if Ray were still alive, pulling the strings of the other players who were still living, and continuing to leave law enforcement stumped. So many clues and tips poured into the FBI and the Albuquerque Police Department, most of which produced no results. People came forward to give statements; some were followed up, but others were ignored because of so many people "crying wolf."

Ray seemingly reached from the grave to touch people in New Mexico, all the way to Kentucky, and even across the globe to Australia. There were so many leads, but most of them were leading nowhere.

In searching for new developments, I spent very many days researching on the Internet and learned so much more about David Parker Ray and his associates than I had expected. All these stories fascinated me: the renewed search for Jill Troia, the FBI's hope for finding a girl named Connie by searching for an acquaintance of hers in Australia, and Jesse Ray's attempt to make a new life in Kentucky.

I felt for Ray's ex-wife, Jesse's mother, who had been

out of his life for very many years, but who still was plagued by his stigma. And I was touched by Jesse's teenage daughter, who coped with the realization of what her grandfather had done by expressing her hope that he had found God before he died.

It is my hope that someone reading this reissue of *Slow Death* might have even a tiny scrap of knowledge that might help law enforcement in their search for the bodies of Ray's victims. Their bodies are believed to be out there, well hidden for all these years. There are so very many dedicated, determined officers and agents who refuse to give up on their searches, and they need all the help and support that we can give them. Please, if you can, lend them a hand. It's the right thing to do.

In closing, I had hoped to write a couple of paragraphs of advice on how to avoid being taken by predators like David Parker Ray. I find, however, that the only advice I can come up with is this:

Don't believe those charming strangers who may approach you in all innocence. Remember not only what happened to those women in the Toy Box, but also to those who rushed forward to help Ted Bundy, with his fake cast and walking cane, seemingly struggling to get into his car. How many women might still be alive, who, instead, met a terrible fate at the hands of someone they perceived as harmless? If only they had been more wary.

For the most part, sociopaths and sexual predators are very skilled in putting their potential victims at ease. Ladies, just because someone may be likeable and seem like a "nice guy," don't let your guard down. Not for a minute. I don't want any of you to be one of the victims I write about in my next book.